Endorsements

'*Project Pearl* is the story of an impossible mission made possible through an ordinary man filled with the heart and power of Jesus. Brother David is a warrior who wrapped himself in zeal as in a cloak. Yet it also tells of the man I have known for decades who was gentle, kind and used the weapons of faith, prayer and wisdom to bring about a miracle for the sake of his beloved China and his wonderful Savior.'

– Jackie Pullinger: Hong Kong pastor and
author of *Chasing the Dragon*

'I consider it a rare privilege to have been considered a true friend by this saintly brother. To me, he has always been "closer than a brother"… Overall, there is no other Christian I can recall in the four decades of my own Christian life who has so consistently exhibited such an absolutely Christ-like attitude towards life and towards other Christians; even his adversaries… Quite simply, he is the most remarkable Christian missionary I have ever met.'

– David Aikman: Journalist, foreign policy consultant and
author of many books including *Jesus in Beijing*

CHINA, LET ME LOVE YOU

(A song from Brother David's heart with words rearranged to music by Sara Bruce)

There is a land whose people hunger,
Who crave the bread which satisfies,
For they've been fed too long on substitutes,
And now I sense their cries –

I hear a billion voices rising
To Him of whom they have not heard;
Oh, will they never speak of Jesus?
Nor have His Word,
Nor have His Word?

Chorus:
China, let me love you,
China, I am weeping for you,
China, oh China, let me love you.

For in that land a shackled people
March on a lonely captive road,
Bound by the chains of ideology
That hold them back from God.

I see a billion faces passing,
Toward a billion Christless graves,
While we have yet still time to turn them
To Him who saves,
To Him who saves.

China, let me love you,
China, I am weeping for you,
China, oh China, let me love you.

project
pearl

BROTHER DAVID
with Paul Hattaway

MONARCH
BOOKS

Oxford, UK, and Grand Rapids, Michigan, USA

First published in the UK in 2007 by Monarch Books
(a publishing imprint of Lion Hudson plc),
Wilkinson House, Jordan Hill Road, Oxford OX2 8DR
Tel: +44 (0) 1865 302750   Fax: +44 (0) 1865 302757
Email: monarch@lionhudson.com
www.lionhudson.com

ISBN: 978-1-85424-853-4 (UK)
ISBN: 978-0-8254-6195-8 (USA)

Distributed by:
UK: Marston Book Services Ltd, PO Box 269, Abingdon, Oxon OX14 4YN;
USA: Kregel Publications, PO Box 2607, Grand Rapids, Michigan 49501.

Unless otherwise stated, Scripture quotations are
taken from the Holy Bible, New International Version,
© 1973, 1978, 1984 by the International Bible Society.
Used by permission of Hodder and Stoughton Ltd.
All rights reserved.

This book has been printed on paper and board independently
certified as having come from sustainable forests.

British Library Cataloguing Data
A catalogue record for this book is available from the British Library.

Printed and bound in Wales by Creative Print & Design.

Contents

Foreword by David Aikman

Project Pearl, which took place on the night of 18 June 1981, was one of the most remarkable incidents in modern Chinese history. Though thousands of Chinese were involved in its implementation, the central corps of personnel was Westerners. They were not involved in a military action, or in any kind of espionage. Rather, Pearl was the delivery of one million Bibles by tugboat and barge manned by twenty dedicated missionaries. The delivery took place right under the noses of the People's Liberation Army and the naval patrol boats and coastal radar of China's Guangdong Province. When the barge was being towed back to its base in the Philippines, three U.S. Air Force fighter jets operating out of the Subic Bay military base in the Philippines circled the returning boat and dipped their wings in salute. They were right to do so. No action by the U.S. government in relation to China, even at the height of the American–Chinese Cold War of the 1950s, had approached the feat of Project Pearl in daring or magnitude.

The man who thought up this astonishing project, carefully planned for it, raised the money for it, recruited the crew and trained them, then led it, was someone who needed to have had military training or its equivalent. And he did. Brother David, then in his mid-40s, had served for six years in the U.S. Marine Corps. He had learned all the essentials of a precise, military operation: preparedness, discipline, obedience to command and the meticulous carrying out of instructions. Brother David, however, was no ordinary former-Marine. He was converted during a Billy Graham Crusade in California in the early 1960s, had felt called to missionary work, and for several years worked in Manila for the Far East Broadcasting Company, a

Christian organization that broadcasts Gospel radio programs to China. It was while he was engaged in printing Christian materials for FEBC that he caught the vision of bringing Bibles into China. At the time it seemed an impossible task, for China was still thrashing about in Mao Zedong's disastrous political and social experiment, the Cultural Revolution (1966–1976), and had closed down all public expressions of religion – including, of course, Christianity – throughout China.

This book tells the story of Project Pearl from beginning to end. It also contains an interesting account of Brother David's own spiritual journey, from self-assured new missionary in the Philippines to the leader of a daring initiative who was ordered, after months of preparation, to call a halt to the operation on the eve of its first scheduled occurrence. There are rich spiritual lessons in the book: the need for utter selflessness in any Christian ministry that is going to bear fruit, the need to forgive, the need to remain humble at all times and the need to acknowledge one's own weaknesses. The book is worth reading for those rich lessons, in addition to the extraordinarily exciting story it tells.

Yet that would not convey enough of Brother David's personality and character. Quite simply, Brother David is the most remarkable Christian missionary I have ever met. His life has not been one of success after success in the process of spreading the Gospel. In fact, although Project Pearl capped a stunningly productive career of getting one million Bibles into China at a time when it was almost impossible to obtain them in many parts of the country, Brother David has undergone deep suffering in his family life (including a failed marriage), his health and his treatment at the hands of other Christians. He has paid a stunningly high price for his obedience to what he felt God was calling him to do. Throughout this, however, he has demonstrated what I can only call an amazing saintliness of disposition. Sure, at times he has been angry or expressed disappointment with people. Overall, however, there is no other Christian I can recall in the four decades of my own Christian life who has so consistently exhibited such an absolutely Christ-like attitude towards life and towards other Christians; even his adversaries.

I first met Brother David when I worked as a foreign correspondent in Hong Kong in the early 1970s. He was one of the very few people who carefully debriefed overseas Chinese Christians who had entered China and returned to tell the stories of the remarkable re-emergence of Christianity there. I first observed that he was a man of amazing kindness and generosity. He once interrupted a missionary trip to Hong Kong for nearly a week to paint the walls of my apartment. Here was a leader in strategic missionary work dropping everything to perform a mundane chore that I should have done myself. Later, he went out of his way to help me make contact with Christians in China when I was starting to gather material for my book, *Jesus in Beijing*.

Even in the 1970s, before Project Pearl, Brother David came under severe criticism because taking Bibles into China without permission of the Chinese government was considered by some Christian groups to be 'smuggling'. There was also jealousy, as this book makes clear. At a time when it was very difficult for Christian groups to get into China, much less do any Christian work there, Hong Kong was at times a snake-pit of missionary rivalries and suspicions. (Thankfully, the situation is much better today.) In all this time I never, ever heard Brother David apply to his critics the same angry criticism they often applied to him.

I used to enjoy eating out with him, not because we shared the pleasure of any particular kind of cuisine – though we both love Chinese food – but because of the startlingly gracious way he treated the people who served him. They were *people*, first and foremost, not waiters and waitresses, and he so frequently would engage them in light-hearted conversation that I became fascinated by how he did it. As a journalist, I learned a lot about relating to people from Brother David.

Project Pearl did have a major impact on Chinese policy towards Christianity. Having dithered in the early 1980s, Chinese printing presses after 1982 made concerted efforts to produce Bibles for the domestic Chinese market of rapidly growing Christians. And, contrary to Bishop Ding Guangxun (who for decades was the 'official' face of Chinese Christianity around the world), Project Pearl was a brilliant success, not at all a failure. Even more amazingly, Brother David visited China after Project Pearl and presented the same friendly face to the Chinese Christian authorities who had initially criticized him ferociously, as he had shown towards the Chinese brothers whom he embraced on the beach of Shantou in June 1981. Despite heart attacks, diabetes, the amputation of toes and near-blindness, Brother David recently made another of his trips back into China, to encourage the brothers and sisters there.

The story of Project Pearl is inspiring to read and the personality of Brother David that emerges from its pages is arresting and memorable. For me, Brother David will always be uniquely memorable. I consider it a rare privilege to have been considered a true friend by this saintly brother. To me, he has always been 'closer than a brother'.

David Aikman is a former Beijing bureau chief for *Time* magazine, an author, journalist, and foreign policy consultant. He has reported for *Time* from more than fifty countries, and interviewed such figures as Boris Yeltsin, Billy Graham, Manuel Noriega and Mother Teresa. He currently resides in Round Hill, Virginia.

Acknowledgments

Many years ago I remember hearing the words of a song that said, 'If you can use anything Lord, You can use me!' This is also my prayer, that the Lord Jesus Christ will use me and continue to use me until the day He takes me home. I would therefore like to start by giving thanks to the Lord for using an ordinary person like me.

There are so many people who have impacted my life over the years that I hardly know where to begin in acknowledging them all. Therefore, to the many co-workers and friends whom I have been blessed to walk the road with over the years, I thank God for you.

Project Pearl was a miracle, and the story behind this book is also a miracle. Looking back, I can clearly see how God wanted me to record His great acts in China, so that His children all around the world could give glory to the Father. This is one of the greatest privileges a Christian has. The Bible says in Psalm 145:3–6,

> Great is the Lord and most worthy of praise;
> > his greatness no one can fathom.
> One generation will commend your works to another;
> > they will tell of your mighty acts.
> They will speak of the glorious splendor of your majesty,
> > and I will meditate on your wonderful works.
> They will tell of the power of your awesome works,
> > and I will proclaim your great deeds.

The idea for this book came as I lay in the Intensive Care Unit after suffering a heart attack. My cardiologist, Dr Mark Vossler, walked into my room and said, 'David, I have a gift for you. It's a dicta-tape recorder! I look forward to reading the Project Pearl story.' Over the years many Christians told me they would love to know more about

Project Pearl, so this little gift became the vehicle for these requests to become a reality.

In 1998 Meiling and I traveled to New Zealand, where we stayed in the home of our dear friends Eddie and Betty Cairns in the town of Tauranga. Through that opportunity we had the chance to meet Paul and Joy Hattaway, a missionary couple who worked in China and other parts of Asia. Little did I know, after much prayer and seven years later, the Lord would impress upon my heart that Paul would be my co-author to write this story, to glorify God, and to bring encouragement and challenge to Christians around the world. God clearly handpicked Paul Hattaway to write this book, and without his involvement the whole project would not have come to fruition.

After returning home to the United States, Sister Lin Jiin-Yun from our church volunteered to help my wife record and transcribe many parts of the story. They worked tirelessly, and through much prayer and the involvement of God-sent individuals, this book you now hold in your hands gradually became a reality.

Finally, it would be remiss of me not to mention my Chinese friends and colleagues who love China. For all of you who have been privileged to witness and even participate in the greatest and most sustained revival in Christian history, *'I pray that out of his glorious riches he may strengthen you with power through his Spirit in your inner being, so that Christ may dwell in your hearts through faith. And I pray that you, being rooted and established in love, may have power, together with all the saints, to grasp how wide and long and high and deep is the love of Christ, and to know this love that surpasses knowledge – that you may be filled to the measure of all the fullness of God'* (Ephesians 3:16–19).

Brother David

Introduction by Paul Hattaway

A pearl conjures up thoughts of beauty, rarity and value. This book is a record of such precious things.

In 2005 I picked up my phone and heard the voice of Brother David on the other end. 'Paul,' he said, 'I believe the Lord wants you to write a book with me on Project Pearl. When can you come?'

A few months later I had the privilege of sitting next to David's bed in his home near Seattle, in America's picturesque northwest. This servant of God, who has lived his life like few other people, appeared to have almost literally burned out for God. After suffering a string of heart attacks, the scourge of diabetes had severely ravaged David's once-powerful frame, now some 100 pounds lighter than at his prime.

This man who traveled the world proclaiming the message of God's love and salvation, now owed his life to a cardioverter defibrillator – an implanted device that kickstarts his heart back into action whenever it stops beating. It had done so several times. Largely blind, and with several of his toes having withered away because of diabetes, David shared the extraordinary story of Project Pearl for day after day as his wife Meiling served us like an angel from heaven.

Sitting at David's bedside reminded me of a story I had heard years before about David Livingstone, the great nineteenth-century Scottish missionary to Africa. In 1857, sixteen years after his first journey into the so-called 'dark continent', Livingstone returned home for a time of rest. He was invited to speak to the students at the University of Glasgow.

It was the custom of the students in those days to heckle visiting speakers. Preachers were especially targeted. The students armed themselves with peashooters, rattles and noisemakers of every kind. Livingstone made his way out onto the platform with the tread of a man who had walked 10,000 miles through the African jungles. His left arm hung at his side, having been almost torn off by a huge lion. His face was lined and marked from numerous bouts of fever and attacks by the natives. He was half deaf from rheumatic fever and half blind from a branch that had poked him in the eyes as he made his way through a jungle.

The students stared at David Livingstone, for they knew they were in the presence of a life that was literally burning for God. Not a rattle moved, and not a word was whispered. The vast audience listened in rapt silence as Livingstone testified to the faithfulness of God, and the fulfillment of a life spent following Jesus Christ.

When the world sees a walking, living sacrifice they know it, and they are silenced. This is the same feeling I had while sitting at the bedside of this gospel warrior, Brother David. Although his body was struggling, his mind and memory remained razor sharp. His recollection of names, dates and details was extraordinary. Moreover, David's spirit reflected the beauty that only someone who has met the Lord in the Most Holy Place can possess. Through decades of being refined in God's fiery furnace, he had experienced fellowship with Jesus Christ in a new, fresh and vital way.

Brother David is not a perfect man. He has made mistakes in his life and experienced much pain, but he has always learned to trust in the Lord and to pour his heart out to Him. In the years I have known David I have noticed that regardless of his health, as soon as the topic of China comes up his eyes sparkle, and his spirit piques. He loves China. Many years ago China opened its arms to receive David, and he welcomed China into the center of his heart. He has now served the Lord Jesus Christ in Asia for more than forty years.

I had heard about Project Pearl before, but as the details of this remarkable event were unfolded, I realized that here was a story that needed to be told to a generation of Christians around the world who are struggling for role-models of what it means to know and serve God. Today there *are* many Christians who want to *give* a message, but few whose lives have been so shaped by the cross that their lives are a powerful message. There are many with theological training, head knowledge and degrees, but so few with a message from the furnace of affliction.

At the start of 1996 Brother David was told he was about to die. He had just experienced four heart attacks in the space of seventy-two days. God, however, had other ideas. When David and his wife established a new mission organization in April of the same year, they appropriately named it 'Love China Ministries'. One of the founding objectives of their new ministry was to provide 5 million more Bibles over seven years to the house churches in China.

Just weeks after I recorded Brother David's testimony for this book, the doctors told him they would have to amputate parts of three more toes on his left foot. This would tend to slow down most people, but not David. Remarkably, in late 2005 he made yet another trip to his beloved China to meet with house church leaders and plan new strategies for the kingdom of God. Months of planning had to go into finding an airline that could accept his wheelchair and walker, hotels in China with ramps and facilities, and a thousand other things. When the Chinese Christians saw him they hugged him dearly and tears rolled down their cheeks. Here was a warrior of the gospel – someone who had been literally willing to die to bring them the Word of God during their darkest hour of suffering. Someone who brought them food when they were hungry, water when they were thirsty, and clothes when they were naked. There are thousands of missionaries working in China today in various guises, doing a myriad of different activities, but those who can claim to have been serving the Lord in China as far back as the Cultural Revolution in the 1970s can be counted on one hand. Brother David is one of them, and the Chinese have long memories.

Interspersed throughout this book you will also find short contributions from others involved with the incidents in the story. These insights will help the reader gain a fresh perspective – and a more complete picture – of this remarkable story.

In many ways this book is also an historical record of what *Time* magazine described as 'A remarkable mission... the largest operation of its kind in the history of China.' Some people, strongly disagreeing with the *Time* description, denounced the whole operation. I have also decided to be open and fair by including many responses – both positive and negative – that came about after Project Pearl. Many of these are written by those who received the Bibles – the house church Christians inside China. Our hope is that these letters and responses will provide the reader with a balanced view of the impact of Project Pearl.

I pray this book will testify to God's greatness and love for people, and will encourage many in the realization that He can use an ordinary person who is willing to take Him at His Word. The great nineteenth-century evangelist D. L. Moody once said, 'The world has yet to see what God can do with a man fully consecrated to him.' Brother David is someone wholly dedicated to Jesus Christ. He has not been ashamed of the gospel, and the God who declared, *'Those who honor me I will honor'* (1 Samuel 2:30), has honored David's faith in extraordinary ways. The paradox is that Brother David is also an ordinary man, with weaknesses like the rest of us. Yet if the King of Kings has been pleased to use him, He can use you and me too.

It has truly been stated, 'It is not great men who change the world, but weak men in the hands of a great God.'

Note: Some of the people involved with Project Pearl continue to serve God in restricted countries today. To protect their identities, their names have been changed in this book to generic terms such as 'Doctor Jim', 'Pablo', 'Brother Joseph', etc.

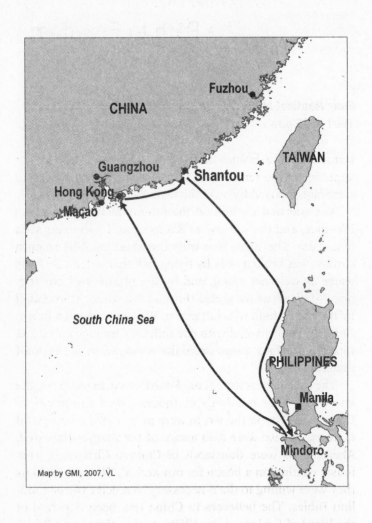

Map by GMI, 2007, VL

Chapter One:
The Path to Freedom

Four Nautical Miles off the South China Coast: 18 June 1981, 8.25 p.m.

I stood on the bridge and looked straight ahead as we approached the rendezvous point. My heart was calm and steadfast, focused fully on the task ahead.

The sun had set behind the mountains of Guangdong Province, and the sea was as flat as glass. I had never seen it so calm. The scene was truly breathtaking. The smooth surface was broken only by flying fish that leapt out of the water as we went along, and by the progress of our tugboat, *Michael*, as we glided through the water, illuminated by the bright light of a full moon. We were towing a barge, *Gabriella*, fully loaded with one million Chinese Bibles: 232 tons of precious cargo carefully wrapped in waterproof material.

The twenty crewmen on board were assured in the knowledge that hundreds of thousands of Christians in China and around the world were praying for a successful delivery, but we were also aware of the dangers involved. Ahead of us were thousands of Chinese Christians, anxiously waiting on a beach for our arrival. They had told us they were willing to die if necessary to receive the one million Bibles. The believers in China had been deprived of the Word of God since the 1950s. At that time most Bibles had been destroyed by the Communists, and more than 10,000 foreign missionaries were forcibly expelled from

China. Hundreds of church buildings had been demolished, and hundreds more were confiscated and turned into government facilities or storehouses.

Years of planning had gone into the operation, which we dubbed 'Project Pearl'. It had consumed my life for the previous two years, and we had seen the indisputable hand of God intervening at many steps of the journey. This was no child's-play. If caught, we faced the possibility of being shot by the Chinese authorities, or at least being imprisoned for a long time. The Chinese Christians faced a similar fate. We had entered Chinese territorial waters without permission, and were planning to deliver God's Word to our hungry brothers and sisters – the very same book Mao and his fanatical Red Guards had spared no effort trying to eradicate from China during the Cultural Revolution just a few years earlier.

As we cut our way through the glassy South China Sea, Captain Bill peered anxiously into the distance. One of the men on the bridge spotted a vessel fast approaching our stern side. 'What's that?' he asked. The captain grabbed his binoculars and his face suddenly stiffened. 'It's a Chinese patrol gunboat!' he replied, 'and it has a mounted machine gun. He's coming to have a look at us.'

The rest of us on the bridge set our gaze straight ahead, trying to appear nonchalant as the patrol boat drew even closer. The machine gun and its operator became clearly visible in the moonlight.

I took a deep breath. 'Lord, there's nothing we can do,' I prayed, the most sincere prayer of my life. 'Only You can take control of this situation. We know you love the believers waiting on that beach and we know how much You desire them to have Your Word.' I calmly ended, 'We rest in Your hands, Lord. We can only stand back and watch you work.'

When I opened my eyes I saw that the patrol boat was still alongside us. It was so close that I could have easily thrown a stone onto its deck. Captain Bill continued to steer straight ahead, his eyes fixed on the coastline. He quietly mumbled, 'If you don't look at me, I won't look at you.'

**

For me, Project Pearl began on the night of 4 September 1963, at the Los Angeles Coliseum. That night I realized for the first time in my life that I had never been honest with God. I had never asked Jesus to forgive my sin and to save me. That night as Billy Graham preached, he said, 'Except you be converted and become as a little child you'll never see the Kingdom of Heaven.' That night I wanted to see heaven. I wanted to get right with God. For the first time in my life I was honest with God. And you know, Jesus did meet me that night at the Coliseum.

I had been raised in a Christian home, but I never had a relationship with Christ until that night in 1963, when I was already 27 years old. I had married several years earlier. My parents did not want us to wed, but we were young and rebellious, so we eloped to Mexico. I remember the hurt on my mom's face when she found out. Things moved fast for us. We soon had three children – two girls and a boy – each one spaced 20 months apart, and our life was full.

I had spent most of my life in southern California, although my birthplace was across country at Norrestown, near Philadelphia, in 1936. My father, Charles, was a military man, and my mother, Marie, worked as the paymaster at Camp Pendelton, a Marine Corps Base located north of San Diego on the Californian coast. My dad's job as a teacher in the military required us to move around, and I still remember as a five-year-old when we drove in my dad's old truck to our new home in Flagstaff, Arizona. During the war years our family was separated for periods of time due to my father's assignments. We later moved to Oceanside, California.

Both of my parents were well educated, so you can imagine their dismay when I struggled greatly at school. By the age of ten I could neither read nor write. I failed third grade and was made to repeat the year. The embarrassment for me was exacerbated by the fact I was easily the biggest boy in my class. The following year I was allowed to enter fourth grade, but I flunked that too, and was forced to repeat another year. School was a humiliation for me, and I was the subject of much ridicule.

During the War years I spent most of my spare time waging imaginary wars on the beach with my friends. There I found the respect I craved, and many afternoons I led my 'troops' on brave and successful raids against our Japanese 'enemies'. We lived near the entrance to Camp Pendelton, and I often saw Marines going off to war. They were my heroes, and I dreaded having to go home each evening. My mother worked hard and my dad was often away. I found my make-believe world much more invigorating and fulfilling than the real life I had been handed.

After the war ended my father came home and for the next two years he taught business administration in various parts of the country. We moved home three times in two years, before finally settling down at Redondo Beach, California. My father was appointed principal of Redondo Union High School in 1959. Three years later he became the assistant Superintendent of three high schools in the area.

At school I was placed in a seventh grade class with boys two years younger and about a foot shorter than me. My new classmates gave me a cold welcome, repeatedly chanting 'David is a dummy!' on the playground. This is when I found my beach military training experience came in handy. I responded to the taunts by fighting, and soon won the respect of my classmates.

I was later diagnosed as suffering from dyslexia, which was the root of my learning disability. I have struggled with this disease my whole life. Dyslexia affects my brain in strange ways. I may start reading a book, but after a while my eyes and mind start trying to read the lines from right to left, instead of left to right. I might write a word and find the order of the letters the reverse of what I intended, or I may drive down to the shops, but instead of turning left I turn right and head in the wrong direction. If you are one of the millions of people around the world who suffer from dyslexia, be encouraged that you can lead a normal and full life with God's help.

My parents were loving and gracious to me at home, always encouraging me to do better. There were many times when I crossed the line and my father's leather belt was applied to my backside. I was always assured that it was for my own good, but it certainly didn't feel like it at the time!

My grades gradually improved, and in the ninth grade a whole new horizon in life opened up to me when I was introduced to American football. At Redondo Union High School I played at every opportunity. Because of my size I was a linebacker, and soon found I was stronger and better than most of my opponents. I revelled in my newfound passion. In the 11th grade we played our rivals, Santa Monica High School, who were the reigning state champions. Although we lost narrowly, I was told I had played well, and that college talent scouts in the crowd had been impressed by my performance. This unexpected news made me feel ten feet tall.

The University of Denver contacted my parents during my final year at high school in 1955. They asked if I would be interested in coming to their fine institution on a football scholarship. I was incredulous, and numb with excitement. My old classmates who used to mock me with their cruel taunts never imagined I would one day go to university, let alone on a scholarship!

After arriving in Colorado the football coach soon

started getting me and my team mates beefed up for the rigours of the season ahead. We were fed T-bone steaks every day, and were put in the gym to lift weights and learn how to pound the wall to toughen us up. I arrived at Denver weighing just 175 pounds, but I soon tipped the scales at 220 pounds.

My first game for the University of Denver was against the Air Force Academy in 1955. It was the very first match ever played by the Air Force. It was an exhilarating feeling to play in front of thousands of spectators, and to represent an institution with a proud history dating back to 1864. In those days players had to play both offense and defense. On offense I was a center (the one who snaps the ball to the quarterback), and I played linebacker on defense.

For the first 18 months in Colorado I enjoyed playing football, but I soon realized I was out of my depth academically and had little chance of passing the exams. I still struggled with reading. My coach suggested I take a semester off and return home to study at a junior college before returning at the start of the football season. Within hours of arriving home my parents' phone had rung three times, as rival colleges called asking if I was available to join their football teams.

My dad, in his normal calm way, asked me what I wanted to do with my life. I assured him my goal was to return to Denver after improving my grades. He told me I would have to wait for several weeks for an opening at junior college, and asked if I would like to take a job as a trainee lithographer at Dunn Brothers, a large printing shop in downtown Los Angeles. I had to face the truth, and it hurt. Despite my love for football and the lifestyle I had become accustomed to in Denver, it was unlikely I would be able to stay at the university because of my poor academic record. I barely knew what a lithographer was, but I decided to take the job and abandon my university career. Little did I know at the time that this choice to enter the world of printing would prove pivotal in my future service for God.

My new job helped me increase my vocabulary, but also exposed me to a deeper life of sin. My workmates introduced me to gambling, and not far behind were the twin temptations of alcohol and girls. I felt I was now a real 'man of the world'. In reality, I was far from God. I spent much energy concealing my lifestyle from my parents. They attended a small Baptist church near our home, taught in Sunday school and sang in the choir.

My parents were genuine born-again followers of Christ. They were dedicated to Jesus, and had devotions at nighttime before going to sleep. I thought their faith and commitment was quaint, and good for them, but I wanted nothing to do with it. On one of the few occasions they managed to get me along to a church service I was asked to make a commitment to their new church building fund. The pastor had even calculated how much I earned in my job and wanted me to give them $5,000 a year! This angered me and I vowed to have nothing to do with the church again.

Several months after starting my new job, I was drafted into the Marine Corps. From the time I was a little boy the military had endeared itself to me and I was thrilled and delighted. I was one of sixty-five new recruits at the Marine boot camp in San Diego. The boot camp was a huge shock to my system. Everything I had experienced in life up to that point was of little help. I was stretched to my absolute limit physically, mentally and emotionally. I was determined not to give up, and the fire to become a fully-certified Marine continued to burn in my heart.

I developed a mean streak during the boot camp. On one occasion the drill instructor shouted at me, 'You're dead!' I was ordered to take on two men, and told, 'They're going to whip your butt!' My time playing football had made me tough and aggressive, and I knocked both of those poor guys out in less than a minute. We were taught the art of killing with your hands. Most Marines receive five hours' instruction, but I received ninety-five. In one session we were asked if anyone would volunteer to try his skills on one of the drill instructors, Sergeant Hall. I came forward and almost killed him. They had to drag me off him. I was an angry young man with a volcano of pent-up emotions ready to explode.

The boot camp came to an end after thirteen excruciating weeks. I then attended a four-week rifle-shooting course, and then traveled back to San Diego for the graduation ceremony. I was now a Marine! More training followed as I was taught how to fight for my country. My parents were filled with pride the first time they saw me in my new green uniform.

In 1963 my six-year stint in the Marines ended, and I returned to my lithographer's job in southern California. When I first received the call up to military service my boss said there would always be a job for me, whenever I needed it. I soon fell back into the same lifestyle of gambling, drinking and girls. The party went on, but inwardly, an uneasy feeling began to gnaw away at me. In rare moments of honesty I somehow knew that my life was hollow and meaningless. To cope, I decided to suppress these feelings and ignore them.

Time passed until one warm afternoon in August 1963. My parents asked if I was interested in going to the Los Angeles Coliseum in a few weeks' time. The massive Coliseum hosted many sporting events, but the event my parents were keen to get me to was quite different. Billy Graham, the Christian evangelist, was conducting a meeting there. My initial response was that it was the last place on earth I wanted to be. For the next few weeks the meeting was brought to my attention again and again, until I finally agreed to go.

September is usually a dry month in southern

California, but on Wednesday 4 September 1963, rain came bucketing down from the sky. As a result, the huge Coliseum – which boasts a capacity of 100,000 – was only about one-fifth full that evening. From where I was seated, Billy Graham appeared like a tiny dot down at ground level, but his words were spoken with great power and authority. He quoted from John 4:23–24: *'A time is coming and has now come when the true worshipers will worship the Father in spirit and truth, for they are the kind of worshipers the Father seeks. God is spirit, and his worshipers must worship in spirit and in truth.'*

The word 'truth' struck me. An inward voice seemed to confront me, 'David, you are not living the truth. You live for your own selfish needs, for your own success. You need to change. You need to start living in truth.'

I tried to convince myself that my thoughts were not those a US Marine should have. I had been trained to show no signs of weakness. I had drunk six cans of beer before driving to the meeting, and tried to convince myself that my crazy thoughts were a result of the booze. The more I tried to justify myself, however, the more uncomfortable I became. I began to realize that my sins had separated me from God. I don't remember if Billy Graham said those words or not, but it felt like a huge magnet was tugging on my heart, pulling me towards God. 'You have to let Jesus become the boss of your life,' the evangelist concluded.

When the invitation to receive Christ was given, a stream of people left their seats all around me and made their way down onto the field. I knew that if I took that step I would have to leave my present circle of friends and start to walk in a completely different way, but I was ready and willing to do so. I felt I had cheated God and lived a lie, and I knew that I had to throw off the false and start living in truth. Right then I heard the voice of Billy Graham cut across my inward struggle. He said, 'God is speaking to someone tonight who is in his late twenties. God is telling that person to be converted and to humble himself like a little child. A little child does not need to understand everything, yet he believes. So should this man believe...'

I was sitting sixty rows back in the grandstand, yet I knew the preacher was speaking to me. I edged my way out of my seat and to the aisle. Then something remarkable happened. It was as though somebody met me and took me down to the field. I realized that 'Someone' was Jesus. Along with hundreds of other contrite people, I bowed my head and repented of my sins, asking Jesus to come and take possession of my life.

That day – more than forty years ago – I met Jesus for the first time in my life. He has never left or forsaken me since.

Chapter Two:
Called to Serve

After meeting Jesus, I went to work the next morning and had such warmth to my personality that one of the women presumed I must have done well gambling the previous night. 'No way!' I replied, 'You'll never guess why I am so happy, so I'll go ahead and tell you. I accepted the Lord. I'm saved!'

At first my workmates thought my newfound religious passion was a joke, but within a few days they knew it was real. My actions and attitudes had been radically transformed. When they saw I had lost interest in gambling they realized I was a 'lost cause'. One of them complained, 'You don't even speak the same, man.' It was true. The swearing and filthy language that had been a part of my identity since the Marine boot camp had abruptly ended. My friends were astonished.

The remarkable thing was that my dramatic transformation in behavior was not something I had to conjure up or force myself to do through my own will power. If it was up to me, I couldn't have done it. Rather, the power to change came from Christ within. It now seemed natural to seek and talk about that which was good and pure, and unnatural to continue in the path I was used to. I had not adopted a new religion, oh no. I had met Jesus Christ! He was alive and well, and He lived in my spirit. The change was tangible. The difference was night and day. I had been inwardly dead, and now I was alive. I knew that for the rest of my life nobody could ever convince me that Jesus was not the Truth, because I had met Him!

I later read that my experiences were exactly what the

Bible says will happen to someone who repents and starts to follow Jesus. God, speaking through the Old Testament Prophet Ezekiel, promised, *'I will sprinkle clean water on you, and you will be clean; I will cleanse you from all your impurities and from all your idols. I will give you a new heart and put a new spirit in you; I will remove from you your heart of stone and give you a heart of flesh. And I will put my Spirit in you and move you to follow my decrees and be careful to keep my laws'* (Ezekiel 36:25–27). This is what happened to me! I had a new heart, and I was overwhelmed with the reality of God's love and power.

In the weeks and months that followed my conversion to Christ I began to read the Word of God on my knees in the evenings and I fell in love with Jesus Christ. I also began to fall in love with the Bible, which had seemed so lifeless and irrelevant to me previously. It now became my most precious possession. The Bible says, *'Therefore, if anyone is in Christ, he is a new creation; the old has gone, the new has come!'* (2 Corinthians 5:17). All things were becoming new in my life. I couldn't get enough of God's Word inside of me. On many occasions I stayed up reading for most of the night, the hours seemingly flying by.

The reality and presence of the Lord was so strong in my life that it was completely natural to want to share Him with as many people as possible. I started sharing the good news with African-American boys in the L.A. suburb of Watts, through an outreach called the Fisherman's Club. This part of the city was poor and ravaged by violence and drugs. The leader of the outreach told me, 'David, the kids there aren't too keen to listen to the gospel at this stage, but they enjoy playing football. Maybe you could go along and help them, and become their friend.' I found that the teenagers accepted me and wanted to know about Jesus after the very first game we played. That day, five of them gave their lives to Christ. The next week two more repented of their sins at the foot of the Cross. Within a month or two, twenty young men met together in a huddle for Bible study and prayer after each game. The same Jesus who had so powerfully captivated my heart at the Billy Graham meeting was also revealing His beautiful character to these precious boys.

As I continued to grow in faith, my knowledge of the Bible expanded greatly. I was excited to read that Jesus said, *'And the gospel must first be published among all nations'* (Mark 13:10, KJV). The word 'published' stood out to me like a beacon. I realized that with the gifts and talents God had given me, I could be involved in helping God's Word become accessible to lots of people who needed to know Jesus. I never thought I could be a preacher. I always felt awkward and embarrassed if called upon to speak in public. But I was excited to think there were other ways I could be involved in God's work.

The more I read the Bible, the more I was attracted to the urgency for all the nations of the world to hear the gospel and know Jesus. I wondered if I might one day be a missionary, but these thoughts were quickly discarded as I thought of many reasons why this was impossible. After all, I was a brand new Christian, and had never attended Bible College. Over the following weeks, however, I just couldn't shake off the idea that maybe God was calling me. My spirit leaped inside of me when I read the final verses in Matthew: *'All authority in heaven and on earth has been given to me. Therefore go and make disciples of all nations, baptizing them in the name of the Father and of the Son and of the Holy Spirit, and teaching them to obey everything I have commanded you. And surely I am with you always, to the very end of the age'* (Matthew 28:18–20). I realized Jesus had said these words to all of His followers. I was one of those, so He was also telling me to 'go and make disciples of all nations'.

A few days later the Bible grabbed my heart again, when I read: 'The Lord gave the word: great was the company of those that published it' (Psalm 68:11 KJV). I started to get the distinct impression that God was directing me through His Word. I went to my pastor, Dr Kelly Walberg, to discuss the matter with him. He told me, 'David, a brother from the Far East Broadcasting Company is coming to speak to our congregation this weekend. Why don't you come and meet with him and share what the Lord has been showing you?'

The Far East Broadcasting Company – or FEBC as they were commonly known – were a well-known mission. They broadcasted the gospel by short-wave radio all over Asia and the Soviet Union, into countries that had officially closed their doors to missionaries and their message. I listened intently to what the brother, Bud Jillson, shared, and heard that they were looking for a worker to help their literature ministry in the Philippines. When I went home that night I couldn't sleep. I told the Lord I was available, and filled out an FEBC application form, asking to be a missionary with their organization. They met with my wife and me, and said that sixteen other people had already applied for the job, but none of them was qualified and they had all been rejected. At the time I had only been a Christian for nine months. I continued to pray, asking God to open the door if it was His will, but there was silence. Thankfully, my church had more faith than me! The missions committee even voted to support me for my first term of missionary service, even though no confirmation had been received from FEBC.

At this time my salary at the print shop greatly increased, and my boss offered me one of the largest contracts they had. This would have assured me of a very attractive future income, but I knew that God had called me to serve Him, so I turned it down. My boss looked at me, and even though he was not a Christian he said, 'I appreciate you, David. I really appreciate you.' He knew that something dramatic and real had happened in my heart, and he didn't want to stand in the way of my convictions.

One day while I was at work I received news that a letter had arrived from FEBC saying, 'Sorry, we can't use you.' I went home and talked to Jesus about it. It just didn't make sense. God had given me so many indications that this was what He wanted, and it all seemed to be lining up. Now all hope was dashed. I cried out to the Lord that night, asking Him to speak with the people at Far East Broadcasting and tell them they had made a mistake.

The very next day we received a phone call from a leader of the ministry, saying that we should disregard the letter because they had found a position for me!

Over the years I have learned that God wants to see if we are serious about serving Him or not. He is serious about us, but He wants to see if we are really serious about Him, or just playing games. It's no good to give up at the first sign of trouble or when things don't seem to go as smoothly as you expected. The Lord wants us to develop a spiritual and emotional backbone, and to teach us things like perseverance and long-suffering.

I have also come to see that the devil will try anything to keep someone from fulfilling his or her calling in God. You may find yourself being offered all kinds of things, even fame and fortune, or you may meet a potential spouse who seems just right for you, but who doesn't share the same call. Perhaps it is the Lord who allows these things to come so that He can test your heart, and see if you are really serious about serving Him. Jordan Grooms once wrote, 'If God calls you to be a missionary, don't stoop to be a king.'

The months flew by as the departure date drew near. It was hard to leave our church family, loved ones and relatives and the teenagers in Watts. As the plane took off from LAX, a mixture of excitement and sorrow swept over me. I didn't know how long it would be before I saw the beautiful shores of America again. It was truly a new start, in a country I had never been to, and among people I had never met.

Chapter Three:

A Heart for Asia

The good people at Far East Broadcasting made our task of settling into life in the Philippines relatively smooth after our arrival on 2 May 1965. The key location for the FEBC work in Manila was called Christian Radio City. This was the name the ministry gave to a 10-acre compound equipped with radio transmitters, recording studios and libraries. At Christian Radio City Filipinos, Chinese, Vietnamese, Burmese, Lao, New Zealanders, Australians, Canadians, Brits and Americans worked together in harmony, broadcasting the good news of Jesus Christ throughout Asia.

The large Marshburn Printing Press was located right next to the main transmitter room. Our three presses could print ten miles of paper per hour. This equated to 40,000 Gospels of John every hour. I was so thrilled to see the machines on my first day at work, but the Lord had some lessons to teach me. After being shown around the facilities, the Filipino foreman told me, 'Brother David, you'll be doing the stapling.'

I thought he was joking. I wondered if he was unaware of my past experience in the printing industry. Anyone could do stapling. They didn't need to bring me from the other side of the world for this. They could easily have hired a local to do the stapling!

God was testing my heart.

I swallowed my pride and began to work, stapling booklets by hand as they rolled off the printing press. For day after day, sweat poured down my face in the intense tropical heat and suffocating humidity.

For weeks I continued in the mind-numbing task of stapling, but with each staple a new realization dawned in my heart about what it meant to serve God, and my attitude slowly became more like Jesus. After all, if anyone had the right to complain, it was the Lord. I complained because I had been trained as a lithographer but was now being asked to do a lesser job. Jesus was none other than the Almighty Son of God, King of the Universe, yet He laid down His crown, left His heavenly throne, and willingly came to the earth as a lowly baby – even being born surrounded by filth and the stench of animal waste after no room could be found for his family at the inn. Imagine it! The Creator of all things was treated like a cast-off.

Over the years I've spent in Christian ministry, I have seen countless men and women with a desire to serve Jesus. Many are skilled and gifted individuals, well-spoken and with impressive personalities and credentials, but I have watched sadly as so many failed to fulfil their calling because they never understood this simple lesson: To serve God, you must first be willing to forsake your reputation and work for the glory of God and the betterment of others. There are many who desire exciting and headline-grabbing ministries in God's kingdom, but few who are happy to see someone else get the credit. God was teaching me the joy of sacrificial service in that sweaty print shop in Manila. He showed me that my heart and motives were more important to Him than any work I could perform. The more I worked, the more joyful I became, for I started to understand that each staple I inserted was my service unto the Lord. My job may have been a small one, but it was nevertheless important to God. There was no other place I would rather be. I understood what the Psalmist meant when he said: *'Better is one day in your courts than a thousand elsewhere; I would rather be a doorkeeper in the house of my God than dwell in the tents of the wicked'* (Psalm 84:10).

If you desire to serve God, you desire a good thing. But

as you step out on that path, read carefully the following admonition from the Scriptures:

> *Your attitude should be the same as that of Christ Jesus:*
> *Who, being in very nature God,*
> *did not consider equality with God something to be*
> *grasped,*
> *but made himself nothing,*
> *taking the very nature of a servant,*
> *being made in human likeness.*
> *And being found in appearance as a man,*
> *he humbled himself*
> *and became obedient to death –*
> *even death on a cross.* (Philippians 2:5–8)

When we first arrived in the Philippines, Papa Lacanilao was handed the responsibility for welcoming us to his nation and people. He was a godly saint who radiated the love of Jesus Christ. He helped us adjust to his culture and patiently showed me how to get around the city of Manila. Each time I went into the city with him, he shared Jesus Christ with people. He had me share my testimony too, which he translated into Tagalog. I saw many Filipinos come to Christ with Papa Lacanilao.

Being around such wonderful people had a tremendous impact on my life and my growth in Jesus Christ. The people working at Christian Radio City were dedicated disciples of the Lord. Every morning we met together for an hour. We worshipped the Lord, and then one of the missionaries or a Filipino would share something from God's Word. Whenever there was a pressing need, we would break into small groups, fervently lifting that need up to the Lord. It was a marvelous spiritual environment to be a part of.

Life was full of many personal struggles for my family and I. We had decided that if we ever had a need, we would ask God to provide, and God alone. We would not ask people, as we couldn't see any examples of this in the Bible.

Due to the erratic postal system in the Philippines, on occasions we went a month or two between receiving letters. Missionaries with FEBC were not paid a salary, but were required to raise their own support from their church and friends before coming to Asia. Not receiving letters meant we were not receiving support. On many occasions we were completely broke, and we even sat down for dinner without any food to put on our plates. Time and again, however, we saw the hand of God supply our needs. Bags of food were left anonymously outside our door, or another missionary would come and drop off some sandwiches, or a can of food, at the time we needed it most.

Once we only had 20 pesos in the whole world. At the time, 20 pesos was worth $5. I heard a knock on our door and found a desperate leper standing outside, asking for help so he could catch the bus to a leper colony in the countryside. I asked him how much the fare was, and he replied, 'Twenty pesos, sir.' I shuddered with the thought that the Lord wanted me to give away all the money in the world we had at that time, but inwardly I knew this was precisely what God was requiring. I gave the money to the man and said, 'God bless you.'

In the kitchen I collapsed into a chair and wept bitterly before the Lord. He had brought us to the other side of the world to serve Him, and we had been reduced to nothing. At least this is how I felt in my self-pity. The next day a letter arrived in our post box. It was from my home church in Redondo Beach. They had taken up a special offering for us, and were glad to forward it to us with much love in the Lord. I opened the paper to find a check for $1,000! God was starting to teach me how to live by faith, a journey that has continued my whole life.

Between 1965 and 1967 we printed millions of books and tracts for FEBC and other mission organizations such as the Pocket Testament League, Wycliffe Bible Translators and Every Home Crusades. It was a great blessing to know that multitudes of people throughout Asia were hearing the gospel and getting to know Jesus like I had done. During these years my responsibilities increased and I was involved with managing the press.

In 1965 I traveled to Hong Kong for the first time, where I was shown around the FEBC studios and familiarized with the radio broadcasting side of the ministry. Hong Kong seemed like another world to me. At the time I had a fear of Chinese food. I had heard that the Chinese eat snakes and drink their blood, and that sent chills up my spine. The first thing my hosts did was to take me to a Chinese restaurant. The meal was delicious, and I have never feared Chinese food again! The following day we went to the border, where we gazed through binoculars across a barbed wire fence into the People's Republic of China. All I could think about was that somewhere beyond the rice paddies and hills lived my Christian brothers and sisters who were suffering dreadfully under the barbaric rule of Mao Zedong.

I was asked to build relationships with the Chinese churches in Manila. This was my first real contact with Chinese people. The city's Chinese community was closely woven together like a beautiful scarf. There were seventeen Chinese churches in Manila, all of which worked together in harmony. Many of these believers became faithful supporters of the FEBC work.

In 1968 I was first asked to go to Vietnam to help solve the missionaries' printing needs. Missionaries from the Summer Institute of Linguistics (SIL) met me at Saigon airport. We immediately bonded together. They were the bravest and most dedicated disciples I had ever met. While the fighting between the North Vietnamese and the Americans was at its worst, SIL missionaries boldly continued their work of translating the Word of God for the many tribal groups living in the jungles.

Each morning before breakfast I joined all the

missionaries in a Bible study and prayer meeting. I loved the fellowship with these dear brothers and sisters who were willing to give up everything so that the tribes would have the Scriptures in their own languages. I learned that all the printing shops in Saigon had been closed because of the war, so the missionaries needed help from the outside. At first I didn't realize the cost these brave warriors had paid. On later trips to Saigon I learned that many of my new friends had lost their wives or their husbands during Viet-Cong ambushes. Amazingly, God's grace and joy had given them strength to stand tall through all the suffering, hurt and pain. Their example of true consecration gave me much strength in the later years of my ministry.

One evening I wanted to take a bath in the mission guesthouse. One of the missionaries took me to a little room where there was a steel washtub, a 50-gallon drum of water and a bucket. He said, 'Stand in the tub in your birthday suit, then take the bucket and pour water over your body and cover yourself with soap.' At the exact moment I was covered with soap, Viet-Cong soldiers attacked the neighborhood. The missionary called me to get out of the washroom immediately. I prayed, 'I am naked, Lord. I need help!' I poured water over my body as quickly as I could, jumped into my clothes and ran for the bunker. The Viet Cong bombed us for the next hour. The SIL missionaries remained calm, for they had been through this experience many times.

The next day was Sunday morning and we drove 25 miles to where more than 1,500 tribal Christians awaited our arrival. I was introduced to the pastor, a precious saint who had lost his eyes after being tortured by the Viet Cong. The missionaries later told me the blind pastor had led over 1,700 people to Jesus Christ, and had baptized most of them right in the midst of the war.

I returned home to the Philippines, and in the coming months all of our machinery, presses, folders, stitchers, binders and staff worked around the clock, printing many tons of gospel literature for Vietnam. We printed and shipped ten container loads of Christian literature for distribution in Vietnam during the war. Each container was 40 feet long. Three months after distribution, we received reports that 3,500 Vietnamese had already believed in the Lord Jesus and been baptized. This news greatly encouraged us and made our work worth all the energy, sweat and long hours we had put in. There was a deep spirit of thanksgiving in the hearts of all staff, glad to know that we were now having an impact in Vietnam as well as in the Philippines.

On one occasion in 1968, after my trip to Vietnam, I started to think about Mainland China. We were not printing any gospel literature for the world's most populated country, and it just didn't make sense to me. China at the time was in the grip of Mao's mad Cultural Revolution. Millions of people were being slaughtered throughout the country, and China's doors were tightly closed to the outside world. Nobody knew for sure what was going on behind the bamboo curtain, but the anecdotal evidence suggested that chaos and evil were reigning supreme. Thousands of mutilated bodies had floated down the Pearl River and turned up in Hong Kong waters.

To the human mind, the prospect of Christian ministry into China did not just seem bleak at the time. It seemed foolish to even contemplate it. Despite all of these thoughts, somehow a little voice deep within seemed to encourage me not to forget China, and I was increasingly challenged by the burden of getting God's Word into that land. A missionary named Bob Padrea often visited me at Marshburn Press. He was amazed to see all the literature being printed and shipped to Vietnam. One day in 1969, as we sat around a swimming pool in Manila, Bob asked me a question that would change the course of my life forever: 'Are you ready with literature for China when the door opens?'

I looked him right into the eye and asked him, 'Don't you know thousands of corpses are floating down the Pearl River into Hong Kong? Mao Zedong has launched the Cultural Revolution. His strategy is to bring revolution to the whole world by launching it in China.' This news did not faze Bob. I thought he was crazy to even mention the possibility of ministering in China, but his question continued to bug me. The fact was, if China did open up, we were not ready to take the Word of God there.

During my next visit to Vietnam and Hong Kong the Lord would not let the question of China leave my mind. After returning to Manila I got down on my knees and asked God two specific questions – 'Is China going to open up?' and, 'Do you want me to get involved with taking Scriptures to China?' I have found that when you get specific with God and you really mean it and don't doubt that you will receive an answer, then He will get specific with you.

I needed the Lord to confirm that this burden for China was something He had given me. A week after my prayer, the Lord woke me at two o'clock in the morning and said, 'My son, go down to your office and I will share with you the answers to your questions.'

I went to the office and He led me in the Bible to Psalm 37. I read, *'Do not fret because of evil men or be envious of those who do wrong; for like the grass they will soon wither, like green plants they will soon die away'* (Psalm 37:1–2). Later in the same Psalm I read, *'But the wicked will perish: The Lord's enemies will be like the beauty of the fields, they will vanish – vanish like smoke.... Those the Lord blesses will inherit the land, but those he curses will be cut off'* (Psalm 37:20, 22).

These words seemed to leap off the pages of my Bible and strike me deep within my spirit. I was so convinced that God was bringing a change to China that I wrote in the margin of my Bible: 'Mao falls. 1969.'

As for whether or not I should prepare for ministry in China, the Lord spoke powerfully to me from Acts 26:16–18: *'Now get up and stand on your feet. I have appeared to you to appoint you as a servant and as a witness of what you have seen of me and what I will show you.... I am sending you to them to open their eyes and turn them from darkness to light, and from the power of Satan to God, so that they may receive forgiveness of sins and a place among those who are sanctified by faith in me.'*

If you have never experienced God's rhema word entering your heart and becoming alive, it will be difficult to understand what happened to me that night in my office. These were not merely Bible verses that I found to justify my ideas. This was a holy time with the Lord, and from that night on I have never doubted my calling to China. I was far from being a Chinese person, and I knew little about their culture, history, or struggles. But that day God burned His love for China in my heart forever.

I knew that God was going to open it up for the gospel and His Kingdom, and He did.

Chapter Four:

Ten Million Bibles for China

When I first shared with missionaries about how God had spoken to me about China opening up, they did not share my enthusiasm, to say the least. In fact, most thought I was crazy! I never doubted that God was going to open China, however, nor did I question that He was calling me to get Bibles to His people there. I learned that just because God has given you a vision it doesn't mean you need to go and share it with everybody else. Joseph received a vision in which he saw his brothers bowing down before him, and he foolishly told his siblings straight away (see Genesis 37:5–11). Not surprisingly, his brothers did not share his enthusiasm, and harm resulted for Joseph.

Nehemiah, on the other hand, received a vision from God to rebuild the destroyed walls of Jerusalem. He quietly set off, saying, *'I had not told anyone what my God had put in my heart to do for Jerusalem. There were no mounts with me except the one I was riding on…. The officials did not know where I had gone or what I was doing, because as yet I had said nothing to the Jews or the priests or nobles or officials or any others who would be doing the work'* (Nehemiah 2:12, 16).

There is a time when we should keep what God has shown us to ourselves, and be very careful and slow to share it with others until the right time. Despite the wave of skepticism, there were a few men who encouraged me in the vision. When I shared with Bob Padrea about how God had spoken to me through His Word about China opening up, he got excited. As Bob and I prayed together on our knees, asking for God's guidance, the Lord showed us the next stage of this calling. It was as if the Almighty was challenging us to trust Him more. Two Bible verses that seemed to leap off the page and into our hearts were: *'Call to me and I will answer you and tell you great and unsearchable things you do not know'* (Jeremiah 33:3); and *'Look at the nations and watch – and be utterly amazed. For I am going to do something in your days that you would not believe, even if you were told'* (Habakkuk 1:5).

God wanted me to catch a glimpse of His greatness, and to allow Him to increase my faith accordingly. After much prayer He burdened me to provide 10 million Bibles for the Christians in Mainland China. We would call the mission 'Project Jericho'.

I knew there was a crisis for China's Christians at the time. Because of the intense persecution, most Bibles had been destroyed, and anyone caught with one suffered severe punishment. Some believers had buried their Bibles in the ground, waiting for the day when things would be better and they could dig them up again. In many instances, Bibles had to remain hidden for twenty years.

The few bits and pieces of news that did come out of China in those days were mostly anecdotal stories from overseas Chinese who had returned from visiting relatives in coastal areas. The great need was for Bibles. New believers had no way to get a copy, and few of the older Christians still had access to the Word of God. Some experts estimated there were approximately 10 million Christians in China at the time, and I prayed many times that God would use me however and wherever He wanted to, in order that these precious believers might once again be fed by His Word.

At the time I didn't really understand what it would cost me to see this vision become a reality. Certainly it was God's work, and He would need to do miracle after miracle to see it come to pass, but in God's wisdom He has decided that His work is usually carried out by ordinary people. He is looking for weak and lowly people to work with, and not the humanly strong and self-confident. Paul described it this way: *'We have this treasure in jars of clay to show that this all-surpassing power is from God and not from us. We are hard pressed on every side, but not crushed; perplexed, but not in despair; persecuted, but not abandoned; struck down, but not destroyed. We always carry around in our body the death of Jesus, so that the life of Jesus may also be revealed in our body. For we who are alive are always being given over to death for Jesus' sake, so that his life may be revealed in our mortal body'* (2 Corinthians 4:7–11).

These days there are many Christians who want to be used in the Lord's work, but they have not learned the secret that God is looking for weak and broken vessels to display His power. He cannot trust those whose motives are impure. Ninety-nine per cent of a person's motive to serve God may be good, but while that one per cent persists that seeks to glorify their own name, God cannot properly use them. He will not share His glory with another. The one per cent of impurity in a Christian's heart can easily grow and take over. Paul warned the church in Corinth: *'Your boasting is not good. Don't you know that a little yeast works through the whole batch of dough?'* (1 Corinthians 5:6).

I had received a vision from God for China, but that was the easy part. The more difficult and painful part was to submit to the process of God to refine and mould me into the kind of person He wanted me to be. Everyone who has been fruitful for the kingdom of God has gone through this process. It usually takes years. The good news is that you don't need to be some kind of spiritual giant to serve God. If that were true, very little would ever get done! It's about whether or not you are available to be broken, to die to self, and to be put back together by God. The Holy Spirit often took me back to the marvelous words in the twelfth chapter of Romans, showing me that my job was simply to give myself to God, to lay my body on His altar and ask Him to take control of me:

> I urge you, brothers, in view of God's mercy, to offer your bodies as living sacrifices, holy and pleasing to God – this is your spiritual act of worship. Do not conform any longer to the pattern of this world, but be transformed by the renewing of your mind. Then you will be able to test and approve what God's will is – his good, pleasing and perfect will. For by the grace given me I say to every one of you: Do not think of yourself more highly than you ought, but rather think of yourself with sober judgment, in accordance with the measure of faith God has given you. Just as each of us has one body with many members, and these members do not all have the same function, so in Christ we who are many form one body, and each member belongs to all the others. (Romans 12:1–5)

Eric Parson, who was responsible for the mission's international news service, was one of my close friends at FEBC. I looked up to him as a man of God. Eric wrote a brochure sharing how the Lord had spoken through His Word that Mao would fall and China would open to the gospel. Provocatively titled, 'China will Open Soon. Are you Ready?' the brochure challenged the readers to be alert and praying for China.

Bob shared this brochure with the seventeen Chinese churches in Manila, while I took copies with me whenever I traveled to Singapore, Thailand, Burma, Vietnam, or Hong Kong. Most missionaries thought we were out of our minds and paid little attention to the vision the Lord had given us.

One day a friend gave me a book and told me I should read it straight away. The title of the book was *God's Smuggler* by Brother Andrew. At first I was hesitant to start it due to my reading problems. I thought if I ever made it to the end it would be a miracle. As soon as I started to read the book, however, I couldn't put it down. I finished it in four days, which was a record for me.

God's Smuggler told how Andrew had been a messenger for the Dutch resistance movement during World War II, helping day and night to sabotage the Nazi control of Holland. Years later God called him to the dangerous task of delivering Bibles to Eastern Europe. The book also described Andrew's first visit to China in 1965.

I thought it would be neat to meet this Brother Andrew some time if I could, as we seemed to share the same heart for God's work. A short time later a letter arrived in my mailbox. There was no return name on the back of the envelope, but I noticed it had been sent from the Netherlands. I tore the envelope open and was amazed to find the letter was from Brother Andrew! It read:

> *Dear Brother David,*
>
> *While passing through Saigon and Bangkok recently, I heard your name in connection with your recent trip to Burma. As you can imagine, I was deeply interested and very much wanted to see you.... Please continue the good work, and let us pray that we can meet soon and discuss the work of getting Scriptures into Red China.*
>
> *Your brother in the great battle,*
> *Brother Andrew.*

I couldn't believe it. I had just finished reading *God's Smuggler*, and here was the very same man encouraging me! For some time I sat down trying to take it in, wondering how on earth Brother Andrew had even heard of my vision for China. I later learned that he regularly traveled with Corrie ten Boom, that wonderful Dutch lady who was interned in a German concentration camp during the Second World War for helping to hide Jews. Her moving story was told in the best-selling book and movie, *The Hiding Place*. As Andrew and Corrie traveled through South-east Asia, my name kept popping up. Various missionaries and Christian leaders who had read our brochure told their Dutch visitors that a former US Marine named David had been traveling throughout the region trying to find depositories where he could leave Bibles near Chinese border crossings.

Unfortunately, we never met during Brother Andrew's trip, so when he returned to Holland he penned a letter to me. I was excited, as it seemed the Lord was putting the pieces of the puzzle together for getting His Word to the believers in China.

***

In December 1969 we returned to the United States for the first time in over four-and-a-half years. My mother and friends gave us a warm welcome home. Unfortunately, my father was no longer with us. Less than a year after arriving in the Philippines I had received a telephone call from California. My mother broke the news that my dad had gone to heaven. He had suffered a massive heart attack and died on the way to the hospital on 2 October 1966, at the age of just 59. My mom had always been a very strong person, both intellectually and spiritually. She held back her emotions while telling me.

I said, 'Mom, I'll catch a plane right away and come home to be by your side.' She replied, 'No, David. Your father and I want you to stay on the mission field and accomplish what the Lord has given you to do. I'll be all right. Many friends are helping me, and Dad is looking down from heaven watching you.'

Now that I was home, I visited the FEBC Headquarters in California and met with the leaders of the ministry. When I shared my vision for 10 million Bibles for China it was suggested I should take a step of faith and go to Europe to meet with Brother Andrew.

I also met with Bill and Cliff Marshburn, and told them

how the Lord was using their press in Manila. The Marshburn brothers were uncles of the late President Richard Nixon. They were the largest growers of carrots in America, and were good stewards of the wealth God gave them. They gave a lot of money to China mission work, and of course funded the Marshburn Press in Manila for the purpose of spreading the gospel throughout Asia. Five years later President Nixon helped normalize relations between the United States and China, and this led to China gradually opening its doors to the rest of the world, and to the gospel.

When I shared with them the vision for 10 million Bibles for China, Bill shouted, 'Hallelujah!' Together the three of us praised and thanked the Lord. Bill asked the Lord to make a way for me to go to Holland and meet Brother Andrew.

Everyone seemed in agreement that I should go and meet Andrew, but there was just one problem. Such a trip could not be paid for by the mission budget, and I had little personal money, certainly not enough for the airfare to Europe and back. My mission leaders had allowed me to go to Holland, but on condition that God provided the funds and I didn't ask anyone for money.

Bill walked me to the gate in his old farmer overalls. When we got to my car, he held out his hand and said, 'Hey, kid, take this. It's enough money to get you to New York. If God is in the Bibles for China idea, He'll make a way for you to cross the Atlantic Ocean and meet Brother Andrew.' I thanked Bill as we hugged goodbye.

I sent Brother Andrew a letter telling him I was coming by faith to meet him in Holland. I received a reply, warmly welcoming me. What he didn't know was that I only had enough money to get to the other side of America, and the rest of the trip would require a miracle from the Lord!

On the way to New York I stopped in Fort Washington, Pennsylvania, where I spent some time with a dear British couple, Neil and Jean MacKinnon, who had served as missionaries in the Philippines. Neil was one of my closest prayer partners. I had learned from him how to intercede before God. We reminisced about our time in the Philippines and about the wonderful things we had seen the Lord do. On one occasion we had held an open-air evangelistic meeting together and seen hundreds of Filipinos come to know the Lord Jesus Christ.

Neil asked me if I had enough time to attend a Full Gospel Businessmen's conference with him in Washington D.C. I did, but was wary about how I could pay the accommodation and food expenses while I was there. I only had $35 in the world, and the Lord had to stretch it to get me to Europe and back! Before I had a chance to say no, Neil interjected: 'David, someone has already offered to cover all your expenses in Washington if you can come.' That settled it.

Our mystery benefactor had booked us in to stay at the plush Washington Hilton Hotel during the conference. One morning a lady I had never met entered the lift I was on and stared straight at me. I felt uncomfortable and couldn't remember if I was supposed to know her or not. She then turned to me and said, 'Young man, we've never met, but the Spirit of the Lord is telling me to empty my purse to you.' She handed me $12 and said, 'This is all I have, God bless you.' I thanked her. That sweet old lady supported the church in China for many years.

At the end of the conference we met another elderly lady who invited Neil and me to a prayer meeting, where she prophesied over us. Without her knowing our background or any personal details, she told me God would use me to reach and bless many people in China. Then she told Neil that the Lord intended to make him a blessing in a ministry to young people. Nobody except Neil's wife and I knew that they were praying about returning to the United

Kingdom to engage in youth work. This God-appointed meeting proved to be a turning point in our lives.

After the conference I headed to New York City to see another family I had wanted to visit, the Olsens. I had come to know them five years earlier. They were now working with David Wilkerson among the gangs and drug addicts on the streets of New York City, and they had even featured in his book, *The Cross and the Switchblade*.

I made my way to the Olsens' stone home in Bethpage and excitedly approached their door. My knock was answered by one of their daughters, Marie. 'Brother David!' she shrieked. I took a step forward, expecting a warm greeting and invitation to come inside, when all of a sudden she turned and left me standing there. I shivered in the cold, wondering what was going on. Then, just as mysteriously, she returned and handed me an envelope.

'Open it,' Marie urged with a smile. The envelope had my name written on it. I tore it open and found $300 inside. I was lost for words. The money was exactly what I needed to get across the Atlantic Ocean and back.

Marie finally broke in, 'Well, don't just stand there. Thank the Lord.'

'Thank you, Lord!' I exclaimed, and then I threw back my head and laughed with joy. Later, over coffee and sandwiches, Marie told me how God had directed her to save part of her tithe for me ever since the day I had left for Manila four-and-a-half years earlier. She had no idea that I planned to go to Holland, or that I had no money to do so. Marie had figured that one day she would see me again, and when she did, she would hand me whatever amount of money she had collected up to that point.

Marie's testimony humbled me, as I realized God had been taking care of me and preparing me for this work much longer than I had known. I was reminded what Jesus had said just before teaching the Lord's prayer to his disciples: *'And when you pray, do not keep on babbling like pagans, for they think they will be heard because of their many words. Do not be like them, for your Father knows what you need before you ask him'* (Matthew 6:7–8).

I headed for Holland sure in the knowledge that the Lord was leading me and His faithful provision was taking me every inch of the way.

Chapter Five:
Dutch Treat

On 2 March 1970, I stepped off my flight and onto Dutch soil for the first time. Four of Brother Andrew's staff members were there to meet me. 'We're treating you to dinner,' they announced.

The dinner proved to be an experience I would never forget, as a traditional Dutch fare of raw herring and raw onions was placed before me. My hosts watched intently as with each bite I prayed harder, every sinew in my body searching in vain for an alternative meaning to Jesus' command: *'Stay in that house, eating and drinking whatever they give you'* (Luke 10:7).

The moment I finished the meal, my Dutch hosts rose as one and gave me a standing ovation. 'Congratulations! David, you're the first non-Dutchman we have seen who has finished raw herring and onions. We thought Americans hated it!'

I thought it was better to come clean with my hosts, so I told them, 'You better believe it. We do hate it. If you want to know the truth, I asked the Lord to help me swallow every mouthful.'

All five of us howled with laughter. Having passed the test, my hosts announced, 'Now our American brother deserves to eat the rest of the dinner.' The cook brought in a hot soup followed by a delicious roast.

When I stepped into Brother Andrew's office for the first time the next morning I instantly knew that he was a man who loved to smile. The laughter lines around his eyes and mouth were well worn and natural. In the days we spent together, I felt very much at home with this godly

Dutchman. I shared my vision for getting the Scriptures to the Chinese Church, and showed him my notes in the margin of my Bible where the Lord had spoken to me that China would open up. After so much doubt and skepticism had greeted me elsewhere, my spirit soared as Andrew nodded in agreement and understanding.

On the second day, Brother Andrew received a call from a young mission leader who was in Switzerland and needed 500 Russian Bibles to take with him to the Soviet Union. We drove down through Holland and France, and met with the young man. His name was Loren Cunningham, and his ministry, 'Youth With a Mission', had experienced explosive growth and was doing many wonderful things for the Lord around the world. I also met a brother named Francis Schaeffer, who was a great theologian and author.

On the long drive back to Holland, Andrew and I encountered a huge snowstorm for most of the way. As we drove together, I described how I had visited countries along China's borders – including Burma, Laos, Afghanistan, Pakistan and Hong Kong – and found people willing to store Bibles. I expected him to be thrilled with the news. Instead, he leaned forward and earnestly said, 'Brother David, that's not enough. You need to go to China yourself.'

The thought of personally going to China had never seriously crossed my mind. America was the arch-enemy of the Chinese Communists, and getting a visa to China was extremely rare. I wanted to explain the reality of the situation to my Dutch friend, but then I remembered whom I was sitting with. Brother Andrew never limited God. His faith seemed boundless, and I recalled the many stories in *God's Smuggler* that told how the Lord had performed the impossible for him. Before I said anything, Andrew interjected, 'If God wants you in China, He'll open the door for you to go through.' 'And brother,' he added, 'I believe the door is already open.'

Brother Andrew shared his deep desire to make contact with the 'underground' believers in China. He yearned to find out whether the church had survived, and what could be done to help and encourage it. He explained, 'When I visited China in 1965, the whole nation was in the grip of fear. I offered a Bible to my interpreter, but she handed it back. She claimed she had no time for reading. In desperation, I tried giving Bibles away to people on the street. People appeared to feel pity for me when they stopped to see what I was offering, and nobody took a single book.'

Andrew was so discouraged by his sole visit to China that he had often wondered if the church in China had perished. 'Brother David, I believe you should find the church in China. Then help it, encourage it, feed it, and love it.'

I remained in Holland for two weeks, enjoying rich fellowship with Brother Andrew, his family, and their co-workers. We spent hours talking, praying and sharing from the Scriptures. Towards the end, I got up the courage to tell Andrew what almost everybody else had ridiculed. 'I'm praying with a friend in Manila for 10 million Bibles for China,' I said, as calmly as possible.

I looked into Andrew's face, straining to discern his reaction. Many others had already assured me it was a foolish and whimsical dream. After much thought, Andrew replied, 'Well, it may sound like a lot of Bibles, but I'm sure from God's perspective it's just a drop in the ocean. After all, 10 million is just one per cent of the Chinese population. Surely we can trust Him to provide such a tiny proportion.' Then Andrew said the words that greatly encouraged and assured me, 'I stand with you in this vision, David.'

It became clear to us that we both had strengths and resources that complemented one another. I worked with printing presses and had helped publish millions of booklets with FEBC, while Andrew had vast experience crossing Communist borders in Eastern Europe and the Soviet Union. 'You are the one who can show us how to get into closed countries,' I said. Once again, Andrew challenged my thinking. 'You're wrong, David. China is not closed. No country is closed. Jesus said, *"I have placed before you an open door which no one can shut"* (Revelations 3:8). All we have to do is obey the Lord, go, and He will show us where that open door is. Right now many people might think you are crazy, but I have found that when you do something for God that nobody else has dared to do, others will soon follow, as long as you don't care who gets the credit!'

Although I was relatively new to all this, Brother Andrew had many years of experience working in Communist countries. He knew a lot about how they worked, and the atmosphere of fear and intimidation they loved to create. He told me an allegory that I never forgot. 'David, tell me,' he asked, 'If we placed a lion and a lamb together in the same enclosure, what would happen?'

'The lamb would be torn to shreds in a moment,' I replied.

'Yes, David, but what would happen if we starved the lion until it was so weak it could hardly raise its head, and we fed the lamb until it became robust?'

'Not much would happen then, I suppose.'

'You're wrong, brother,' Andrew said. 'The lamb would be the conqueror. He could even step on the lion and claim the victory.'

As I struggled to come to grips with the meaning of the story, my Dutch friend explained, 'You see, the lion is Communism, and the lamb is the persecuted church. If we feed the lamb, it will grow strong. The emptiness of atheism is destined to weaken the Communist ideal as people realize it will never fill the spiritual void they feel in their hearts. In due time, the lion will be weakened and the lamb will conquer!'

The truth of this allegory seared itself into my mind and heart, and I thought what a great privilege it would be to feed God's lambs in China.

I greatly enjoyed my trip to Holland, and I found in Brother Andrew a man with a similar passion to my own. I left knowing that God had planted something deep within my heart. As I boarded my flight back to America I was excited and passionate about the vision God had called me to. My perspective had changed. Now the prospect of getting Bibles inside China didn't just seem possible, it was inevitable. It was time to find out how God would open the door to China.

Chapter Six:

God's Little Red Book

For the next year I continued in my work with FEBC, but the constant call and burden for China gnawed away at my heart. I became frustrated because of the lack of progress in the vision God had given me. The hope I had when I met with Brother Andrew six months earlier had evaporated and I felt hopeless and inwardly ill. The Bible puts it this way: *'Hope deferred makes the heart sick, but a longing fulfilled is a tree of life'* (Proverbs 13:12).

The thing that had got me down more than any other was all the negative responses I received from just about the entire mission community whenever I shared my vision for China. Many of the older missionaries looked down their noses at me and sighed, as if to say, 'Young man, you are new to this work and impetuous. Just be patient, and you will change and become like us.' Even some of those brothers and sisters who had encouraged me in the vision earlier now seemed to think it was a foolish dream.

One Sunday morning I watched a Christian television show from America. The preacher talked about bitterness, and how it often springs up from discouragement and can choke both our lives and our vision if we let it grow. Nobody benefits when bitterness is present. The Bible warns, *'See to it that no one misses the grace of God and that no bitter root grows up to cause trouble and defile many'* (Hebrews 12:15). I realized that over the last six months I had become increasingly bitter because of my frustration.

Discouragement can be like a disease. It can strip you of all your energy and peace, and cause you to become cynical. Dis-courage-ment is just that. It breeds the oppo-site of courage, making us weak and fearful. When your hopes and dreams have been crushed it is a terrible thing. The Bible says, *'A cheerful heart is good medicine, but a crushed spirit dries up the bones'* (Proverbs 17:22). In countless places throughout the Scriptures, the Lord exhorts His people to 'Be strong and courageous'. We all need to be encouraged, and we are blessed indeed if the Lord has sent someone into our life who can hold our hands up in the battle and share the burden with us.

My spiritual life had plummeted since my visit to Holland. I struggled to pray, and had little joy or strength to serve God. I felt like a small boat with a broken engine, being tossed around on the sea with no sense of direction. I got on my knees and asked the Lord to forgive me and to remove all the poison and bitterness from my heart. As I did, the Holy Spirit helped me to relax and the chains that had started to grip my spirit fell off.

In May 1971 I traveled to America on work-related busi-ness. While I was there, Brother Andrew sent me a letter saying he was concerned because he hadn't heard any more news about my vision to get God's Word into China. The simple answer was that I had nothing to report. Andrew was traveling to the States, and sent me a ticket so I could go and meet with him during a one-day stopover he had in New York.

I told my Dutch friend what had happened to me since our last meeting more than a year earlier. He encouraged me and we prayed together and talked extensively about the challenges of getting God's Word into China. The coun-try was practically shut off from all outside influence, and was in the grip of the Cultural Revolution.

Mao Zedong had somehow transformed himself from a political figure to being a god to the masses, who eagerly hung on his every word. His 'Little Red Book' was read reli-giously by people all across China. It contained his favorite sayings, and outlined his goals for the nation. Those goals did not allow for the existence of God. All other books were looked down upon, and the fanatical Red Guards – teams of young cadres who zealously carried out Mao's orders – burned millions of books. The most hated of all books were religious Scriptures, and anyone caught with a Bible was brutally treated.

Brother Andrew reminded me of how nobody would take his Bibles when he visited China in 1965. It was obvious that people there now would not accept anything that looked like a normal Bible. During our prayer time, the Lord seemed to show us the way forward. The answer was so simple that I was amazed nobody had thought of it earlier. Mao's book was approximately the size of a Chinese New Testament. We should print New Testaments with red covers, just like Mao's book, and in the same size, shape and format. Christians would be able to carry and read God's Word without arousing suspicion!

The second thing we decided during our meeting was that we needed to organize a conference for all the various Christian leaders and organizations interested in China. No inter-denominational meeting focused solely on China had taken place since the 1940s.

I flew out of JFK Airport with new vigor and an order from Brother Andrew to print 25,000 Little Red New Testaments for the church in China. The Lord had answered my prayers, and my direction was clear once again. That day was like a fresh breeze in my soul.

**

To print 25,000 Chinese New Testaments was a giant leap of faith, as at the time we didn't have any contacts inside China. After obtaining two of Mao's Little Red Books, we carefully copied the dimensions and appearance so that our books would appear identical on the outside. I watched excitedly as the first of the books rolled off the Marshburn Press in October 1972. They were shipped to Hong Kong, India, Laos, and Thailand.

From all four locations, God's little red book began to penetrate the bamboo curtain. From India and Thailand they entered Burma and then across the mountains on the backs of donkeys and men into China's Yunnan Province. From Hong Kong, copies of God's Word were carried across the border into Guangdong Province by Chinese believers visiting their relatives. At the border crossings they encountered no problems, even when the officers opened their bags and saw the red books. They waved them through, thinking they must have been ardent Communist Party members!

The most effective location for getting the books into Mainland China was from the small country of Laos, bordering South-west China. Laos at the time was a free country (it became Communist a few years later in 1975), and many of the Bibles entered China through our contacts there. We also successfully delivered 50,000 Gospels of John into China at this time.

Our main contact in Laos was a Chinese pastor named Ling, who had fled into Laos after being cruelly persecuted by the Communists. From Laos he constantly risked his life in order to get God's Word to his brothers and sisters in China. When I first met Ling his physical appearance took me by surprise. He had a huge scar across his face, and when I reached out to shake his hand, I discovered his right arm was missing from below the elbow.

This saint preferred to speak about the goodness of God rather than his own experiences, but I later learned how the Communists had arrested him in Hunan Province in 1952, sentencing him to five years in a prison labor camp because of his Christian faith. The authorities warned him to stop telling others about Jesus, but Ling could not help himself. After his release from prison in 1957 a revival broke out in his hometown and this infuriated the Communists. Ling was again dragged off to prison. As punishment for his obstinacy, he was tied up against a wall with his arms outstretched. Two soldiers stood in front of the faithful pastor. One suddenly bashed Ling with his rifle butt, slicing his face open. As blood gushed out, the soldiers released the defenseless captive from the rope that held him by cutting off his right arm at the elbow.

After meeting Pastor Ling and others like him, I gained a fresh understanding of the level of sacrifice and commitment so many Chinese believers had endured. To them, the cross was not a fashion accessory to be worn on a chain around the neck. The cross was real, and it was painful. They could say with the Apostle Paul, *'Let no one cause me trouble, for I bear on my body the marks of Jesus'* (Galatians 6:17).

The benefits of suffering in the lives of these believers was evident for all to see. The persecution they had endured produced an acute awareness of their own brokenness and their need for Christ. This resulted in them having a level of intimacy in their relationship with Jesus that made them a joyous blessing to all those they met. Paul knew of this special blessing and spoke of it this way: *'I want to know Christ and the power of his resurrection and the fellowship of sharing in his sufferings, becoming like him in his death, and so, somehow, to attain to the resurrection from the dead'* (Philippians 3:10-11).

The Word of God was trickling into Communist China and getting into the hands of the believers. I was thrilled to know that the vision God had given me was finally becoming a reality. The small number of Bibles making their way into China hardly suggested 10 million copies would flood the land, but it was a start. A tiny trickle can turn into a mighty river if Jesus stands in the water with you. The largest tree in the forest was once a tiny seed. We should never *'despise the day of small beginnings'* (Zechariah 4:10).

In the early 1950s, many people believed it was impossible for a man to run a mile in less than four minutes. Roger Bannister proved them wrong, becoming the first to break the mark in 1954. Within a year, more than a dozen other men had broken the four-minute barrier. Often all it takes is someone to do the 'impossible' and others will follow. I have seen a similar dynamic taking place in God's family. After the Word of God started going through the bamboo curtain into Communist China, and reports trickled back that Christian brothers and sisters were being nourished by it, people's perspectives started to change. Some of the missionaries who had belittled my vision now began to ask, 'If he can do it, why not us?'

In the Bible there are many examples of men and women doing the 'impossible', against all human odds. When young David was told to take some lunch to his brothers on the front lines, he arrived to find the entire army crippled with fear because of the taunts of Goliath. The Bible records that, *'Saul and all the Israelites were dismayed and terrified'* (1 Samuel 17:11). David was not afraid of the giant, for he had spent much time with the Almighty God, and he knew that Goliath was no more than a flea in comparison. As you know, David boldly advanced on the Philistine, God gave a great victory and David cut off Goliath's head. Have you ever noticed what happened next? The Bible says, *'When the Philistines saw that their hero was dead, they turned and ran. Then the men of Israel and Judah surged forward with a shout and pursued the Philistines to the entrance of Gath and to the gates of Ekron. Their dead were strewn along the Shaaraim road to Gath and Ekron'* (1 Samuel 17:51–52).

Just minutes earlier the Israelite soldiers had considered the prospect of beating Goliath to be impossible, and were terrorized by his taunts and blasphemies. Now the impossible had happened, and their perspective experienced a dramatic shift. One bold act of faith in the kingdom of God can result in a flood of believers experiencing a breakthrough into a new freedom and sense of victory.

If you know that God has called you to something, be bold and courageous. Ask Him to send you someone who will encourage you in the fight. Although it is good to have advice and counsel, be careful about submitting your plans before too many committees. You might just find that those 'mature' members will try to bring the kiss of death to your God-inspired plans. Do not give up or shrink back. Jesus didn't give up on His plan to save you. The Bible says, *'My righteous one will live by faith. And if he shrinks back, I will not be pleased with him. But we are not of those who shrink back and are destroyed, but of those who believe and are saved'* (Hebrews 10:38–39).

Chapter Seven:
I Will Build My Church

At the start of 1973 I felt uneasiness in my heart because by focusing on what God had called me to do, I found myself with less time to spend on my job at FEBC. One night I was so troubled that I decided to stay up and pray to the Lord until He showed me what I should do. I opened my Bible and knelt on the wooden floor, reading God's Word and praying intermittently. I asked the Lord to search my heart and give me direction. Seven hours later I rose from my knees with the peace of God in my heart. The struggle was over. Through several passages of Scripture in Isaiah, I believe the Lord showed me it was time to leave FEBC and start working full-time on this new vision for China.

Although I was sure of the way forward, it was still difficult to leave FEBC, who had treated us superbly since we joined them. I loved the work, and my family and I had developed many wonderful friendships with other families on the compound. It would have been more comfortable to remain in what we were doing, but the Lord had another plan, and that was the way we had to go.

I didn't know whether I should approach Brother Andrew to see if we could join his ministry, or if we should start a new work. I sent a letter to my Dutch friend, praying that his answer would be a confirmation about what we should do. A few weeks later a reply arrived from Holland. Andrew greatly encouraged me that I had taken the correct step, and concluded, 'Welcome to the ministry!' I stepped down from FEBC, and was warmly received into the ministry of Open Doors. I was soon appointed leader of

Open Doors Asia, and continued to operate from our base in the Philippines.

Many of the missionaries who had worked in China in the past held little hope that the Chinese Church would survive the onslaught of Communism. Pessimistic articles appeared in their newsletters, lamenting that if the door to China ever reopened, missionaries would need to bring the gospel and start again from scratch. Mao's wife, Jiang Qing, told foreign visitors, 'Christianity in China has been confined to the history section of the museum. It is dead and buried.' After a Christian delegation from the United States visited China, they reported, 'There is not a single Christian left.'

In 1973 and later, however, an altogether different picture began to emerge from the lips of the overseas Chinese Christians who had visited their relatives. It became clear that the church in China had not only survived the decades of cruel oppression, but had actually flourished and grown in the midst of hardship! The earliest estimates suggested the church in many places had grown 400 per cent since the advent of Communism in 1949. We needed to confirm if this was true, and if there were believers left inside, we needed to find out how many there were, where they lived, and how we could best help them. We prayed frequently, asking the Lord to lead us to the right people. I traveled to Hong Kong to conduct some research. At the time visas for Westerners wishing to enter China were virtually non-existent, whereas Chinese people living in overseas countries were allowed to visit their relatives inside China.

I met a Filipino-Chinese, Brother Joseph, who had just returned to Hong Kong after visiting China with his Uncle Liu. Little did I realize it at the time, but Brother Joseph was to play a large part in my life and work for years to come. After we spent much time together praying and discussing how to help the believers, they both agreed to help find contacts inside China. Joseph and Liu put aside their busy lives in the Philippines in order to help the brothers and sisters in China. These were dark times in China, and there was the potential for great danger to these two faithful servants of God. Many other Christians warned them not to enter China, outlining the dire consequences if they were caught doing Christian work.

To begin with they spent months in Hong Kong trying to get information from Christians returning from across the border, but the situation was so tense under Mao's vicious dictatorship that nobody would share any information with them. The Communist Party encouraged all citizens to report on any activity that seemed out of the ordinary. The atmosphere in China at the time was charged with paranoia and danger, so it was not surprising that Christians didn't want to provide the names of their relatives. After praying and persevering for six long months, Joseph and Liu were finally given the name of just one Christian contact in China.

Joseph and his uncle travelled into China at the start of 1974. They took with them 16 copies of our Little Red New Testaments. On the day before they crossed the border I sent a coded message to Brother Andrew in Holland saying, 'Apples are on their way'. Understanding what I meant, Andrew sent an urgent prayer request throughout Open Doors offices around the world and thousands of people started to pray for their trip.

The next day, when Joseph and Uncle Liu crossed the border from Macao into China, the customs officers ordered them to open their suitcase. Lying right on top of their clothes were the 16 red New Testaments. One officer said, 'It looks like we have a Party member here,' but when he thumbed through the pages he found no mention of Chairman Mao. All he found was Jesus Christ and the Word of God. He asked the two couriers, 'Are you Christians?' With rapidly beating hearts, they thought, 'If we deny that we're Christians then Jesus will tell the Father in heaven. But if we admit that we are Christians, we will be in trouble too.' Joseph and his uncle told the officer, 'Yes, we are Christians.' The officer asked, 'Tell me, how did this happen?' For the next 25 minutes the two Filipinos shared Jesus Christ with that man and a group of ten more customs officers who came over and listened intently as they flicked through the New Testaments. At the end, each officer took a copy for their 'personal use' and allowed the rest into China!

The duo continued on their way. Joseph and his uncle not only found the one contact that had been given to them after six months of prayer, but they met many Christians who were alive and strong in the Lord. In Guangdong Province they visited one house church that had come through the furnace of affliction and persecution, and was connected with other small fellowships throughout their province, and even in other parts of China. They then traveled to Shanghai with the name of another believer, whom they had not been able to contact in advance. When Joseph and Liu knocked on her door, the old saint warmly welcomed them inside as though she was expecting them. She explained that God had given her a vision earlier that morning while she was praying. In the vision she saw that two men would visit her later in the day, and Joseph and his uncle matched the description.

In town after town, Joseph and Liu met with Christians in small groups of ten or twenty believers. Although restrictions were tighter in the larger cities and towns, they were told that in some rural areas hundreds – and even one or two thousand – believers regularly met together to worship the Lord and hear the teaching of God's Word. Each group of Christians the travelers visited told how God had sustained them through the storm, and that their greatest need was for Bibles. Some of the believers gave Joseph and Liu all the money they had in the world – usually just a few dollars – in the hope they could somehow get them a Bible.

The Word of God for them was not something to put on the shelf and read from time to time. Rather, they were so desperate and hungry that for them the Bible was life and death.

In later years many testimonies came out of China telling of the level of intense hunger for God's Word that existed in those days. Brother Yun, in his book, *The Heavenly Man*,* told how as a new believer in 1974 he prayed for a Bible until his own family thought he was losing his mind. One hundred days later the Lord answered his desperate cries in a remarkable manner. The love and respect the Chinese believers held for God's Word reminded me of what David had written long before: *'They are more precious than gold, than much pure gold; they are sweeter than honey, than honey from the comb'* (Psalm 19:10).

The Chinese Christians also said how much they appreciated and needed the daily gospel radio broadcasts coming into China on short-wave radio. It was considered a serious crime for anyone to tune in to broadcasts from overseas, yet many of the believers listened to their radios secretly under their blankets with the volume turned down to a minimum. When I heard this I greatly rejoiced, and couldn't wait to share it with my colleagues at FEBC.

In one location near the coastal city of Shantou – where missionaries had first brought the gospel in 1847 – our coworkers were told a remarkable story of God's provision and power. An elderly brother had believed in the Lord for many years when the Communists took control of the area. The 'Old Man', as the other believers affectionately called him, came from an impoverished family, and he had never learned to read or write properly. Despite these impediments, after he received the Lord Jesus, the old man

---

* Brother Yun with Paul Hattaway, *The Heavenly Man: The Remarkable True Story of Chinese Christian Brother Yun* (London: Monarch Books, 2002).

70

proved to be a powerful evangelist, leading hundreds of people to faith in Christ throughout the district.

Because of his extreme poverty, the government decided to make a show by giving the old preacher the best house in the village and a generous supply of food. In the early 1950s they also made him Chairman of the village's Communist committee, thinking that when the old man abandoned his religion he would become a shining example of the goodness of Communism to the rest of the population.

The elderly brother, however, belonged to Jesus Christ first and foremost. He used the large house he had been provided with to hold house church meetings, and distributed the food he was given to those believers in need. After some time the government saw that their plan was badly backfiring. They issued an ultimatum to the 'chairman'. He had to choose between his faith and the new lifestyle and status he had been afforded by the authorities. Although he knew that he would be consigned back to a life of extreme poverty and hardship, the old Christian man did not hesitate for a moment. 'I choose Jesus!' he boldly declared.

The enraged officials threw him out of the house. He had nowhere to go, but another believer was able to provide him with a small room on the side of his shack. China at the time was suffering terribly from Mao's disastrous economic experiments, and millions of people throughout the countryside were starving to death. Even though the old man now had his tiny room, there was no food available to give him. All of the meagre crops were taken by the government, and the other Christians were too poor to help him.

For some days the old man wasted away in his tiny room, with no food passing his lips. He grew weak and ill, and knew that his life would soon be snuffed out. One morning he awoke to find a hole in the bottom of the wall. He didn't know what had caused it, and repaired the damage. A few hours later he found another hole, and started to wonder if these strange occurrences were from the Lord. While he was still pondering it, a large rat came through the hole, with some food in its mouth. After entering the room, the rat dropped the food on the floor and then left. A short time later it returned and did the same again. A small collection of nuts and vegetables lay on the dirt floor!

Each morning the rat paid a visit to the elderly brother who, like Moses, had *'regarded disgrace for the sake of Christ as of greater value than the treasures of Egypt, because he was looking ahead to his reward'* (Hebrews 11:26). In response to his commitment, God saved the old man from starvation by instructing a rat to feed him! This miraculous provision continued for several months. On some days the rat brought more food than usual. These were the days when the old man was expecting a visitor! As our co-workers listened to this story, the other believers smiled and nodded their confirmation that it was true. Brother Joseph smiled, and said, 'Well, if God can use ravens to feed Elijah [see 1 Kings 17:1–6], I guess He can use a rat just as easily!'

When they reached the large city of Fuzhou in Fujian Province, Joseph and Uncle Liu found that a revival had recently broken out there and hundreds of people were coming to faith in Jesus Christ. The revival in Fuzhou had started after two little old ladies started to meet together for prayer, asking Jesus Christ to visit their city in power and might. One day they prayed for a young girl who was deaf and mute. The Lord healed her instantly, and news spread quickly that Jesus was still alive in China. Soon their little meeting of two grew until more than 200 people met in their home.

One day, while a meeting was in progress, a captain in the Chinese army heard all the noise coming from the house where people were praying and worshipping God. He knocked on the door and demanded to know what was going on. 'Oh,' one of the old ladies replied, 'These people here all have needs and God is meeting them.' He mockingly asked what kind of needs God was meeting. 'Well, some are sick and have no coupons for medicine. So we have been praying to our God and He has been touching and healing them. Others have no food or clothes, so we have been praying to our God and He has been providing for them.'

The captain pointed at his nose, which had a cancerous growth protruding from it, and asked, 'Do you think your God might be able to help me too?' The Christians invited the captain in, laid their hands on him, and earnestly asked God to heal him. The man felt no different and went home. That night, as he lay on his bed, his nose began to tingle. When he woke up the next morning the cancer had disappeared and he was completely healed. The captain was so excited he returned to the house and told the two old ladies what had happened. He asked, 'Who is this God of yours?' They shared Jesus Christ with him, and the man opened his heart and received the King of Glory.

The army captain immediately started to spread the gospel throughout the city, and dozens more people found the Lord. When our co-workers arrived at Fuzhou in February 1974, there were already 1,200 people worshipping the Lord in those house meetings.

God was conquering the devil's plans in China. Mao's wife was wrong! Christianity had not been consigned to the museum; it was alive and well because Jesus is alive and well. The church had learned not to fear what the Communist Red Guards could do to them, but to fear God. They understood the meaning of Jesus' words, *'I tell you, my friends, do not be afraid of those who kill the body and after that can do no more. But I will show you whom you should fear: Fear him who, after the killing of the body, has power to throw you into hell. Yes, I tell you, fear him'* (Luke 12:4–5).

The Communists had tried to ban Jesus from their country, but found it impossible. As countless tyrants and dictators have discovered through the centuries, the course of human history belongs to God, and not to man. The Almighty God was once again proving that *'The king's heart is in the hand of the Lord; he directs it like a watercourse wherever he pleases'* (Proverbs 21:1).

Two thousand years ago Jesus told His disciples, *'On this rock I will build my church, and the gates of Hades will not overcome it. I will give you the keys of the kingdom of heaven; whatever you bind on earth will be bound in heaven, and whatever you loose on earth will be loosed in heaven'* (Matthew 16:18–19). The gates of hell had tried to do all they could to hold out the advance of the kingdom of God in China, but they had begun to give way. Just as Brother Andrew had predicted, the lion was becoming weaker, and the lamb was growing stronger by the day. In the midst of the darkest struggle, a blinding light had burst forth and a voice had again thundered from heaven: 'I will build my church!'

***

Following Brother Joseph and Uncle Liu's groundbreaking visit to China in 1974, a small trickle of letters started to come in from some of the believers they had visited on their trip. Just before Christmas, a touching letter arrived. It said:

Christmas is here. May we adore Him with our heart, like the shepherds in the wilderness during the cold night. They were alert and went to worship the Lord. At the same time in the town of Bethlehem, all the Pharisees and the Scribes were asleep. They could not see the birth of Jesus. Only the alert shepherds were able to hear the Good News proclaimed by the angels and were directed to go and see the baby Jesus. We who are awake will see the second coming of Jesus. May the Lord be with you.

Another letter, from Fujian Province, said:

> *Although Christians in the Mainland at the moment are not able to go to church and worship God, we can gather about ten people to worship in our homes and to have fellowship and prayer. Please pray for us. May God call His own people to work for Him and to proclaim the gospel that He so loves the world.*
>
> *I have asthma, and am physically very weak. I am already 68 years old and my days in the earth are not many. I am waiting for Him to take me home. Please pray I will not be empty-handed when I meet my Lord. May our Heavenly Father save sinners, and give faith and love to all people.*

When each letter arrived we treated them like manna from heaven. They greatly encouraged me, especially seeing I had still not been able to visit China myself. They inspired me to continue to work tirelessly to find ways to help our brothers and sisters in the underground church.

Chapter Eight:
Love China '75

When I met Brother Andrew in New York in 1971, we agreed that a conference needed to be held at which all interested Christian ministries could attend, to pray and strategize about ministry into China.

As more information emerged about the needs of the church in China, it made sense for the different parts of the Body of Christ to meet and see how we could share resources. If we could agree to work together where possible, for the sake of the kingdom of God, so much more could potentially result. In his great chapter on the unity of the Body of Christ, the Apostle Paul wrote, *'The body is a unit, though it is made up of many parts; and though all its parts are many, they form one body. So it is with Christ…. In fact God has arranged the parts in the body, every one of them, just as he wanted them to be. If they were all one part, where would the body be? As it is, there are many parts, but one body'* (1 Corinthians 12:12, 18–20). It made no sense for those of us interested in Chinese ministry to do our own thing without the others knowing.

Open Doors agreed to sponsor the conference, which we called 'Love China '75'. The dates and location were set from 7 to 11 September 1975, in Manila, Philippines. This vision had taken four years to come to fruition, and involved the efforts and planning of many staff members. Hundreds of letters and invitations were sent to Christian leaders around the world, asking if they were interested in discussing the need for Christian work in China.

More than 430 delegates from twenty-three countries gathered in the Philippine Village Hotel in Manila. They represented fifteen Protestant denominations and fifty-five mission organizations. My friend and *Time* magazine correspondent David Aikman called it, 'the first full-scale gathering anywhere in the world of evangelicals concerned about the Christian witness in China since the Communist government gained power in 1949.'

On each day of the conference, different speakers shared on subjects related to the task of advancing the kingdom of God in China. Brother Andrew was one of the first to speak. He addressed the need for Christians to take the offensive against the forces of evil in China. He explained one of the foundational beliefs of Open Doors: that Christians were not called to sit back and wait for God to open countries that had closed their doors to Christianity, but that He has commanded the church to go into all the world and proclaim the gospel, regardless of whether we are invited or allowed to enter a certain nation or not. While Christians wait, millions perish without having heard the offer of Christ's salvation.

Brother Andrew was not just spouting an idealistic theory. He spoke with authority and everyone knew he had personally placed his life at risk for many years while delivering Bibles behind the Iron Curtain to the Soviet Union and Eastern Europe. He often taught that Christians should not wait for further permission to go anywhere, since Jesus had already commanded us to 'go'. We needed to step out in faith, and God would open the doors. It was the Lord who had once told His church, *These are the words of him who is holy and true, who holds the key of David. What he opens no one can shut, and what he shuts no one can open. I know your deeds. See, I have placed before you an open door that no one can shut'* (Revelation 3:7–8).

After challenging everyone present, Andrew concluded with these powerful words: 'By faith in Christ and by prayer to God, by obedience to the Holy Spirit, by courage, by determination, and by supreme sacrifice we can accomplish the task of evangelizing China in our generation. But we'd better hurry. We've got to begin somewhere, but begin we must. And the answer is obvious: We have to live a life that is more revolutionary than that of the revolutionaries.'

Dr Samuel Moffett, a missionary in Korea at the time, echoed these thoughts: 'The Chinese Communists have out-disciplined us, out-worked us, and out-committed us. Unless we are willing to match their commitment in our service for the Lord, we are never going to make a difference in China.'

William Willis, who as a young boy had come to Christ during the great Welsh Revival of 1904, spoke on the subject of intercessory prayer. He had spent fifty years as a Salvation Army missionary in China and Korea. Brother Willis defined an intercessor as 'a man who prays and weeps in the secret place of prayer until God stoops down and dries his tears'. He not only taught on prayer, but he demonstrated it. Each time he prayed it felt like heaven came down into that conference room.

Although many of the messages at the conference were inspirational, it seemed that some of the participants believed they could do nothing for China as long as it remained a 'closed' country. A common feeling was that as long as Chairman Mao remained in charge of China it was fanciful or even absurd to consider Christian work there. It is sad when we try to limit God through our own small ideas of His greatness. It has correctly been said, 'If you set your goals low, you will surely reach them.' It's always easier to sit back and wait for circumstances to change before we do God's work. But this is not biblical at all. We are instructed to resist the forces of evil, and to prayerfully and practically obey the Great Commission, even if it places us at personal risk.

Overall, I felt the conference was extremely successful and much good resulted. Some of those who attended later played key roles in helping the church in China. Two attendees, one Chinese and the other Japanese, consecrated themselves to serve the Lord during the conference and have worked in China to the present day.

***

After the Love China conference concluded, William Willis traveled to Hong Kong with some co-workers and me. The white-haired Welshman was a great intercessor, often praying for seven hours or more each day. He told me that when we pray we should pour out our soul before the Lord. He offered many biblical examples. Eli had even presumed Hannah was drunk as she prayed from her heart. She told Eli, *'Not so, my lord.... I am a woman who is deeply troubled. I have not been drinking wine or beer; I was pouring out my soul to the Lord'* (1 Samuel 1:15).

Brother Willis asked me, 'Young lad, what do your prayers cost you?' I thought about this question. What did my prayers cost me? King David had told Araunah, *'I will not take for the Lord what is yours, or sacrifice a burnt offering that costs me nothing'* (1 Chronicles 21:24). I examined my own heart, and asked God to search my motives. Was my motive for working in China really to see God glorified, or did I also revel in the attention that it brought me? Did my offerings and sacrifices carry a personal cost?

My times with William Willis revolutionized my prayer life. During times of intercession he always prayed, 'Lord, break me! Break me! I'm not broken yet.' He would continue praying until the Lord would break him by the Holy Spirit and move him to tears. William Willis was truly a broken vessel in the hands of God. He told me, 'Young man, when God breaks you and the tears finally flow, Jesus comes down and scoops up your tears and then you know that your prayers have been answered.' On many occasions since I have been brought to that place of brokenness before the Lord, pouring my soul out in intercession for the lost millions of China.

My time in Hong Kong with Brother Willis was eye-opening. Sometimes it was also a little frustrating. He spent so much time in prayer that we never knew when to ask if he wanted to join us for a meal, as we didn't want to disturb him. He usually prayed in his bathroom, on his knees with the door shut. One day he came out of his prayer closet and announced, 'The Lord has shown me something. I want you to take me to the China border, and when we look into China I will let you know what the Lord has shown me.'

We traveled the thirty miles or so out to Lok Ma Chau, where we gazed out across barbed wire fences and rice paddies into Mainland China. At that moment, Brother Willis declared, 'Very soon, China is going to open up! You will see it happen, and it will never again close to the gospel of Jesus Christ until He returns.'

On 9 September 1976 – exactly one year after Love China '75 – Mao Zedong died and a new era commenced in China. The advance of the kingdom of God owes much to saints like the late William Willis.

Chapter Nine:
Entering the Land

Although it was difficult for Westerners – especially Americans – to enter China in the mid-1970s, I didn't lack for trying. I visited the Chinese travel offices in Hong Kong at least thirty times, only for my visa application to be turned down on each occasion. I also applied at Chinese embassies and consulates in all the countries I visited throughout the region. Each time I was met with curiosity as to why I wanted to visit China, followed by a polite rejection.

By 1976 I was working long hours, traveling extensively, and not getting enough rest. I was under a lot of stress, and suffered a heart attack while in the Philippines. I was just 39 years old at the time and it was a real shock to my system in more ways than one.

Five days earlier I had taken a flight from New Delhi, India, back to Manila. On board I picked up a *Reader's Digest* magazine and read an article called 'Ten Symptoms of Having a Heart Attack'. I thank God for this article; because when I started to experience the same symptoms I immediately knew I was suffering a heart attack. I was taken to St Luke's Hospital in a taxi, and put into the Intensive Care Unit. When the cardiologist, Dr Calleja, came to see me the three nurses in my room got very excited. Afterwards I asked them about their reactions and they replied that I was very lucky, for Dr Calleja was the most famous cardiologist in the Philippines, and was the personal doctor of President Ferdinand Marcos.

As I lay on my bed a few days later, the words of a beautiful song, 'China, Let Me Love You', just flowed out of my spirit. A visiting friend wrote the words down on a piece of paper. In many ways the words (which are at the start of this book) represent the deepest longings of my spirit. Years later, when I shared this song with Sara Bruce, she was inspired to compose music to the words.

Ten days after my heart attack I was released from hospital and decided to take a vacation with my family to Turkey. It was our first real break from the mission field in six years and we enjoyed visiting the various New Testament sites. When we were in Ephesus, the familiar, precious voice of the Holy Spirit took me by surprise. I was scheduled to visit Holland, and the Lord told me that when I arrived there I should tell Brother Andrew that I wanted to go to Romania. This idea was not from my own mind, for I had never thought about visiting Romania before in my life. As I prayed, asking the Lord for the reason I should visit the Communist nation, I again heard His gentle voice saying, 'When you get to Holland, tell Andrew what I have said, and he will tell you why you should visit Romania.'

I realize that many people, including some Christians, probably think I am crazy to claim to be able to communicate with God in such a direct manner. Some believers have been brought up to believe that such claims are a dangerous breeding ground for deception and should therefore be avoided.

Of course the main way God speaks to people is through His written Word, the Bible. Any direction He wants to give someone will never contradict His Word. In my years of following Jesus, however, I can scarcely imagine all I would have missed out on if I did not believe God wanted to speak directly with His children. I am not talking about some kind of bizarre claim to a higher spirituality, but rather I'm talking about being able to discern God's small, still voice in your spirit. This comes only from walking with Christ intimately as Lord and friend.

I believe God wants to lead and direct His children in

specific ways as they follow Him. This occurred through-out the New Testament, such as when Paul was directed in his travels. In one place he was *'kept by the Holy Spirit from preaching the word in the province of Asia'* (Acts 16:6), only to then receive a vision of a man from Macedonia begging him to come and help (Acts 16:9). On another occasion Paul proclaimed, *'And now, compelled by the Spirit, I am going to Jerusalem, not knowing what will happen to me there. I only know that in every city the Holy Spirit warns me that prison and hardships are facing me'* (Acts 20:22–23).

How was it that the Holy Spirit directed, compelled, and warned Paul? Was it solely as a result of him reading the Scriptures? Surely Paul was in constant fellowship with the Father, and heard His voice guiding him along the way. Isaiah prophesied that a day would come when the people of God would be guided by His voice: *'Whether you turn to the right or to the left, your ears will hear a voice behind you, saying, "This is the way; walk in it"'* (Isaiah 30:21).

The Bible is full of examples of God's people hearing and following His voice. Indeed, Jesus seemed to indicate that hearing His voice was a mark of all who follow Him: *'The watchman opens the gate for him, and the sheep listen to his voice. He calls his own sheep by name and leads them out. When he has brought out all his own, he goes on ahead of them, and his sheep follow him because they know his voice. But they will never follow a stranger; in fact, they will run away from him because they do not recognize a stranger's voice.... My sheep listen to my voice; I know them, and they follow me'* (John 10:3–5, 27).

A few weeks after our vacation I flew into Amsterdam's Schipol Airport. When I saw Brother Andrew again, our hearts reconnected like brothers. I told him, 'I believe the Lord showed me that I should go to Romania, but He did-n't tell me why.' Andrew leaned back as if he remembered something important. 'Of course, David,' he enthused.

'Romania is one of the few allies China has in Eastern Europe. All the other countries are aligned with the Soviet Union. If you go to Romania, I'm sure you will have no problem getting a visa to China. There is even a flight from the Romanian capital, Bucharest, to Beijing.'

A few days later I was loaded down with a heavy suitcase of Bibles, and boarded a flight to Romania. On the drive to the airport I had seen two rainbows. It was as though the Lord was reminding me that His promises are good and trustworthy. The Bibles were successfully delivered to the underground Christians in this needy nation, and I had few problems arranging my first ever journey into China. Five days later I boarded a plane in Bucharest, Romania, headed for Beijing, China! The flight took a circuitous route, stopping over in Pakistan on the way.

After years of tireless attempts to visit China, my hopes were almost snatched from me. I became gravely ill during the stopover in Pakistan, and for two-and-a-half days I writhed in agony. My stomach felt like it was full of lead and the battle left me physically and mentally exhausted. I vomited almost unceasingly, and had never felt so sick in all my life. My mind was besieged with doubts, and it seemed the devil attacked me in every way possible. I wondered if I would ever get to visit China in my life. As I lay there, God reminded me of how He had led me to Romania. This gave me confidence that I was in His will. I managed to drag myself to the floor and knelt in prayer. Thanking Jesus for His great victory on the Cross, I prayed for healing and deliverance from the violent sickness. Almost immediately I felt a change, and within a few hours I had returned to normal!

The next evening I went to the airport and boarded my flight across the majestic Himalayas into China. I saw beautiful Mt Everest illuminated by the moonlight, and the next morning as we crossed Chinese territory my heart was dancing. Peering through the window, I saw rice fields and villages below, and could scarcely believe that my long-held ambition to visit China was about to be fulfilled.

We touched down at Beijing Airport. I looked out of my window, with my eyes wide open, and the first thing I saw was a huge portrait of Chairman Mao staring back at me. I was ready to take my first steps on Chinese soil, but another surprise was in store for me. When the doors of the plane opened, two soldiers boarded and asked everybody to show their passports. I was sitting near the back of the plane, and when the soldier nearest me inspected my passport he said, 'Sir, we have been waiting for you. Please follow me right now.' I was the first person taken off the plane. My mind was racing, wondering what this meant. Perhaps the Chinese had heard about my plans to spread the gospel in China? Maybe I was in trouble?

A Chinese immigration official, speaking surprisingly good English, welcomed me to the People's Republic of China. He then said, 'I'm afraid you can only stay in China for eight hours. You must stay in the airport during this time. You can walk around, but we are unable to accommodate any visitors in Beijing because all buildings have been evacuated due to the earthquake. Everyone is sleeping on the streets."

The day before, on 28 July 1976, a massive earthquake measuring 8.2 on the Richter scale had struck northern China, centered on the town of Tangshan. Beijing also took a huge hit. It has been estimated that up to 750,000 people were killed, in what is one of the worst disasters in world history.

I watched in hopelessness as hundreds of wounded, bleeding people staggered around the airport in a daze. Most of them had lost everything they owned in the world. The whole place was in a state of shock, and people were weeping everywhere I looked. In those few hours that I was allowed in China, God deeply touched my heart for the Chinese people. I had loved them before I had seen them, but now that I had seen them in their most vulnerable and desperate state, I knew there was no sacrifice too great for me to make to see the salvation of China become a reality.

For thousands of years the Chinese people had believed natural disasters were a sign of heaven's displeasure, and a portent that change is about to take place. It was later reported that many people in China believed the earthquake was a sign that Mao's reign was about to end. He died just six weeks later. When reports of Mao's death reached me, I remembered back to what the Lord had shown me from Psalm 37, seven years earlier. Now that Mao had been removed from the scene, I wondered if China would soon open its doors to the outside world, and the gospel, once again.

Just eight hours after my long-awaited arrival in China, I boarded a flight out. The clerk at the airport assured me that I would be welcome back to China any time. I took him at his word, and returned to China just three months later with a friend. This time it was a land crossing from Hong Kong, and I carried 20 Bibles with me. As I prayed silently, the customs official waved me through without opening my bag.

We arrived in the city of Guangzhou on 6 October 1976, and immediately sensed that something important was going on. Firecrackers were being let off all over the city, and the streets were filled with armed soldiers who were busy erecting posters on every street corner. For the second time, something extraordinary was taking place on the day I arrived in China. This time the Gang of Four had been toppled. The four Communist leaders, including Mao's wife Jiang Qing, had been arrested and were made the scapegoats for much of the mayhem that took place during the Cultural Revolution. Jiang was the one who had mockingly told a delegation of foreign visitors that Christianity was dead and buried in China and had been confined to the history section of the museum. Now, just a short time later, I was in China gazing at posters of drawings which showed her hanged and quartered, and being roasted over a fire in the same way that pigs are cooked in China.

In 1969 God had told me that He would bring about change in China and that Mao would fall. I just never expected that I would get to personally experience these tumultuous events!

Chapter Ten:

The Ethics of Smuggling

Over the years I have met many good Christians who were strongly opposed to our ministry of providing Bibles for believers in Communist countries. They believe it is completely wrong for a follower of Christ to do anything against the laws of a government, and often cite Romans 13:1 as their favourite verse: *'Everyone must submit himself to the governing authorities, for there is no authority except that which God has established.'* In some people's minds this one verse provides them with a sense of self- justification for their own inaction for Christ, while others genuinely believed we were doing wrong to carry Bibles into China, because by so doing we were violating the 'laws of the land'.

Having such a rigid view based on one verse of Scripture can be very dangerous. Using this same principle, it would have been wrong for Corrie ten Boom and her family to protect the Jews from the Nazis. After all, the Nazis were the 'governing authorities' at the time. Should the blacks in South Africa have accepted the apartheid system? After all, it was a law instituted by the government. The same warped reasoning can be used in countless examples around the world today.

If you live in a Western nation, then most likely abortion is legal, and countless millions of innocent lives have been butchered in cold blood. Is it therefore wrong to try to prevent such slaughter? Do Christians need to 'submit to the governing authorities' when it comes to abortion?

Of course Brother Andrew had been dealing with this kind of argument for years, especially after the publication of his best-selling book, *God's Smuggler*. The criticism became so strong that Andrew wrote a second book in response. The fierce criticism from other Christians must have seemed very strange to him, as it seemed strange to me. I didn't understand how the critics could take their stand on one or two Bible verses so strongly, while ignoring so many others.

I was more motivated by the command of Jesus to 'Go into all the world,' and the desperate needs of my brothers and sisters in China. They were hungry and thirsty for God's Word. They longed to be clothed in His righteousness, and they were begging and pleading for Bibles. God was performing miracle after miracle to help His Word get to His needy children, and yet many Christians in the West were strongly opposed to such activity, claiming it was better to leave the suffering believers alone because as Christians we had to submit to the governing authorities.

Such views persist among some sections of the Body of Christ today, although in less force than thirty years ago.

As a fellow believer, the very least I can do is to want to help my family members in China as much as possible. I don't want to be one of those to whom the Lord says, *'Depart from me, you who are cursed, into the eternal fire prepared for the devil and his angels. For I was hungry and you gave me nothing to eat, I was thirsty and you gave me nothing to drink, I was a stranger and you did not invite me in, I needed clothes and you did not clothe me, I was sick and in prison and you did not look after me'* (Matthew 25:41–43).

I agree that the motivation for all our actions should never be one of opposing the government or purposely wanting to disobey the law, but rather of obeying God and preaching the gospel. We should be most concerned about obeying God, for He is higher than any government. In many things the laws of God and the laws of the land do not contradict one another, but in certain things the two clearly clash. At such times we must always obey God.

A clear conscience before God is a wonderful thing to possess, even if it means we have offended the earthly authorities in the process. When Peter and John were seized, the Sanhedrin *'commanded them not to speak or teach at all in the name of Jesus. But Peter and John replied, "Judge for yourselves whether it is right in God's sight to obey you rather than God. For we cannot help speaking about what we have seen and heard"'* (Acts 4:18–20).

After my initial visits to mainland China, a great sense of urgency and purpose swept over me. I knew we had to act quickly to get the Word of God into the hands of the starving Chinese believers, and that whatever work we did now for the Lord was vital for the kingdom of God in the world's most populated nation.

General Douglas MacArthur once wrote, 'The history of failure in war can be summed up in just two words: "Too Late!"' Each follower of Jesus Christ is involved in a war being fought in today's world. It is taking place in a valley spoken of long ago by the prophet Joel, who cried, *'Multitudes, multitudes in the valley of decision'* (Joel 3:14). In China, there are still multitudes in the valley of decision today. A battle over the eternal destiny of souls is underway and we need to get involved immediately. So often we act too slowly. Tragically, we might even be too late to help the multitudes in the valley of decision.

We need a change in our perspective. Too often we think nobody is interested in the gospel, when in fact Jesus said, *'Do you not say, "Four months more and then the harvest"? I tell you, open your eyes and look at the fields! They are ripe for harvest. Even now the reaper draws his wages, even now he harvests the crop for eternal life, so that the sower and the reaper may be glad together. Do not say, there are four months, then comes harvest. I tell you, lift up your eyes and see the fields are already white for harvest'* (John 4:35).

Jesus said this after the disciples returned to find Him talking with a Samaritan woman at the well. The Jews hated the Samaritans. They were considered lower than dogs, and the Jews were forbidden to eat with or have anything to do with a Samaritan. They believed to do so would cause them to become contaminated. No doubt the disciples believed the Samaritans would never receive God's salvation. Jesus, as he usually did, turned the disciples' perspective upside down, telling them to open their eyes, for the harvest was ready now!

How about you? Have you given up on your community, your country, and your own family? Have you convinced yourself that people's hearts are hard against the gospel, and they will never accept the Lord? Through the riches in God's Word, we can give the multitudes a choice in that valley of decision. A personal encounter with the Bible will give them the chance to choose Jesus, His salvation and His eternal life.

Can we ignore China? Is it too far away for us to care about a billion lost souls? We need to move now; on our knees, on our feet, and with our hands. There is not a moment to lose. We have the supernatural power to do so. But have we the will to move?

I believe there is such a thing as ethical 'smuggling'

for a Christian. When we hear the desperate cries of God's children, and we choose to block our ears and ignore them, we place ourselves in danger of God's judgment. The Bible warns us, *'Rescue those being led away to death; hold back those staggering toward slaughter. If you say, "But we knew nothing about this," does not he who weighs the heart perceive it? Does not he who guards your life know it? Will he not repay each person according to what he has done?'* (Proverbs 24:11–12).

In his book, *The Calling*, Brother Andrew explained his firm belief that Christians in the free world are called to overcome the obstacles that keep people in closed countries from receiving the words of Scripture. He stated that the methods used may be legal or illegal according to the laws of that particular country, for believers had to "obey God rather than man." He acknowledged that such a position could be, and in his personal experience has been, challenged by other Christian believers or organizations. Still, he firmly urged free Christians to take the initiative—it is their responsibility to go and to proclaim the message of Jesus Christ, even if it should invariably trigger a confrontation.

Let's open our eyes and ears to the needs of other Christians in China, around the world, and right wherever we live. If our hearts are so hard that we cannot be bothered to reach out to them now, how can we hope to live with them in heaven for all eternity? The Apostle John put it this way: *'This is how we know what love is: Jesus Christ laid down his life for us. And we ought to lay down our lives for our brothers. If anyone has material possessions and sees his brother in need but has no pity on him, how can the love of God be in him? Dear children, let us not love with words or tongue but with actions and in truth'* (1 John 3:16–18).

Dear friend, let's work for the Lord while we have the opportunity.

Just two words, MacArthur said: 'Too Late!'

Chapter Eleven:
Papa and Mama Kwang

In 1974 we learned about a Christian couple, Papa and Mama Kwang, who were connected to hundreds of house churches throughout China. The Kwangs were to play a key role in my life and in the work the Lord had called me to do.

Papa Kwang was a brilliant man. He was one of China's leading mathematicians and professors, but when the Communists commenced their campaign of destruction, he was forced to carry boulders for many years in a prison labor camp. In the evenings, the wicked guards often entertained themselves by torturing Papa Kwang because he was a devout follower of Jesus. On many occasions they forced him to bend forward and they placed live poisonous snakes around his head and neck. The guards would shout at him, 'Denounce Jesus Christ and acknowledge Chairman Mao as your leader!' He refused. Over time, Papa Kwang found that he grew stronger and stronger. Not once did he acknowledge Chairman Mao, nor did he deny Jesus Christ. And not once did a snake bite him.

Mama Kwang had been in prison three times for the sake of the gospel. Despite enduring great hardship, there always seemed a smile on Mama Kwang's face, and her eyes seemed to sparkle whenever she talked about the Lord. Her knowledge of the Scriptures was extraordinary, and she had memorized many parts of the Bible so that she could meditate on them while in prison.

Mama Kwang faithfully shared the gospel with many

people before and even during the Cultural Revolution. She was a gifted evangelist and thousands of people had met the Lord through her ministry. On one occasion she was arrested and confined in a tiny cell measuring four feet wide and four feet high. It was more like a box than a cell. She couldn't even sit upright, and the cell stank from human waste. Despite the deplorable conditions, she often liked to say that there was room for someone else to join her in that cell. Jesus Christ came and comforted her in the midst of that terrible environment.

I came to know the Kwang family well. They had suffered so much. One of their sons had been savagely beaten and later died of malnutrition and disease while both of his parents languished in prison. The Communists allowed Mama Kwang to temporarily leave the prison when her son was close to death. The little boy told his mother, 'I see Jesus! I see Jesus,' and then went to be with Him.

In 1978, after both Papa and Mama Kwang had been released, they contacted us and asked us to bring 1,000 Bibles into China for them. Up to that time we had successfully taken in between 50 and 100 Bibles each time in suitcases. But when they asked us to bring 1,000 Bibles, our faith was stretched and we had to depend on God to do it. Six of us commenced preparations to carry a total of 900 Bibles across the border in suitcases. We only had the faith to take 900 in. The other 100 would have to be delivered later. I went through the customs area without being stopped, but I looked back and saw my friend James standing there with the officers going through his suitcase, touching the Bibles. James told me later he was praying under his breath, 'Lord Jesus, let them feel the Bibles but don't let them take any of them.' Moments later I saw the suitcase zipped up and the customs officer waved James through into China.

Although all 900 Bibles had been delivered successfully, and we had seen the hand of God, I realized that these were like a drop of water spilled into a sandy desert. They were a help, but the need was so vast. I wished we had been able to take in a truckload of Bibles. A short time later we received the following letter of appreciation from China:

> We have received the Bibles you sent us. My happiness, love and warm tears mixed together. The love of the Lord flows toward me like a river from His throne, and makes me leap with joy. The deepest part of my heart is completely filled with living water, and the Holy Spirit has made me brave. Whether I live or die means nothing to me. God is enlarging His territory inside of me.... Those who know Jesus are spreading everywhere like water in the ocean. This is the wonderful work of the Lord and the answer to our prayers.

The Kwangs' nineteen-year-old son, Daniel, was the first family member to leave China for Hong Kong in 1977. Daniel was praying on Christmas Day, 1975, when the Lord said He would take him to Hong Kong so that he could be a witness of the suffering church in China to Christians around the world. The Lord gave Daniel a precise date – more than a year later – when he should apply for a passport and exit visa. Many countries require a visa for people to get in, but such was China's paranoia and control of their people that they also required a visa for any of their citizens who wanted to get out!

Daniel Kwang went down to the local authorities on the appointed day, and requested the forms to apply for a passport and exit visa. The woman at the office knew he was the son of hated house church Christians who had brought thousands of people to faith in God. Both of Daniel's parents were convicted criminals of the worst kind – counter-revolutionaries and traitors in the eyes of the Chinese government. The woman screamed at Daniel to get out, and ordered a guard to beat him for his trouble.

After being badly beaten and bruised, Daniel was left slumped outside on the ground, confused about what had happened. He reminded the Lord that he had obeyed His voice, and had come to the office on the very day he had been instructed to. As the guard who had beaten him strode back towards the office, he suddenly spun around for no apparent reason and asked, 'Are you Daniel Kwang?'

'Yes, I am,' the teenager replied.

'Then come with me.' The guard took Daniel back inside and helped him complete the application form.

When Daniel returned home, his parents rushed out to meet him and asked what had happened. They explained that 300 believers had gathered for a meeting in their home that afternoon, and after the meeting concluded they were returning to their own homes when suddenly the Holy Spirit stopped each person and told them to return to the meeting place to pray for Daniel, because he was in trouble and needed help.

All 300 Christians returned and cried out to God to deliver and protect Daniel. Some even prayed that he would be granted permission to travel to Hong Kong, even though they knew nothing about the plan. Daniel had only told his immediate family and a few close friends. After fervently interceding for the young man, the believers suddenly sensed that God had answered their prayers and they returned home.

In 1979 the rest of the Kwang family came out of China and were allowed to settle in Hong Kong as refugees. I was startled when I heard this news and flew to Hong Kong immediately to meet with them. They were living as squatters in terrible conditions, with no running water, toilet, or shower. Despite the environment, their faces shone with the presence of Jesus and they had quite a story to tell.

Several years earlier, the Lord told Mama Kwang that she and her family would leave China to testify about the Chinese Church to the rest of the world. Leaving China was impossible for anyone with a prison record, but that did not prevent Papa and Mama Kwang from filling out an application form and trusting God. For several years they heard nothing from the authorities. Then one morning in the spring of 1979, while Mama Kwang was kneeling in prayer, she sensed God telling her that they would leave China in one month.

The Kwangs immediately started to train other leaders to replace them in the ministry. Confident that they had heard the voice of the Lord, they made plans for their departure. Nobody bothered to contact the authorities to check on the progress of their application. They had heard from the Lord Himself, and that was all the confirmation they needed. On the last day of the month they held a special service where new leaders were commissioned to continue the work. The very next day a government official came to the village and told the Kwangs, 'Come with me to the police station. Your exit papers are waiting for you.' A few days later the Kwangs arrived in Hong Kong.

I asked Papa and Mama Kwang how the church was doing in China. They replied, 'We have been through many years of darkness and death, but the Lord has breathed His life on our dead corpses and today we are alive again!' I asked if the believers in China had any needs. They answered, 'Yes, we need 30,000 Bibles right away.'

It took me a moment to compose myself. Amazingly, the previous week I had placed an order for 30,000 Chinese Bibles from the Hong Kong Bible Society. I had placed the order in faith, believing we would deliver these across the border over time. When I told this to the Kwangs they laughed out loud and declared, 'Now then, God is with us. All we have to do is let Him show us how to get them in.'

I asked the Kwangs if the 30,000 Bibles would meet the need. They looked me in the eye and said, 'Oh no! That's not enough, David. They will fill our immediate needs, but what we really need is a million!'

Trying to keep a calm demeanour, I made a request: 'Let's begin with 30,000 first, please.'

***

Mama Kwang shared a story that greatly encouraged me. She said that in 1974, during her third time in prison, she had received a vision from the Lord. She saw thousands of Christians, both Chinese and from around the world. They were working alongside one another and digging a trench. When the trench was large enough, water began to flow into it. This water, the River of Life, flowed across all of China, and after that it flowed into other nations of the world.

This vision so encouraged Mama Kwang that she started to take her eyes off the filthy conditions and dire surroundings of the prison, and began to pray daily for the fulfilment of the vision. She prayed that God would raise up believers from other countries to come and work hand-in-hand with the Chinese Church, laboring together in such a way that a trench of living water would flow throughout China and attract millions of people into God's kingdom. She then personalized the story for me. 'Brother David, 1974 was when you were just starting out in your ministry for China. You are one of the answers to my prayers!'

I thought about how great God is. He had been guiding and preparing me for this work all along, even when I was discouraged and had no clue how to advance. Now I realized that God had me in the palm of His hand the whole time. This work was not something being *invented* as I went along. Rather, it was being revealed piece by piece. This is the same for all who follow and serve Jesus. He has a work for each person, a work He has already prepared for us. The Bible says, *'For we are God's workmanship, created in Christ Jesus to do good works, which God prepared in advance for us to do'* (Ephesians 2:10).

Up to that moment I had only thought of the ministry and encouragement the Western church could give to the suffering church in China. Now I understood that their ministry to us was much greater than what we could offer them. There was so much to learn from their love, passion and wisdom. The 'River of Life' had a two-way flow.

***

At the time, the only news coming from Christians in China was from representatives of the government-approved 'Three-Self Patriotic Movement'. The political thawing that had taken place in China since Mao's death in 1976 resulted in the reintroduction of the Three-Self movement, which had been birthed in the 1950s but was put aside during the Cultural Revolution. 'Three-self' stands for the movement's three guiding principles: self-propagation, self-support, and self-governance.

The main spokesman for the officially-recognized church in China was Bishop Ding Guangxun (also known as K. H. Ting), who traveled widely around the Western world, informing Christians that there was nothing to worry about, that a new era had dawned for the church in China, that they had plenty of Bibles, and that persecution was a thing of the past. All this would have been great, if it was true. The fact was that house church believers – those who refused to register with the Three-Self – were still being brutally persecuted throughout China. Hundreds of brothers and sisters were imprisoned for their faith.

While the government was boldly announcing a new day of religious freedom had dawned in China, the house church believers smelled a rat. The fact remained that the bedrock of Communist ideology is atheism. When news emerged that the government was advising Three-Self preachers what they could and could not preach from their pulpits, the suspicions of the house church believers were confirmed. Certain subjects were considered taboo in the Three-Self churches. Preachers could not speak on the Second Coming of Christ, about marriage between believers and unbelievers, on healing, anything from the Book of Revelation, and so on. It was also strictly forbidden for anyone under the age of 18 to attend one of these 'liberated' churches.

Most house churches refused to have anything to do with the Three-Self Church. They believed that to register with the government would be akin to denying Christ. The general feeling was that the Three-Self Church was little more than the government's insidious attempt to control and kill off genuine Christianity. They didn't mind if the churches were filled with old ladies, but any attempt to bring young people into the kingdom of God was strongly opposed, and any sign of the life of Christ flowing among its members was quickly extinguished. That way, so the government thought, the 'plague' of Christianity would gradually die out as the elderly believers passed away.

Many house church Christians had spent years in prison labor camps for the sake of the gospel, and hundreds had been martyred during the 1950s, 1960s, and 1970s. Many Three-Self pastors, on the other hand, were widely known to have betrayed Christ during the Cultural Revolution. Some had even helped the government identify and persecute their flocks. A clear division developed between those Christians who joined the official church, and those who refused to do so. This line of demarcation remains to the present day, although it has become a little more blurred in recent years as China has slowly allowed more religious freedom.

The Three-Self Patriotic Movement also refused to acknowledge any Christian expression not under its control. Bishop Ding seemed to downplay the size and scope of the church in China, and poured cold water on any reports about the revival that we knew was going on among the house churches. He told believers in the West there was no need for them to help or come to China, or to bring Bibles, for they had it all under control.

A few months after arriving in Hong Kong, Mama Kwang wrote a touching letter on behalf of 'The Suffering Church in China'. This was the first clear statement to come from a house church representative, and was widely circulated. The nature of Mama Kwang's letter was totally different from Bishop Ding's statements, and brought edification and inspiration to many Christians around the world. She spoke of the intense joy the Christians had experienced, and the goodness and faithfulness of God in the midst of years of persecution. At the time, many Christians outside of China imagined the Chinese believers to be suffering, beaten-down individuals who had managed to grimly hold onto their faith despite the storms of Communism. Mama Kwang's letter changed the perspective of many. She wrote:

Thank God for His wonderful grace. He has called us from the four corners of the earth to be His children together. Love binds us together in the Lord and we become like one big family. We have been given the glorious mission to spread the gospel all over the world and to let all men hear and come to know the Lord Jesus Christ, Saviour of Love, until the end comes. When we think of the approaching time of His glory, our hearts continually dance and sing with joy.

We, the whole family, come from the suffering Church of China. In the past 30 years, although we went through many trials, sufferings and adversity, the Lord kept us dependent on His grace and enabled us to overcome. During those years, the many wonderful deeds the Lord performed cannot be described or expressed in words.

Recalling those hard days, the eyes of the Lord were upon us, watching and protecting us. His powerful arms, which can shake the whole world, helped us to do His work and to rebuild the Church. He used the miracles and wonders in our lives to prove that the gospel will reach millions of people. Many have witnessed His deeds and have believed in the gospel. The Name of the Lord has been glorified.

In China, where the schemes of the anti-Christ are strong, people are not allowed to believe in Jesus. Preaching the gospel is unlawful. I and our co-workers and the whole family, have suffered heavy persecution for preaching. My eldest son was killed during persecution, and my husband was sent to a re-education prison camp because he wouldn't forsake Jesus' name. He suffered all kinds of torture. I, myself, have been put into prison three times. I suffered all kinds of torture and adversity, hunger and beatings. But all this cannot remove the faith in our hearts. We depend on the power and courage that comes from above. We will continue to preach the truth whether inside or outside prison.

Many people, compelled by the Lord's love, have been motivated and touched and have come to believe in the Lord Jesus Christ. Hallelujah! The gospel of the Lord is finally being proclaimed. Today in China there are thousands, even millions, of pastures all around us. The tidewaters of the gospel are flowing everywhere, filling up the land like the ocean. Now we are able to advance forward, with our eyes focused beyond the horizon. The harvest is ripe and ready for reaping. We deeply feel that the coming of the Lord is near.

Chapter Twelve:

Rainbow to China

In 1979 we held our annual Open Doors meeting in Manila. Brother Andrew and the other leaders came together to plan what God had in store for us in the coming year and to identify what the needs were. The work of Open Doors was diverse, covering many countries in Asia, Eastern Europe, the Soviet Union, Africa, and Latin America. When I stood up to report on Asia, I started by asking all the leaders from Open Doors to help carry the 30,000 Bibles into China. This was no small task to do by suitcase, for that many Bibles weighed two-and-a-half tons.

Some of my co-workers thought that we were trying to 'bite off more than we could chew'. It was suggested that we lower the risk by taking in a smaller number of Bibles now, with the rest to be carried in over time. This sounded logical, but God does not necessarily operate according to our logic. I thought about how I had already ordered that exact number before the Kwangs had mentioned it. The church in China had requested 30,000 Bibles immediately, and that is what we would deliver, with God's help.

We were too small a mission to accomplish this task alone, so my co-workers and I went to seventeen other missionary organizations based in the Philippines and invited them to join us by providing couriers. The operation was a huge undertaking, and we realized we needed a lot of prayer cover. In the United States alone, Open Doors sent out 90,000 prayer letters, asking for prayer support while not mentioning any of the specific details of what we were planning to do. Countless thousands of believers prayed for us around the world, and of course in China.

The Christians in Japan were such a blessing. They sent couriers over to help us. Although there was a language barrier, in their shining eyes I could see a love and willingness to serve their persecuted brothers and sisters in China. I recalled my youth, and the war games my friends and I had staged on the beach in California against our imaginary enemy, the hated Japanese. The Lord reminded me that His love could transform anyone, from any nation. These days many in the West see Muslims as our enemies. As Christians, we need to be careful that our own prejudices don't limit our understanding of what God wants to do. Jesus loves the Muslims so much that He willingly bled and died for them, and He has wonderful plans to bring His salvation and life to those who have lived so long in darkness and as captives of the devil.

In October 1979, over a period of ten days, eighteen small teams of couriers successfully carried a total of 30,000 Bibles into China in suitcases. We timed our trips to coincide with the dates of the Canton Trade Fair. Many foreigners were expected to enter south China to attend the fair, and we hoped to take advantage of more relaxed borders at the time. Just two individuals were stopped and their Bibles confiscated. Everyone else made it through successfully.

We dubbed the operation 'Project Rainbow', although afterwards I heard that some of the couriers who lugged those heavy suitcases referred to it as 'Project Hernia'! I crossed into China with two Chinese Christian ladies, an Indian brother named Sam who had a broken foot, another man who was as skinny as a chopstick, and a large man like me who was chairman of the board of Open Doors in North America.

Altogether we had five trunks and seventeen suitcases full of Bibles, which we loaded onto huge baggage trolleys and wheeled into the customs building. When we got to the inspection desk, the customs officers wanted to take a look inside our trunks, but Sam had recently broken a bone in his foot and started to complain about the pain. This diverted the officers' attention, as they gathered around and asked him what the problem was. After a few minutes a leading official ordered the customs officers to move the trolleys through the building and to get back to work.

Our role was to carry the Bibles into China and let the local believers come and take them off us. They would then be taken to a depository, and other Christians came later and moved them to their final destinations. This way the risk for the Chinese was greatly lessened, as they would have minimal direct contact with us. China was full of watching eyes. Such was the volume of Bibles we had brought into China, that Sam and I had to wait in our room at the Dong Fang Hotel for three days, while the two overseas Chinese ladies on our team made contact with the local believers. We didn't want to leave the Bibles unattended for a moment, so for the whole time we stayed in our room and had our meals brought up to us until the local believers came and took our gigantic load of five trunks and seventeen suitcases away, one at a time.

One of our couriers, a medical doctor, had such a heavy load that when he got to the customs area he set his suitcases down on the floor. The officer waved him on through, but when the doctor reached down to lift his luggage up, he found he wasn't able to budge it. He thought, 'Dear me, what am I going to do now?' and he prayed, 'In the Name of Jesus, rise.' He reached down, picked the suitcases up, and walked 200 metres out of the building and set them down inside China. It took three Chinese men to lift each suitcase onto the back of a cart. He found power in the name of Jesus Christ.

Thanks to the mercy of God, not one of our suitcases or trunks used in Project Rainbow was opened. Our couriers pushed our trolleys across the bridge that separates Hong Kong from the Chinese town of Shenzhen. That bridge was known as the 'Bridge of Weeping'. Thousands of desperate people in those days tried to escape the nightmare of life in China by walking across the mountains or swimming through the dangerous shark-infested waters into British-controlled Hong Kong. Many were sent back to China, and were often literally dragged across this bridge by the Communist border guards. Thousands were never seen alive again. We thanked God that the pain, misery and death that this bridge represented was now the very same structure that helped us bring the joy, blessings and life of the Word of God to China.

A few weeks later we received word that every single Bible had reached their final destination, and were now in the hands of the long-suffering believers. I asked my team-mates what it was like to participate in Project Rainbow. They said, 'It was like the day when the Red Sea opened up and the children of Israel walked through on dry ground.' Our faith was greatly strengthened by seeing God move in such a powerful way. His power and greatness became a reality, which affected the rest of our lives.

The Word of God was now in China.

The Chinese believers were praising God and so were we. I asked Papa and Mama Kwang what was next, and they repeated, 'We need a million Bibles.'

***

In the weeks and months following Project Rainbow, we received letters from house church leaders who had taken delivery of the precious scriptures. Many of these loving letters touched our hearts and once again showed us the depth of their need for Bibles. Here is a selection of the precious letters we received:

Brother Ji, 3 November 1979:

Thanks to the special grace of the Lord, the food of life you have brought to us has made our hungry hearts full. We received your precious gifts, and embraced them for a long time, not wanting to put them down. Thanks to the grace of our Lord and your loving work, our tears are gushing forth, and we dance and sing Hallelujah!

Now that we have received the Word of the Lord, our spiritual lives have been oriented in the right direction and we have revival. The Word of the Lord awakened many prodigal sons, found the lost sheep, saved many lives from drowning in the bitter sea, and released many who were bound by sin and Satan.

In recent days, family members from Jiangxi, Jiangsu, Shanghai and Shanxi and other places have come and taken the gifts back to their homes. May the Lord give you His power so that you will not become weary. In this place the number of saved people is increasing and sheep are being added to God's flock every day, so more spiritual food is needed.

Sister Yin, 13 November 1979:

We were very thirsty and hungry, not because we had no bread to eat or water to drink, but because we lacked the precious Word of God. When we were filled, we were like camels drinking at an oasis. Our hearts are filled with unexpressed joy! Thank you so much. Although my heart-felt thanks cannot be expressed in mere words, still I wanted to write this note to express my gratitude.

May God's blessings flow endlessly!

Brother Wu, 16 November 1979:

First, let me – a tiny, lowly child – give thanks to the Father, and my gratefulness for your love. You have taken care of the poor in the Father's house. We had lost the Bread of Life in the past, but today, through your help, our cupboards are full!

Your love for the Lord and for His people overwhelms us. You shouldered a heavy responsibility, travelling over land and water, mountains and valleys to overcome many hardships, just to take care of us poor and needy children. God has now made us rich and full! Since we received the Bread of Life, we have continually given thanks to our Father with our arms upraised, at the same time our hearts have hungrily feasted on the bread. It has empowered and equipped us to fight the good fight of the faith.

Brother Tian, 18 November 1979:

I received the spiritual food you sent, thanks to the grace of the Lord. Once again we saw the wonderful will of God in operation, and He let all the food arrive safely.

You were entrusted to deliver the food to us. How happy our hearts were! The Lord has taken care of us lowly children, even during the years of adversity when our hearts were so dry. We need the Word of the Lord very much, just as we need His rain to moisten our dry hearts. The Lord has listened to our begging, and has opened a way for us. God used you to bring the truth, life, and light of God to us. We are deeply touched by your love and cannot stop crying.

Mama Kwang, December 1979:

The Light of truth is shining inside China again. The Bible is the store house of truth, the true description of life, the only way to see God, the living testimony of Christ, the source of living water, the mirror that reflects people's hearts, the sword of the Spirit, the bread of life, the standard for our faith, the heavenly law, the lamp unto our feet and the light unto our path, and the way that leads us home to heaven.

The Church in China has endured a great wave of persecution that was stirred up by that roaring lion, Satan. Not only were the churches closed, but precious Bibles were burned. The believers were bitterly persecuted. Some were killed and others imprisoned. Their homes were ransacked and they suffered all kinds of harsh persecution and torture. Satan did all he could to destroy the Church, but the wiles of the enemy have led to the fulfilment of God's purposes. All these persecutions have in fact brought even greater glory to God. In the midst of tribulation God has purified His Church, adorned His bride and raised up thousands of brothers and sisters who are faithful unto death and steadfast in the Word and who fight the great battle for truth. They have established house meetings all over the country and the gospel is being spread to all parts. When people hear the good news of our Lord and receive the heavenly hope, their sense of hopelessness disappears and darkness changes to light. Heavy burdens are stripped away and sorrow turns to joy.

People from all walks of life have realized their need for Jesus and have believed the truth. The numbers are increasing daily but they have no Bibles. This is the biggest problem: they have no Bibles. Before the Bibles were burned the Lord showed me to take my Bible to a sister in a rural village. She hid it and so the Lord preserved that Bible for me. Night and day I have copied it by hand to meet the needs of my co-workers, but the demand is greater than the supply. When our hunger and thirst became most acute we could only go to the secret place of the Most High and look up to Him, asking Him to supply us with precious Bibles. We even sang a hymn asking for Bibles.

Thanks be to the Lord. Our songs and prayers reached His ears and He stretched out His hand of mercy to help us. He placed the burden of delivering Bibles to the churches in China upon foreign brothers and sisters who love the Lord. In May 1978, Brother David, who neither fears death nor hardship, came to China to meet us. As a result, our long yearning to meet with brothers and sisters from outside China at long last became a reality. We had sweet fellowship in the Spirit and told of the Lord's wonderful works of salvation in China and how He has given us an open door that no man can close. David showed deep compassion and at the same time told us how many brothers and sisters overseas are deeply concerned about the suffering church. He told us many are praying for us and they are thinking of all kinds of methods of delivering Bibles to China to satisfy our spiritual hunger. This is the Lord's powerful work. When I heard this, I bowed my head and worshipped the true and living God. Tears ran down my cheeks and I was deeply touched. I couldn't stop praising God.

In October 1978 the Lord used His faithful servants to deliver 900 Bibles to us. As a result, 900 house churches were able to receive spiritual food. Hallelujah! At the time of our most critical suffering, God helped us to do great and difficult things through His powerful strength, which moves the whole world. He has given our overseas brothers and sisters faith to cast mountains into the sea. At last, God has opened a door for delivering Bibles into China, a door that had been tightly closed and securely locked but which now He has opened and no man can close. Hallelujah!

God's Word is full of power. The living water is springing up in China and flowing out to all hungry and thirsty hearts. The brothers and sisters receive the Bibles like someone receiving a priceless treasure. Their joy and exultation cannot be suppressed. Deeply moved, they offer thanks. However, there are still many brothers and sisters who do not yet have a Bible. There are many places where believers have never even seen a Bible. Praise the Lord; He has once again placed the burden upon our overseas brothers and sisters. May God bless them and fill their hearts with the abundance of His riches. Above all, I pray that the work of delivering Bibles may go smoothly, and that every believer in China may have a Bible to read and that the light of truth may shine again throughout our country, leading those who sit in the dark shadow of death onto the path of peace. Amen.

Chapter Thirteen:

An Impossible Dream

After we completed Project Rainbow in October 1979, I waited upon the Lord to see what He wanted us to do next. Papa and Mama Kwang, on behalf of the underground churches in China, had said they needed one million Bibles. This was not an arbitrary figure plucked out of the air, but one based on extensive discussions with their network of Christian contacts throughout the country.

A short time later we received an official request from the church leaders in China. It read:

Right now China needs one million Bibles. Even this is not enough for a country with a population of one billion.

Before 'liberation' the Church was neither hot nor cold. But during the past 30 years it has suffered much persecution under the Communists.

Now the Church is 'hot'. The Lord is blessing His Church because of its faithfulness to Him during those hard years. More and more people are seeking the Lord. Students in the high schools and universities are finding the Lord. Patients in hospitals and those in distant villages are turning to God. There is a mighty revival going on in China right now, but there are not enough Bibles. We need Scriptures for those who have been Christians for many years, and we need Bibles for those who are trusting Christ by the thousands this year.

During the Cultural Revolution, the Communists destroyed all the Bibles they could find. So right now, we request one million Scriptures to supply the needs in China.

This figure staggered us. One million! We sent a Chinese co-worker into China to do research, to see if it was realistic. There would have to be enough believers ready and able to receive a million Bibles. After months of research, we found that the real need for the Body of Christ in China was for much more than a million Bibles. It would help, certainly, but revival was underway in many parts of the country and there were millions of hungry believers without God's Word. Researchers at the time believed there were between 10 million and 30 million Christians in China.

As we meditated on the request for a million Bibles, we felt so hopeless. We saw the expectation, hunger, and desire of the Chinese believers for God's Word, but the size of the need was greater than the size of our faith. We realized that Open Doors could not do it. Brother Andrew could not do it. I could not do it. None of us could do it. Gradually, a new sense of purpose and realization started to dawn in our hearts. Jesus could do it!

Not only *could* He do it, but we began to get a strong sense that He *wanted* to do it. I thought about how the Lord Jesus had taken us step-by-step, increasing our faith and expectation along the way. The process started with Brother Joseph and Uncle Liu carrying just sixteen New Testaments into China in 1974. Then we took in suitcases with forty or fifty Bibles at a time, followed by the delivery of 900, and Project Rainbow with 30,000. Along the way God had provided everything we needed to succeed, and had graciously taught us many lessons. Regardless of whether it was one bag or one million Bibles, I had learned we must never trust in our own strength to do God's work, or we are doomed to failure. God wants us to be humble and trusting children, relying on Him in prayer at every moment. If there is one scripture that best sums up the approach needed for God's work, it is, ' "*Not by might nor by power, but by my Spirit," says the Lord Almighty*' (Zechariah 4:6).

I now believed that God wanted us to work with Christians all over the world to take a million Bibles into China. We saw that our Chinese brothers and sisters had the faith and desire for a million Bibles, so why not us? At the time, both missionaries and the believers inside China had a real sense of urgency. We were convinced that God had allowed China's doors to open for a brief time, and that we had to act quickly and decisively to get Bibles in while we had an opportunity.

An undertaking of this size was simply impossible. Many Christians in those days were too scared to carry a single Bible with them when they went into China, and now we were praying about delivering a million! In our own strength, we could do absolutely nothing and the whole idea was ridiculous from a human perspective. With God's help, guidance, protection and provision, it could be done. When we looked at ourselves, we got discouraged at this impossible dream. But when we looked to Jesus, we had faith that *'What is impossible with men is possible with God'* (Luke 18:27).

Many people in the Bible were asked by God to do the impossible. When Jeremiah gained a revelation of the greatness of God, he proclaimed, *'Ah, Sovereign Lord, you have made the heavens and the earth by your great power and outstretched arm. Nothing is too hard for you'* (Jeremiah 32:17). God reiterated Jeremiah's statement by asking, *'I am the Lord, the God of all mankind. Is anything too hard for me?'* (Jeremiah 32:26). A short time later the Lord spoke to Jeremiah again, with a wonderful invitation: *'This is what the Lord says, he who made the earth, the Lord who formed it and established it – the Lord is his name: "Call to me and I will answer you and tell you great and unsearchable things you do not know"'* (Jeremiah 33:2–3).

Throughout the entire Bible, God did the impossible and allowed normal people to see great things done in His name. The same God who created the universe by the power of His Word, who parted the Red Sea and let the Israelites escape Egypt, and who raised His Son from the grave, possesses limitless power. He could do it! Our role was to find out if, how and when the Lord wanted to do it, and try to follow His leading each step of the way.

As I asked the Lord for direction, He gave me the name 'Pearl', from the Scripture: *'The kingdom of heaven is like a merchant looking for fine pearls. When he found one of great value, he went away and sold everything he had and bought it'* (Matthew 13:45–46).

I also thought about Pearl Harbor, and how the Japanese had managed to spring a complete surprise on the United States. I knew that if we were ever to successfully deliver a million Bibles to China, all the planning and operation from start to finish would have to take place in complete secrecy. If one person had 'loose lips', the whole plan would be sunk. I started to pray that God would send me people I could trust. God knew who could be trusted and who couldn't. I asked the Lord to bring in those He had handpicked for the project, and to remove those who were not meant to be involved.

In December 1979, before the vision for Project Pearl had really been birthed, the Lord spoke to me from the Gospel of Mark: *'I tell you the truth, if anyone says to this mountain, "Go, throw yourself into the sea," and does not doubt in his heart but believes that what he says will happen, it will be done for him. Therefore I tell you, whatever you ask for in prayer, believe that you have received it, and it will be yours. And when you stand praying, if you hold anything against anyone, forgive him, so that your Father in heaven may forgive you your sins'* (Mark 11:23–26).

Preachers often use the first part of what Jesus said – about having faith to pray for the impossible – but rarely mention it in connection with the second part, that if we hold anything against any person we must forgive them. You may have a large need in your life that never seems to go away. As you pray about it, ask the Holy Spirit to search your heart and reveal if you are holding any bitterness or unforgiveness against another person. If so, you may find that when you forgive those who have offended you, the blockage you have struggled against for so long will also be cast into the sea.

From that point on, the Lord told me that I would never see Pearl succeed unless I maintained a witness of walking in forgiveness in front of every person involved with the project. Only by doing this would the Lord's blessings be upon us, and only if I were able to walk in humility and reconciliation would the other participants in the vision follow my example. If I failed to do this, I felt it would be impossible for other people to catch the fire and have the same vision for Project Pearl. We had to make sure there was no sin blocking our walk with the Lord, because if there was, anything we tried to do would be doomed to failure.

I also had to show the others involved that I believed the project would succeed. This was in obedience to the first part of the scripture in the Gospel of Mark, which says, *'I tell you the truth, if anyone says to this mountain, "Go, throw yourself into the sea," and does not doubt in his heart but believes that what he says will happen, it will be done for him.'* There was no point in me being unsure if the whole thing was from the Lord, or doubting that we would succeed. The Lord required me to be resolute and not to doubt. Only if this happened would the other men be committed to the task ahead of us. The Bible asks, *'If the trumpet does not sound a clear call, who will get ready for battle?'* (1 Corinthians 14:8). Part of my role was to sound the trumpet clearly to all those involved with Pearl, so as to prepare them for battle.

***

In January 1980, the famous house church leader Wang Mingdao was released after a total of twenty-three years in prison. When I heard this, I traveled with two colleagues and met this old saint at his home in Shanghai.

Wang Mingdao was first arrested and imprisoned in 1955. Being a key leader in the Chinese Church, he was cruelly tortured by the authorities. After fourteen months he was unable to bear any more, and in a moment of weakness Wang agreed to sign a paper admitting that his opposition to the Three-Self Patriotic Movement had been a misjudgment.

Even in his weakness, Wang would not entertain the thought of denying Jesus Christ, but his confession stated that he no longer believed in heaven. Wang reasoned that this was not the same as denying the Lord. He returned home unannounced, much to the surprise of his wife. She knew something was wrong and immediately asked him why he had been released. When he told her that he had not denied Christ, but had signed a statement indicating he didn't believe in heaven, Wang's wife was filled with righteous anger. 'Get out of here!' she shouted, 'I don't want to live in the same house as a man who doesn't believe in heaven!'

Wang Mingdao's mind was wracked with remorse and he returned to the police station where he had made his confession. He asked to see his written statement, and the officer duly obliged, thinking Wang had come to add some more words to it. As soon as it was given to him, the preacher shoved the paper into his mouth and ate it. In this dramatic fashion, he retracted his confession.

The authorities rearrested Wang Mingdao and sent him back to prison. He remained there for the next twenty-one years and eight months. When I first met him, Wang leaned forward and told me, 'I have been a Peter, but I have never been a Judas. Now there is only one thing I fear. I fear God. So long as I do not sin against Him, and I remain faithful to Him, then I am afraid of nothing.'

The life and testimony of Wang Mingdao and his wife had a great impact on me. Years later I was privileged to write a book on my experiences of meeting him.*

_____

* Brother David with Lela Gilbert, *Walking the Hard Road: The Wang Ming Tao Story* (London: Marshall Pickering, 1989).

Chapter Fourteen:

God Searches Our Hearts

We had committed to deliver one million Bibles to China, but the details of just how that would happen still had to be worked out.

Teams of couriers from many nations came to Hong Kong, and were loaded down with Bibles to carry across the border into China. Many prayers were uttered along the lines of, 'Lord, when you were here on the earth you opened blind eyes. Now we ask you to blind open eyes as we take your Holy Word to your children in China.' Team after team returned to Hong Kong with their faith enlarged and their passion for Jesus ignited. A thousand different things happened, one never the same as another. On countless occasions they saw God help them at the exact moment they needed it. Guards were often distracted and looked away as one of the Bible couriers approached the inspection desk. On numerous occasions a whole line of tourists would be stopped and thoroughly searched one by one, only for the Christian's bag to be waved through. One courier reported that an officer had been fully alert and checking bags, but when he approached the desk, the man suddenly closed his eyes and dozed off! Others said that for some strange reason the officers just didn't seem to see them at all, so they just kept walking through the customs inspection area and into China.

On those occasions when Bible couriers were caught, the Bibles were taken from them and a receipt issued. When that person left China, they would go to an office in the customs building, reclaim the Bibles, and take them back to Hong Kong. The same Bibles would be repacked and taken across the border a short time later. The end result was that the large majority of couriers successfully delivered their Bibles into China, and the church was being blessed and strengthened with each bag and suitcase that made it through. These were exciting days, and when other mission organizations based in Hong Kong heard about it, they too started to mobilize teams to carry Bibles into China.

Open Doors began to openly advertise our plan to take one million Bibles into China. This was a deliberate decoy, so that the Chinese government would think the million would come in bag-by-bag, suitcase-by-suitcase, by foreigners crossing the borders. We began to share the vision for Project Pearl around the world, in Japan, Australia, New Zealand, Holland, Italy, France, Britain, Latin America, Africa and North America. People began to respond, saying they would pray and believe with us. Some sent finances to help with the printing of the one million Bibles that would go into China.

One of the key figures in Project Pearl was Dr Edward Neteland, who was the Vice-President of Open Doors International at the time and also the Director of Open Doors USA. He was an integral part of Pearl from the beginning, and was responsible for spreading the vision for the project around the world. Ed became one of my dearest friends and co-workers. He went to be with Jesus after suffering a fall at his home in 2006. Heaven is richer and this world poorer for the passing of Ed Neteland.

A number of large teams came from around the world. Twenty people came on one team, thirty on another, and fifty on the largest team. Some of them were caught at the border and all their Bibles confiscated. This did not bother us, because we knew their efforts were helping Project Pearl. If they got the Bibles across, great! God's Word would bless the believers. If they were caught at the border, great! The decoy that we planned to deliver one million Bibles by suitcase would be reinforced in the minds of the customs officers.

While teams of couriers continued to come, we were wrestling with a larger question: Just how should we take a million Bibles to China? God started to reveal the plan step by step. At times we felt His presence strongly as we planned and prayed about Project Pearl. We studied some scriptures that Chinese believers in Shanghai had sent us. They quoted from Psalm 104. As we read through the Psalm we were most struck by the many verses that spoke about God's glory being shown on the water or sea:

> He wraps himself in light as with a garment; he stretches out the heavens like a tent and lays the beams of his upper chambers on their waters. He makes the clouds his chariot and rides on the wings of the wind.... There is the sea, vast and spacious, teeming with creatures beyond number – living things both large and small. There the ships go to and fro, and the leviathan, which you formed to frolic there. (Psalm 104:2–3, 25–26)

Was this a message from the Lord about the type of Bible delivery we should do for Pearl? We felt so, and committed ourselves afresh before the Lord. Later, the Kwang family verified that the best method for the delivery of one million Bibles would be by ship.

In January 1980 I was in Sydney, Australia, when I fell ill with chest pains and was taken to hospital. I was diagnosed with angina, brought about by the stress of the whole project. While I was recovering, an elderly couple visited and gave me a paper about Joshua and the story of when the sun and moon stood still for almost twenty-four hours (see Joshua 10:1–15). God spoke to me through this booklet, and I knew that just as Joshua and the Israelites had seen the mighty power of God that day, so we also could ask the Lord to manifest His awesome power and presence to help one million Bibles be successfully delivered into the hands of His starving children in China.

After recovering from my illness I left Australia and flew to Hong Kong and met with the Kwang family. Without sharing what the Lord had shown me in Australia, I asked them, 'How is it going to be when we take a million Bibles into China?' They replied, 'It is going to be like the day in the Bible when the sun and moon stood still for Joshua.'

A short while later I traveled to Holland to lay these plans before Brother Andrew and the international directors of Open Doors. While on the plane, my Bible reading brought me to the account of when the Israelites sought the Lord's protection from the Egyptians. The story concluded, *'Throughout the night the cloud brought darkness to the one side and light to the other side; so neither went near the other all night long'* (Exodus 14:20). Brother Andrew was excited about our plans for the delivery by boat. He told me that if I had the faith, I could do anything to complete Project Pearl and I should trust the Lord to bring all the pieces together.

Later, after returning to Hong Kong, my co-worker Keith Ritter and I met with Papa and Mama Kwang at our hotel. They had just returned from several weeks of prayer and fasting with the believers inside China. 'Our brethren are praising God for the wonderful news of Project Pearl,' Papa Kwang reported. 'They send you their love and are praying for the delivery.' Mama Kwang added, 'They know it will take a mighty act of God to see one million Bibles in their land. And brothers, the miracle will not end with the delivery itself. After that there will be many lives touched by the Bibles.'

Mama Kwang reached for her Bible. 'Brother David, we believe the Lord has given us a verse regarding what He will do on the night of the delivery of the Bibles. We received this while in prayer with our brethren inside

China.' She thumbed her way through her well-used Bible. As I waited eagerly for what she was about to share, I remembered that the Chinese Christians have a saying: 'Dirty Bible, clean Christian. Clean Bible, dirty Christian'. Mama Kwang's Bible had obviously seen thousands of hours of use.

'Ah, here it is,' she exclaimed. It was from Exodus: *'Throughout the night the cloud brought darkness to the one side and light to the other side; so neither went near the other all night long'* (Exodus 14:20). I nearly fell off my chair when I heard this! It was exactly the same verse the Lord had shown me on my way to Holland. When I explained this, we all wept with joy, thanking God for giving us such clear confirmation of His will.

A deep realization dawned on me that this delivery would only succeed if we saw a series of miracles as God's power energized us and swept us along. Perhaps this is what the Apostle Paul referred to when he wrote, *'To this end I labor, struggling with all his energy, which so powerfully works in me'* (Colossians 1:29).

The Bible also says, *'In his heart a man plans his course, but the Lord determines his steps'* (Proverbs 16:9). We realized we could make all the plans we wanted to, but if God were not personally involved, directing and empowering the whole project, it would be a disastrous failure. God was bringing us to a place where we had to utterly depend on Him for success. This was not a game. Our lives, and the lives of our Chinese brothers and sisters, might depend on it. We couldn't turn to any human source for help. We could only turn to Jesus Christ. *'This is what the Lord says: "Cursed is the one who trusts in man, who depends on flesh for his strength and whose heart turns away from the Lord"'* (Jeremiah 17:5).

We also meditated on the story about when the disciples were out on the Sea of Galilee and were suddenly swamped by a storm. When Jesus climbed aboard, however, *'immediately the boat reached the shore where they were heading'* (John 6:21). This was a crucial lesson for us. We had to make sure Jesus was in our boat if we were to be successful.

Throughout history, God has worked in ways that bring glory to His name. When God's children trust Him to do something that is completely impossible by mere human effort, all the glory goes to the Lord. We were convinced that God wanted to glorify His name and display His power through our lives and through Project Pearl.

So much Christian activity seems to be mere human plans being accomplished by human strength. Only those things that have been initiated and empowered by God will remain. The rest of our efforts and activities will be of no eternal consequence. I wonder if this is one of the meanings of what Paul wrote to the church in Corinth: *'But each one should be careful how he builds. For no one can lay any foundation other than the one already laid, which is Jesus Christ. If any man builds on this foundation using gold, silver, costly stones, wood, hay or straw, his work will be shown for what it is, because the Day will bring it to light. It will be revealed with fire, and the fire will test the quality of each man's work. If what he has built survives, he will receive his reward. If it is burned up, he will suffer loss; he himself will be saved, but only as one escaping through the flames'* (1 Corinthians 3:10–15).

***

In March 1980 I called all the various Open Doors leaders who wanted to be involved in Project Pearl to come to the Philippines for prayer and planning meetings. Fifty of us met together at the famous Manila Hotel, which General Douglas MacArthur had once used as an operations base for fourteen years. The fifty leaders were paired up two to a room. At the time, they didn't know about the plan to deliver the one million Bibles by boat, all at one time. They assumed that we would try to expand the successful suitcase deliveries that had helped us take 30,000 Bibles into China.

Most people arrived in Manila on a Saturday, and unpacked their bags in readiness for the meetings ahead. A few days before the meetings I knelt in prayer one evening, asking the Lord for guidance. Then I went to bed. In the middle of the night the Holy Spirit woke me up and I quieted my heart before Him. I then heard the small, still voice of the Lord speak in the depths of my spirit: 'You are to change hotels on Monday, to find out if they will really be obedient to you.' Without telling the incoming Open Doors leaders, I asked my Filipina secretary to go across town to the Plaza Hotel and book the same number of rooms, twenty-five, for Monday until the end of our conference.

On Sunday evening we had a time of prayer and worship at the Manila Hotel, and everyone caught up with one another. The following morning I stood up and taught about the Israelites when they marched around Jericho. I read how Joshua commanded the people to be quiet until they had completed the seven days of marching around the city (see Joshua 6:10). I then told everyone, 'Right now, all of you need to keep your mouths shut. And don't open them again until I tell you. You have forty-five minutes to go to your rooms, pack up all your belongings and bring your bags down to the lobby. Check out of your room, then go outside and get onto one of the two buses that will be waiting for you. Keep your mouths shut during this whole time. There will be people on the bus watching you.'

Everyone did as I asked, and our two buses drove off. We purposely took a circuitous route around the city of Manila until we finally arrived at the Philippine Plaza Hotel, where a sign said, 'Welcome to the Master Consultants group'. At the Manila Hotel we had been booked in as Open Doors. As this was a well-known missionary group, I thought it posed a security risk to our operation, hence the change to a generic name. We all went into the conference room at the Philippine Plaza Hotel, and we continued our meeting.

I told the gathered brothers and sisters that due to the nature of the operation, complete secrecy was required. On a board in the conference room I wrote in capital letters: 'NEED TO KNOW'. I explained that information would be given to them strictly on a need-to-know basis. If they needed to know something, they would be told. If not, then they would not be told. It was as simple as that. I continued with the Bible study from Joshua and when I reached the point where the Israelites were commanded to shout, I told the group that they could now open their mouths. Everybody shouted 'Hallelujah!'

In an operation as large, complicated and potentially dangerous as Pearl, we needed people who were willing to work in secrecy, otherwise we would have no chance of success. We needed to retain the element of surprise. If the Chinese authorities discovered what we were planning it would have disastrous and deadly consequences.

Throughout this whole process, people were always given a choice of staying with the project or leaving. They were free to go home at any time. Nobody was forced to stay against their will. This was the way God led Gideon to deal with his army as they prepared to fight the Midianites (see Judges, chapter 7). The Lord sifted the men, until the number of those who fought against the huge Midianite army was reduced from an original 32,000 to just 300! The rest were told to go home. God gave Gideon and his men a great victory that day as the 300 routed the enemy.

If you are starting out in any form of Christian ministry, let this be a lesson for you. Force of numbers does not impress God. He doesn't need large numbers of people to do things. You shouldn't merely pray for people to join you.

Rather, you should ask God to handpick and send the right people to serve with you in the vision. It may be many or it may be few, but God knows how to piece together a team that can achieve what He has asked you to do.

I believe the Lord told me to change hotels in Manila so that we could discern who should be involved with the project, and who should not. Most people passed the test, but one lady was particularly upset with me because of the sudden and unexplained change. With tears streaming down her cheeks she told me how rude I was. I didn't care in the slightest, because I wasn't interested in winning a popularity contest. I sent her back home to America and she played no further part in Project Pearl.

I have found that many Christians are not used to receiving instructions at all. The church in their minds is some kind of a happy social club, where nobody requires anything of anybody else. I guess it has something to do with my time in the Marines, but I knew that if Project Pearl was to be a success we had to have a clear chain of command. The stakes were too high for anything else. The worst-case scenario was to be out on the high seas with a million Bibles, with crew members who wanted to discuss every order so that we could all reach a consensus before proceeding. No! We needed a crew that understood when they were told to do something; they needed to do it without hesitation. Anything else would never work.

Before I had told any of the fifty people in Manila about how the delivery would take place, Eddie Cairns from New Zealand came to me and excitedly declared, 'David, I've already seen it!' I looked at him quizzically and asked, 'What do you mean?' He replied, 'The Lord showed me how it's going to happen in a vision! I saw a whale going up onto a beach, and it spewed all the Bibles out onto the sand.'

I asked Eddie if he had told anyone else about his vision, and he assured me he hadn't. I pleaded with him not to tell a soul. This was also a confirmation to me that we were on the right track. Eddie is a precious brother, who later played a crucial role in Project Pearl. You could write a whole book about all the visions and dreams the Lord has shown him over the years. They tend to be remarkably accurate in a way that unmistakably reveals the mind of God. When Eddie promises to do something, it always gets done. He also possesses a shepherd's heart, literally. Once I was driving with Eddie from his home in Tauranga to New Zealand's largest city, Auckland. All of a sudden he pulled the car over to the side of the road and got out. He leapt over a fence and ran into the middle of the field, where a lamb was stuck in a pool of mud. Eddie picked the freezing lamb up in his arms and hugged it until he was sure it would survive.

Our meetings in Manila concluded, and everybody went home. Some of them had the task of raising finances for the project, while others were involved in a variety of different ways. Only a small core of several people had been informed that the Bibles were to be delivered by boat. The remainder still believed they would be taken across the border by teams carrying suitcases.

Chapter Fifteen:

Outcome, Methods, Resources

We believed that God had spoken to us about delivering one million Bibles to China by boat. This was a huge undertaking, and we hardly knew where to begin.

A core group of six men emerged who were to be the only people with the full picture of what Project Pearl involved and how we planned to deliver the Bibles. This group, which I called the 'inner circle', consisted of Brother Joseph (from the Philippines), Pablo (an Open Doors leader from Canada), Keith Ritter (a former American Marine then living in Japan), Bill Tinsley (an American living in the Philippines who captained the boat), Dr Jim (an American who provided invaluable technical input and strategizing expertise), and myself. Each of us had various strengths and weaknesses, but the Lord used us to complement one another. The only member of our inner circle who wasn't on the boat for the delivery was Dr Jim, but he was an indispensable part of the whole operation.

The six of us had many meetings together, sometimes for a week at a time. We spent hundreds of hours together in prayer, and we planned and talked until our voices were hoarse. During one meeting Daniel Kwang, the son of house church leaders Papa and Mama Kwang, told us about a beach near the city of Shantou (formerly called Swatow) in southern China. We immediately asked Brother Joseph to visit the beach and take pictures so we could get an idea of what it looked like.

Jim told us that whenever the military plans an

operation, they first create an O.M.R., which stands for 'Outcome, Methods, and Resources'. The reason for this was to set clear goals for the mission, and to examine how to achieve them. The big difference between us and the military, of course, was that we had few or no resources at our disposal, so we had to trust God for everything.

I spoke first on the desired outcome of the project: 'We want to see a million Bibles delivered safely on the beach. We want to go in and come out without losing a man or even being discovered.' The other men sat in silence, letting the reality of our mission impact on them. I continued, 'We want to see the power of God go with us and before us. And we want Him to receive all credit for the success of this whole thing.'

When we looked at the resources needed for Pearl, it was obvious that it would cost millions of dollars. It emerged that there were only a few thousand dollars at our disposal at the time! After a long discussion, I again spoke up: 'Look, if we are going to trust the Lord for a million Bibles, then surely we can trust Him for the funds and equipment to deliver them.'

Four objectives were expressed for the outcome of the delivery, and these became the main focus of our prayers:

1. First and foremost, we prayed for a successful delivery of one million Bibles.

2. We prayed that when news of the enormous need of the Chinese Church reached the West, thousands of Christians would get involved in bringing Bibles to China.

3. That God would use the delivery to increase the profile of the house churches in China, and give them a voice around the world. We believed they had a vitally important message for believers everywhere.

4. We prayed the delivery might prompt Deng Xiaoping and the Chinese government leaders to avoid similar deliveries by legally printing Bibles for the Christians in

China. At the time the Three-Self Church had begun to print Bibles, but only in very small numbers, and only for their own members.

At one of our earliest planning meetings in the Philippines we tried to estimate exactly how much space one million Bibles would require, and how much they would weigh. We estimated that each Bible would weigh approximately half a pound, which meant a total of around 500,000 pounds, or 232 tons. For size, we took the dimensions of each Bible to be 5.5 inches long, 3.5 inches wide, and 0.75 of an inch thick. There was silence as we started calculating. Pablo was the first to speak, 'That appears to be a stack about 20 feet square, or about the size of a two-story house.'

One of the original ideas we discussed was to have a great big landing craft with trucks, cranes and forklifts on-board, and to land right on the beach and simply drive off with the Bibles. Another plan to emerge was to do a sea transfer, lifting the Bibles off our vessel with cranes and loading them, while out at sea, onto a vessel operated by the Chinese Christians. In the end, the believers in China told us they were only able to do a beach delivery.

Dr Jim was well connected with some of the most qualified engineers and strategists in the world. He asked me if he should approach his contacts for their input into how a group of people could secretly move 232 tons of cargo onto a beach within a two-hour time frame. The suggestion of the 'think tank' was to place the cargo into 50-gallon drums, and pull them to shore by rope.

Instead of using 50-gallon drums, I thought we could design a water-proof block with a certain number of boxes of books on it, fitted in such a way that it would float. I made some suggestions, and Dr Jim took them to his 'think tank'. They did their calculations and declared, 'It won't float'. We went away and come up with another design, and again their response was, 'It won't float'. This process continued several times until finally Bill and Dr Jim designed a block with an 18-inch freeboard at the bottom. This addition made the blocks substantially more stable, and almost impossible to sink. This is the design we went with.

We now had a plan of how to float the Bibles in the water, but we needed direction from the Lord about how to haul such a massive load across the ocean, how to unload it, and what kind of boat we would need to achieve this in the fastest and most efficient manner possible. At Captain Bill's suggestion, we made plans to build a submersible barge. The rest of us had never even heard of such a thing before.

***

Captain Bill Tinsley:* I met my old friend David for breakfast one morning in the Philippines, and he asked me what I was involved with at the time. I explained that I had a new research project to bring rare species of fish from the South China Sea, with the aim of repopulating the inland seas around the Philippines. David listened attentively and said, 'That's interesting, but the challenge I want to share with you now is much larger.' I asked, 'What do you have in mind that could be bigger than moving tons and tons of live fish across a thousand miles of sea?'

'How about moving a few hundred tons of Bibles across that same sea to our brothers and sisters in China?' David replied. This set me back, and when he explained the vision God had given to take a million Bibles to China, I asked if he was serious. After assuring me that he was, I expressed my interest in getting involved, and promised to pray about it.

When I returned home that day, I was not thinking

---

* Bill Tinsley included an account of Project Pearl in his autobiography. See William K. Tinsley, *Sea Dog: An Autobiography* (Taipei: Living Stone Press, 1984).

much about moving fish. I wondered if David was really serious or if he was just speculating. It was a really crazy idea, but I had known David for many years and he was known for taking impossible leaps of faith.

Over the coming weeks, the Lord clearly directed me from His Word, confirming that I should get involved with Project Pearl. I prayed more than I had done for years. For about ten days in a row, Bible verses about the sea leapt out of the Bible to me. God's direction was as clear as a bell. He also led me in the Bible to King David's experience when he moved the Ark of the Covenant (see 1 Chronicles, chapters 13 to 15). David had attempted to move the sacred box in two different ways. One way was wrong and ended in a terrible disaster. The other way was God's way and was a great success. Similarly, I knew that moving the scriptures to China would be a sacred trust. It had to be done the Lord's way; otherwise it would result in disaster.

At the time I thought I would be just one of a group of experienced crewmembers. I never imagined I would end up being the only person on-board with any experience at sea, or that I would be appointed captain. I even ended up designing the barge that we used. There were only six of us involved in the planning in the early stages. We spent many hours discussing and praying together, and we understood the need for absolute secrecy if it was to succeed.

At one of our planning meetings, David set a delivery date in April 1981 – just seven months away. This was equivalent in my mind to Elijah pouring water on the sacrifice before the prophets of Baal. 'We have no money or equipment. All we have is a plan. How can we possibly do this job in seven months?' I objected. Others agreed with me. Brother David just as stubbornly reminded us, 'What is impossible with man is always possible with God.'

After considering what kind of barge we would need to best deliver such a massive cargo, I realized the ideal design would be a semi-submersible barge that could sink far enough below the surface of the water to allow the cargo to float off.

I went to the Engineering Equipment Yard at Batangas, Philippines, and told the manager that we needed a barge built from scratch in just a few months. He thought I was crazy, but agreed to hire more men to help build it. The barge we needed would be 100 feet long and 37 feet wide, and have two 10-inch gate valves, which when opened would allow the cargo-deck to sink five feet underwater, yet still retain her stability. This would allow the blocks of Bibles to float free and be pulled by smaller boats onto the beach.

We asked Brother Frank to oversee the construction of the barge for us. A talented engineer, he supervised the Filipino workers for the entire length of time it took to build the barge. Although he didn't make the final delivery team, Frank was an invaluable part of the whole project, and was a blessing to everyone who knew him.

Chapter Sixteen:
The Miracle Tugboat

Work on a semi-submersible barge large enough to carry the Bibles was underway, and we were moving forward in total reliance on the Lord. We had nothing, and there was no way we would ever see this plan come to fruition unless God sovereignly involved Himself in every step of the process. We moved forward by faith. At one time our barge consisted of just sheets of metal for the hull. We had no money to even start building the sides!

While we were trusting Jesus to provide for the barge, we still didn't know where we could find a tugboat to pull the barge across the South China Sea. We decided we might as well start to look, so we went to inspect an old tugboat that was for sale in Manila Harbor. It turned out to be a piece of junk. I gave Pablo the responsibility to find a suitable tugboat, and we sent him to Taiwan, Hong Kong and Singapore. He didn't find one in Taiwan or Hong Kong and he didn't go to Singapore, as everyone told him tugboats were not made or sold there. For the next few months all avenues to buying a tugboat were dead-ends. There was a growing sense of frustration, and it seemed that for some reason tugboats had become as scarce as hen's teeth in South-east Asia.

In January 1980 Todd Martin, an Open Doors leader, and I traveled to New Zealand, to speak at a mission conference. After arriving, I asked one of our hosts, Eddie Cairns, how much a cow cost to buy in New Zealand. He replied, 'Approximately a thousand U.S. dollars'. The next day I told the audience what the Lord had impressed on my heart to say: 'We need New Zealand to give 500 cows to help get a million Bibles into China.' I didn't want to tell the New Zealanders that we needed half a million dollars, as that seemed too overwhelming for people. But by saying we needed 500 cows, people were able to better grasp and understand the size of the need.

Eddie got us out of bed one night at 1.30 a.m. Bleary-eyed, we gathered together. Eddie and another New Zealand mission leader knelt down in prayer and committed to raise half a million U.S. dollars, or 500 cows, for Project Pearl.

New Zealand was the newest Open Doors office at the time, and was considered the 'baby' of the ministry. When other Open Doors offices around the world heard about their generous commitment, they were amazed. Australia also committed to give half a million dollars, and the United States became more heavily involved from this point on.

Open Doors leaders decided that the first money given to Project Pearl should be personal donations made by them and their staff members. This way, they would not be asking anyone to give to something that they themselves had not given to first. After this, donations started to come in from all around the world. It was really amazing to see the Lord bring them in. Many were small amounts of a few dollars each, and these were precious to the Lord. A grandmother knitted sweaters, sold them at her local market, and gave the money to Pearl, and we received reports of children emptying their piggy banks to bless the Christians in China. Other gifts were large. In Australia a farmer gave $200,000 to Project Pearl, while one church with just thirty members in Melbourne sent a gift of $100,000. We were amazed after receiving this gift, and were wondering how a small church could manage to send such a large amount when a second gift of $100,000 arrived from them!

I traveled to Germany for the first time and was amazed to see the generous response there too. I stayed in the home of Waldemar Sardaczuk, the head of a mission called Aktionskomitee für Verfolgte Christen, or AVC. He and his wife fed me split pea and oxtail soup with French toast. I came to like it. A couple of days later, Waldemar told me he and his board had prayed, and had decided to give $200,000 towards the cost of the Bibles for Project Pearl.

Several months after I had challenged the believers in New Zealand to provide 500 cows, I returned to Auckland to check on their progress with the board of Open Doors. During the meeting I told them about the tugboat we were looking for. Everyone in the room dropped to their knees and prayed to the Lord, asking Him to provide the right tugboat, and to show us where to get it. As we were praying, Eddie Cairns suddenly had a vision. He said, 'I see some sheds in Singapore painted like a rainbow. There is a line of trees at the entrance to the facility, which is covered with wire netting. Behind a fence next to the building is a tugboat, hoisted out of the water. That is the tugboat the Lord has provided for you.'

I had known Eddie long enough to realize he was a man of God, and I had yet to hear him share any direction from the Lord that turned out to be false. Eddie was the one who had come to me in the Philippines and told me the Lord had shown him a vision of a huge whale depositing Bibles onto a beach in China. I was excited and believed the Lord had provided an answer to our many prayers. Then a series of strange and remarkable events unfolded in quick succession, which to this day ranks as one of the most amazing experiences of my life.

I was due to leave New Zealand the following day, but Qantas Airlines went on strike and I couldn't return to Manila through Sydney as planned. Qantas reassigned me to an Air New Zealand flight, going through Singapore. The flight arrived in the afternoon and was too late to get a connecting flight to Manila that day, so I was required to stay overnight in Singapore.

As soon as I checked into my hotel room in Singapore I looked through the Yellow Pages for boat manufacturers and wrote down a list of names and addresses. Then I prayed and asked the Lord to direct my path. I went downstairs and got into a taxi. The driver asked me where I wanted to go and I showed him my list of boat manufacturers that I had collected from the telephone book. The driver asked me what kind of boat I was looking for; I told him, 'A tugboat'. Looking at me in his rear vision mirror, he said: 'Tugboats are not made by any of the manufacturers on your list, but I can take you to where they build them. It's only ten minutes from here.'

All of a sudden, as we traveled along the beautiful tropical road, I saw a building painted like a rainbow. I asked the driver to pull over and stop, and I went up to the gate and asked the guard if the company sold tugboats. 'Yes, we have tugboats, but I can't let you see them tonight,' he insisted. 'You will have to come back tomorrow morning.'

I looked the guard in the eye and said, 'Sir, I want to buy a tugboat but I am leaving Singapore tomorrow morning. Please let me have a look.' He opened the gate and there I beheld a wonderful sight: Two brand new tugboats hoisted up on blocks.

I could hardly sleep that night as excitement and awe surged through my body. God was doing a great miracle, and I could hardly wait to see the next step. I flew back to Manila and told Pablo and Bill to drop whatever they were doing and come with me back to Singapore. The next day we arrived back in the prosperous island nation. We checked into the same hotel that I had stayed in during my stopover, and as soon as we had put our bags inside our rooms I took my brothers to the shipyard. Their eyes got big with excitement when they saw the two new tugs sitting there. We were allowed to climb the ladder and stand on the bridge. Captain Bill asked the workers to lower the boat into the water so he could see how the engine ran. He was thrilled by the quality of the vessel and declared, 'This is it!'

The three of us discussed what we should do next. We decided Bill would return to the Philippines while Pablo and I would remain behind in Singapore to negotiate the price of the tugboat.

The next morning we met the owner and asked him how much he was selling the tugboat for. He wrote a figure on a piece of paper and handed it to me: 'US$750,000'. I told him, 'Sir, sharpen your pencil!' He asked what I meant, and I replied, 'There's no way in the world I'm going to give you $750,000 for that tugboat. I'll give you $450,000.'

The owner immediately acted like my offer was an insult, and said he had never had a Westerner bargain over a price before. He looked at me and asked, 'Do you have Chinese blood in you?'

In the end, after protracted negotiations, we agreed on a price of $480,000. He told us, 'You have to put a $100,000 deposit down and then you will have ten days to pay the balance, otherwise you will lose your deposit.'

The next morning Pablo and I returned to his office to sign the contract.

There was just one problem. We didn't have any money to buy it!

I asked Pablo, 'Do you have the faith to sign?' He replied, 'If you have, I have,' and together we signed on the dotted line.

Back at the hotel, I phoned some of our Open Doors leaders around the world and told them that we had found a tugboat. I asked if they had any money that they could wire to us in Singapore to help us pay the deposit. Brother Roly said the New Zealand office had $25,000 to send. Then I phoned George Conner in Australia. He said he would wire $50,000 immediately. Both men sent the money directly into the Singapore shipyard's bank account.

I then called Keith Ritter in Japan and told him we

needed $25,000 immediately. He said this was impossible because Japanese banking regulations meant it would take several days for the money to be cleared before it left Japan. Hearing what was going on, one of Keith's staff members, a Japanese lady named Sachiko-san, provided a solution. The restrictions on sending money out of the country did not apply to personal accounts. She graciously volunteered to send $25,000 of her own money to us in Singapore, and she immediately went down to the bank and arranged it.

The next day, Pablo and I told the boat owner that the $100,000 was on its way. Now all we needed was $380,000 more in ten days, otherwise all of the deposit money, collected from hundreds of generous individuals and given for the work of the Lord, would be forfeited.

***

Eddie Cairns: Brother David came to New Zealand and shared the vision to deliver one million Bibles into China by boat with me. David and I had known each other since 1976, when we found that we shared the same vision of providing the Word of God to persecuted Christians. Our hearts were immediately knitted together. We prayed and wept together for China, and since that time we had often been in contact.

David told us that a barge was being constructed in the Philippines, but they had struggled to locate a suitable tugboat for the operation. We prayed together and a colleague, Maurice, suddenly said, 'I believe God is telling me that this boat is in Singapore.'

David was surprised. He explained that he was leaving New Zealand, going through Australia, and returning to the Philippines. He didn't have an opportunity to visit Singapore. As we continued to pray, a vision appeared before me. In it I saw a large tugboat in its cradle on the waterfront behind some sheds painted like a rainbow. The area was enclosed by high wire netting, and at the entrance to the facility stood some trees.

While I told this to the group, a young lady from the office entered the room and told Brother David that Qantas, the Australian airline, had stopped flying because of a strike, so she had rerouted David through Singapore on Air New Zealand instead!

We all looked at each other and smiled. This was the hand of the Lord.

Two days later I received a phone call from an excited David. 'I found it!' he said. 'It was just like you described. I got off the plane in Singapore, took a taxi, and asked the driver to take me to the shipyards. I told him I was looking for a tugboat. We approached the waterfront. I saw the trees, the rainbow buildings and the wire netting, just like you said!'

Chapter Seventeen:

God's Work, Done God's Way...

After we signed the contract for the tugboat, Keith Ritter asked me to come to Tokyo as soon as possible. I arrived two days later. Keith and I had a wonderful Japanese dinner together and afterwards I went to my room and fell asleep. At three o'clock in the morning my phone rang. I answered it and found it was the treasurer of the Open Doors USA office on the other end. He said, 'David, I hear you're purchasing a tugboat.'

I replied, 'Yes sir.'

'Well, we don't have the money for it!' he said, 'and who gave you the permission?'

I told him, 'Brother Andrew told me that if I had the faith I could do anything to complete Project Pearl.'

He insisted, 'Well, you should have talked to me first!'

I assured him, 'I have been talking to the Lord.'

Again, he asked, 'But why not me?'

I replied, 'Because you are not God!'

I hung up the phone and went back to sleep.

In the morning I woke to find a telegram had been pushed under my door. It was from the chairman of the board of Open Doors USA, ordering me to fly to America and explain my actions at a board meeting scheduled for a few days' time.

I have come to see that when God is moving in miraculous ways and opening doors of opportunity, it is often difficult for those not directly involved to come to grips with it.

The next day Keith and I met together to pray about

how the Lord might provide the $380,000 needed to complete the purchase of the tugboat. We now had just seven days left to get it.

While we were praying, Keith had a distinct impression that he should call Chuck Smith, pastor of the large Calvary Chapel in California. Keith had known Chuck for a number of years, so I encouraged him to go ahead and call. When Chuck answered the phone, Keith told him that we were coming to America and would like to meet with him. Chuck replied, 'I know. The Lord told me that you're coming.'

***

Keith Ritter: When I first heard about the idea to deliver a million Bibles by boat to the Christians in China, I felt the Lord was behind it so I never doubted that it would be done. We were careful to determine whether this was our own desire or God's will. Once it was clear that God had actually spoken, it was a matter of just watching Him do what He said He was going to do.

I had known Brother David for many years. I knew that he was someone capable of hearing God's voice, and I recognized the anointing that God placed on his life for this particular project. I was living and working in Japan when the project commenced. The Lord clearly spoke to my heart, telling me to leave the ministry in Japan and stay by David's side until the project was completed.

The financial needs were enormous, way beyond our ability to do anything about. God would have to provide all the money. We needed $480,000 to purchase the tugboat. All of our bases around the world managed to muster up the $100,000 deposit, so we needed an additional $380,000 in ten days or the purchase would fall through.

We prayed a lot, and during one of these times I got the distinct impression that I should go and present the project to Chuck Smith, pastor of the Calvary Chapel in

California. I had known Chuck for many years, and I knew that he was extremely careful how he spends money that has been given to the church as offerings and donations. He feels a deep responsibility to see the money used for the purpose of God's kingdom.

I called and asked if we could come to California and meet with him a few days later. I said, 'Chuck, we have a project that will help the suffering church in Asia. We need help financially. In fact, we need quite a large sum of money. David and I would like to come and see you about it. We're coming to the U.S. tomorrow and we're wondering if you could set some time aside to meet with us.' Chuck issued an enthusiastic invitation, saying he would set aside the whole morning for us. We immediately jumped on the first available plane and were in California the next day!

We arrived at the church on a Friday morning at nine o'clock. Chuck led us to a private room and we set up our presentation. We showed him a large picture of the beach where we intended to deliver the Bibles, and pictures of the tug and barge. We presented details of our research and planning, and went through our budget. We even took along a pair of 'hot goggles' – military style infrared equipment that would help us see in the dark. We turned the lights in the room off and let Chuck try them on.

I remember that when Calvary Chapel first began in the mid-1960s, the church couldn't afford to pay Chuck anything. He was so poor that he couldn't even afford to buy shoes for his children to attend an athletics meeting. At that time I went to a Bible bookstore with Chuck and saw a little leather pocket Bible. It was just what I needed. The Bible cost $8, but I was so poor that I had to reluctantly put it back on the shelf. Chuck noticed this and bought it for me, even though it was a real sacrifice. Later, we used that same pocket Bible of mine as a model to help design the size and dimensions of the Project Pearl Bibles. It's amazing how the Lord works. Today many people know about the huge Calvary Chapel in Costa Mesa where Chuck Smith continues to lead tens of thousands of believers, and the thousands of churches around the world that the movement has established, but few realize its humble beginnings.

I think Chuck was impressed with the amount of thorough planning and research that had gone into Project Pearl, both inside and outside China. He knew this was not some vague idea, but all the pieces were in place except for a few major ones.

We finished talking at around lunchtime, and Chuck excused himself and went into another room to pray about it. He told us he would need to speak with the members of his church's board, and that we should return to our hotel room for some rest. At six o'clock in the evening the phone rang. I was out visiting my daughters but David answered. It was Chuck Smith. He said, 'I just wanted to let you know that you can come by tomorrow morning and pick up your $380,000.'

The next morning we returned to the church, amazed at God's provision and praising Him from the bottom of our hearts. We had a wonderful prayer time together with Chuck Smith, Greg Laurie, Mike McIntosh and some other friends. Chuck told us, 'You know, if you are able to pull this thing off, I believe it will go down as one of the great events in church history.'

Because we were running out of time, the money ended up being wired directly to the boat company's bank account in Singapore. Incredibly, before the ten days were up, they had received full cash payment of $480,000 for the tugboat. The owner later told us we were the first people who had ever ordered a boat from them and paid for it on time. I guess they thought we were wealthy businessmen. Little did they know that we were not rich men, but our Father does own the whole universe!

***

Brother David: When Chuck Smith called our hotel room and broke the news, I was so excited that I shouted, 'Hallelujah! Praise the Lord! Thank you, Pastor Chuck, and thank you Calvary Chapel! I don't know what more to say.'

Chuck said, 'David, you have said it all. I'll see you tomorrow morning.'

A few minutes later, Keith arrived and I told him the good news. We thanked the Lord Jesus from the bottom of our hearts, but our celebrations were short-lived because we had to leave and go to the Open Doors board meeting that I had been ordered to attend.

When we walked into the room the atmosphere was tense and you could hear a pin drop. There was fire in the eyes of some of the men there, who were unimpressed that we had the audacity to 'waste' $100,000 of donations as a deposit on a boat, when there was 'no possibility' of us getting the remainder. One of my closest friends on the board, Sealy, arrived. I took him aside and whispered in his ear, 'The tugboat is paid for.' He leapt into the air with excitement, but didn't tell the others.

The board meeting commenced. After prayer, I was asked to give a report on Project Pearl and to update the board members with all the latest news. When I got to the part about Chuck Smith and the $380,000 gift, those gathered momentarily had looks of utter disbelief on their faces, before the atmosphere changed to one of loud rejoicing. The whole room was enraptured with the power and goodness of the Lord Jesus Christ. The same faces that had deep furrows of concern just minutes before were now full of happiness and relief.

The next morning we met Chuck Smith in his office at nine o'clock. His countenance shone like a star, as he took down all the information and wired the $380,000 to the

Singapore boat builder that day. Before we parted he prayed for us and wished us, 'God Speed!'

We flew from Los Angeles to Singapore and met with the owner. He told us, 'I have sold about 50 tugboats before, but this is the first one to ever be paid for before the due time!'

He didn't realize that this was God's tugboat.

Before leaving America we had called the Philippines and asked Bill to get all his crew to Singapore as quickly as possible. Dr Jim and Captain Bill shopped around and purchased the best sonar and satellite navigation equipment they could find. After it was installed we climbed aboard and tested the Lord's new boat in Singapore Harbor.

It had been a hectic week, yet we had seen God move powerfully before us, and we had been swept along in His glory. I was reminded of a principle the great China pioneer missionary J. Hudson Taylor had discovered more than a century earlier: 'God's work, done God's way, will never lack God's supply.'

***

Captain Bill Tinsley: When I first laid eyes on the tug I knew it was exactly what we needed, and what I had specified in our planning meetings. I had prayed for a tug with a high bow to take the big waves. It also needed to be between 90 and 100 feet long, and would need 1,000 horsepower engines. God had answered all of these prayers. It was perfect.

In the following weeks we worked hard with all the many details required to undertake a sea voyage. We had to register the vessel, get licences for all the crewmen, take medical exams and countless other things. The Lord helped all of it to come together.

Chapter Eighteen:
Michael, *Gabriella* and a Million Bibles

After we purchased the tugboat in Singapore we needed to get it registered. On an earlier trip to south China we took more than 700 photographs of ships and tugboats pulling barges up the Pearl and Huang Pu Rivers. We noticed with great interest that most of the boats flew the Panamanian flag. We decided in order to look as inconspicuous as possible, we should register our boat with Panama. To the present day, many ship owners around the world choose to register as Panamanian vessels, as foreigners registering a ship with Panama are not subject to income tax, and the whole process is fast and efficient. Jim went to the Panama Embassy and registered our boat, and also secured seamen's licenses for all the crewmen.

We set up a training base at Puerto Galera on the Philippine Island of Mindoro. A group of initial crewmembers came from around the world and Captain Bill put them through a strenuous training regime. New equipment was purchased to aid our operation. Two large Boston Whalers were a welcome addition. These powerful vessels were used extensively during the training, and sat hoisted up at the back of the barge during the delivery. They were extremely fast across water, and if things went wrong during the Bible delivery, we planned to use them to quickly flee back to international waters.

We also purchased three Zodiac, or 'Z' boats from a distributor in California. These super-fast rubber speedboats were an integral part of the operation. We planned to attach the blocks of Bibles to the Zodiacs, which would then pull the blocks right onto the beach in China, and into the hands of waiting believers.

The whole of Project Pearl was now moving along rapidly. We named the tugboat *Michael*, after the archangel of the same name. From the Bible we saw how Michael fought on behalf of God's people (see Daniel 10:10–21 and Revelation 12:7–9 for example). When the construction of the huge submersible barge was completed we named it *Gabriella*, after the archangel Gabriel. We didn't name the barge *Gabriel* because we didn't want anyone to guess we were a Christian organization.

The archangel Gabriel appears in passages like the eighth and ninth chapters of Daniel, when he was instructed to give *'understanding and insight'* to the prophet. Centuries later, Gabriel appeared to Zechariah in the temple and foretold the coming birth of Jesus Christ, and then went up to Nazareth to tell Mary that she would give birth to the *'Son of the Most High'* (see Luke 1:11–38).

We felt that just as these two archangels came to the aid of God's people at vital times in history, we also needed their help for Project Pearl. We needed all the understanding and insight from the Lord that we could get.

Just how much we needed God became apparent during her maiden voyage from Singapore to the Philippines. Our crewmembers flew into Singapore and boarded the new tug for the journey. Except for the captain, this was our first experience working at sea, and our complete naivety was soon revealed through several comical incidents. During one training session, Captain Bill gave the order, 'All hands on deck!' The men started to run to the deck as instructed, but Brother Joseph ran around in circles with a confused look on his face. He finally asked, 'Where is the deck?'

On another occasion someone was trying to tie a knot with a large rope and Captain Bill yelled, 'No, not like that!

Do it like you did last time.' Finally the person replied, 'But I've never tied a knot before!'

During this time when God was providing the resources we needed to take a million Bibles to China, we were also busy working on one rather important part of the project – the Bibles themselves! First we needed to know which version of Chinese Bible the Christians in China wanted. We sent seven different versions to believers in 40 different locations, and every one replied that they wanted the Union Version, in Simplified Chinese script. This is the version still used by almost all Christians in China today. I went to the Hong Kong Bible Society and asked them to redo the old Union version Bible and typeset it in the new simplified script.

Next we researched printing companies in Japan and Hong Kong to see where we could best print the Bibles according to our specific needs. I then made a special trip to Nashville, Tennessee, and met with Sam Moore, the President of Thomas Nelson Bible Publishers. Before sharing anything about our need for one million Chinese Bibles, I asked Sam to agree to complete secrecy. He could not tell anyone of our plans, whether they ended up printing the Bibles for us or not. He agreed.

I sensed the meetings at Thomas Nelson were really appointed by God. One of the main things I needed to find out was whether the binding adhesive would be strong enough to hold the Bible together during the potentially rough beach delivery we were planning. Without saying a word, Sam Moore picked up one of their Bibles and threw it across his office. It crashed against the wall and fell to the floor. The binding remained perfectly intact. He had made his point!

He then got one of his most trusted employees to shrink-wrap each Bible and place them inside a box, which was then shrink-wrapped two more times. They placed the box into a bathtub full of water, and it floated. We then went out for lunch, and when we returned the Bibles were still floating. We opened the box and found it completely dry inside. This gave me great confidence that our Bibles were both durable and could be made waterproof for the delivery.

I placed the order for one million Chinese Bibles. The dimensions we used were an exact copy of the pocket-size Bible published by Zondervan in Britain. Each full leather bound Chinese Bible was 629 pages in length. After being printed, 90 Bibles were placed in each box, which was then shrink-wrapped in plastic. The printing and packaging of each Bible cost $1.25 each. That might not sound like much, but it meant we had to trust the Lord to provide $1,250,000 to pay the bill! When all the transportation and other costs were included, the total was $1.4 million. Thomas Nelson Publishers graciously agreed to accept payment later when we had the money.

At the end of 1980 I received a precise prophecy during a prayer meeting. At the time it seemed a bit strange. It said that the Bibles would be printed in the first fifty-five days of the new year, and within the second fifty-five days of the year the Bibles would be delivered to Asia, and that it would be done in the resurrection power of the Lord.

Only later did I understand what that meant. The Bibles arrived in Hong Kong just before Easter Sunday – the 109th day of 1981.

After the Bible printing was completed, they were placed inside twenty-five containers and transported across America in a fleet of eighteen-wheeler trucks to San Francisco, where they were repacked into the floatable blocks that we planned to deliver them in.

Along with several other key leaders of the project, I flew to San Francisco to watch the first block being built. It was an exciting and awesome experience. What we had prayed about was now becoming a reality before our very eyes. The 18-inch base of each block was made out of hard blue plastic, which was hot sealed. Then an inch-thick plastic rope was wrapped around the boxes of Bibles numerous times to hold everything in place. A thick coat of plastic shrink-wrap was then applied around the whole block, making the Bibles waterproof.

We took the first block down to San Francisco Harbor to test its buoyancy. It was around midnight at the time, so we would have been a strange sight to anyone who saw us, but we didn't care. We placed the block into the water and a man jumped on top. The block sank about an inch. A second man climbed on, and it didn't sink any further at all. A third man hopped on, and it sank another inch. With the additional weight of three men on top of the Bibles, the block had only sunk two inches into the water and it remained strong and compact. We knew that all our calculations had been accurate. We had a design that worked.

Our original plan was to ship the Bibles from San Francisco to the Philippines, where they would be loaded onto our barge and delivered into China. One day, however, a Chinese man who was one of the leaders of the facility where we were building the blocks asked me to come to his office. He closed the door and told me, 'We cannot ship the Bibles to the Philippines, because the Chinese Communists know about the plan. They have been watching us work and load the Bibles.'

This news startled us, and we prayed about what to do. The Chinese had spies everywhere, and they would follow the shipment's progress all the way to the Philippines and undoubtedly wait to see what we intended to do with them after that. Instead, we decided on an even more daring plan. We secretly arranged for the one million Bibles to be shipped directly to Hong Kong. Our plans had changed. Now we would have to take our empty barge to Hong Kong and load up there, right on China's doorstep.

***

Keith Ritter: After the one million Bibles were printed they were trucked across country and loaded into containers for the trans-Pacific journey to Hong Kong. A friend in San Francisco organized a group of about thirty young Christian hippies to come and help do the packaging. This was during the time of the 'Jesus people' movement, when thousands of drug addicts, hippies and those whom society labelled 'misfits' came to faith in Christ. These were the kind of people Jesus frequently associated with, but whom the church tragically so often rejects.

I'll never forget one little Mexican boy, who was covered in tattoos. He told us, 'I'm a brand new Christian but I want to help.' We all held hands and prayed together. He removed his cigarette and prayed with us, and when we were finished he made the Catholic sign of the cross. He told David, 'You know, I really want to send a message to those people over there in China, to tell them how much we love them.' He wrote a letter and put it inside one of the boxes.

We were using a binding machine to wrap the boxes in plastic. In the middle of the night the machine broke down. This was bad news as trucks were constantly arriving with more Bibles to unload, and we had no way of getting a new binding machine until daylight. Some of the teenagers who were helping us said, 'Since we can't buy a new binding machine, why don't we lay our hands on it and pray for it?' They all gathered around and laid their hands on the metal band protruding from the machine. They bowed their heads and prayed, asking God to intervene. Straight away it started working again!

The next morning we went out and purchased two new binding machines. The moment the new machines were brought in, the old one shut down, permanently this time. We loved the simple faith of these teenagers. They prayed for a metal object and believed God would fix it. And He did.

Chapter Nineteen:

Counting the Cost

On the night before Jesus chose his twelve disciples, he *'went out to a mountainside to pray, and spent the night praying to God'* (Luke 6:12). We also prayed a lot before choosing the crew members for the delivery. We were scheduled to depart Hong Kong on 18 April 1981, delivering the Bibles on to the beach in Shantou three days later. We settled on twenty men. Most of them were recruited from Open Doors offices around the world, and they came from a wide variety of backgrounds. We had farmers from Australia and New Zealand, mission executives from America, Canada, Cyprus, Holland and Japan, a former tennis professional, an airline steward, a man with a heart condition and two Filipinos.

The crewmembers included a brother named Jerry, whose specialty was building racecars. He made a tremendous contribution to Pearl by overseeing the packing of all the Bibles that were shipped to Hong Kong. Jerry was a 'jack of all trades' and an integral part of Pearl.

Art was a flight steward who worked with Qantas – the national airline of Australia. He worked hard during the project and was a great encourager to the rest of us. Mark, a teacher from New Zealand, was both an encourager and a prayer warrior. He answered the call to join the crew at short notice, and I praise God for his important involvement.

My eighteen-year-old son Douglas also joined the crew. Despite his youth he contributed greatly and experienced the presence of God in a mighty way.

Our crew changed during the months of the project. Several men withdrew and were replaced. One brother from Holland had to be sent home after he compromised the security of the operation by speaking openly about it with some missionaries in the Philippines.

The only crewmember with any experience at sea was the captain. The rest of us were complete novices, but we had a heart to serve and to work hard. Most importantly, we all loved the Lord Jesus. This was our true motivation for joining the crew. Each man had a clear testimony of how God had called him to participate, and they were willing to count the cost.

Captain Bill put the crew through its paces in the Philippines as the Bibles were being shipped across the Pacific Ocean from America. When it came time for the tugboat and barge to make their way across the South China Sea to Hong Kong, the stark reality of life at sea dramatically struck home. Twenty-foot waves mercilessly battered the vessels for most of the three-and-a-half day journey. All of the landlubbers on-board were sea sick, as we yearned to step foot on dry land.

The floor of the tugboat's kitchen turned into a disgusting mixture of salt water, instant coffee and watermelons, as well as smashed dishes and utensils which broke loose from the pounding we received from the huge waves.

There were many funny times as we prepared for the delivery, but there was also a very serious element too. Each crewmember had to sign a document, stating that we were fully aware of the risks involved, and absolving Open Doors from any responsibility if we were killed, captured or injured during the delivery. Many of the older men wrote out their wills in case they did not return to their families.

Not only did the crew members have to count the cost, but our wives and family members also had to be convinced that this was God's will, and then bring themselves to a place with the Lord where they were able to accept the risk of losing their husbands. We had to make sure every man's wife was 100 per cent behind their husband's participation. Once they had agreed, we then had to ensure that each wife be sworn to total secrecy. They could not tell their pastors about the project, nor could they tell their extended family members or anyone else. The fewer people knew about it, the safer we would be.

***

Keith Ritter: As the project unfolded, and the long hours of work and amount of stress involved became apparent, I started to worry because I had a heart condition. At the time I was taking twelve pills each day for my heart, and when the delivery took place I brought enough pills for a month in case we were arrested. I didn't want to have a heart attack on the boat, so I prayed hard, again asking for God's confirmation that I should be a crewmember. I also didn't want to slow the other men down if I died. My wife and I agreed that if I died at sea, my body would just be dropped into the ocean so the others could continue with the task.

During the training phase, all of the crewmembers had to count the cost of their involvement with Project Pearl. We had to come to realize that we might die, either from the dangers of the sea journey or the dangers of being caught by the Chinese military. There was also a chance of a long prison sentence if things didn't go according to plan. Each crewmember had to make peace in their own hearts that they were obeying God, and be willing to pay the price if things went wrong.

We also discussed what would happen if anyone died during the delivery. We had no way of refrigerating a corpse on the boat, so we agreed that any remains would have to be dumped overboard to feed the fishes. We also discussed what would happen if someone was badly injured or had a limb cut off during the actual delivery. As it would be several days before our boat would reach the Philippines again, and we had no doctor on board, it was agreed that a badly injured crewmember would be left on the beach in Shantou, and the local believers would see that he was taken to the hospital. This idea carried serious implications, as the person would be in big trouble for having entered China illegally and being involved in the delivery, but we agreed that the consequences were better than bleeding to death on board the boat as we tried to return to safety. These precautions may seem over the top, but I can assure you the dangers and risks were very real to each one of us. We had to be willing to literally lay down our lives for the sake of the gospel.

***

Brother David: Everything seemed to be falling into place so smoothly. In a mere seven months we had gone from having no money or resources to owning a brand new tugboat, a specially designed barge and a million Bibles. They arrived on 15 April 1981, just three days before our scheduled delivery to China. On the following day our men began the long process of loading the Bibles onto the barge. There were 232 blocks, each weighing a ton. Cranes and forklifts were used to bring the blocks out of the shipping containers and on to the barge. The men guided them into position on deck, packing them together as tightly as possible. It was a typical hot and humid Hong Kong day, and we were all soon covered in sweat. The men removed their shirts as they continued the heavy work.

After several hours, a shocking realization hit us. The 232 blocks were simply not going to fit into the space provided on the barge! We couldn't believe it. A team of men skilled in such calculations had spent hours checking their measurements, and all were convinced the Bibles would fit onto the barge. Now we feared there had been a serious miscalculation. Speculation began to circulate that perhaps we had not allowed for the bulk of the blue waterproof plastic wrapping. We even measured the barge again but found it had been built exactly to the specifications we had given the builders in the Philippines.

As we continued our work that day, we concluded that we would need to put 20 of the one-ton blocks into storage in Hong Kong. Each block contained 4,320 individual Bibles, so this meant a total of 86,400 Bibles would need to be left behind. Some of our team members thought this was okay, as our courier teams would be able to take them into China by suitcase over time.

Something didn't sit right with me, however. God had clearly instructed us to take a million Bibles to China. On several different occasions, and in various ways, He had confirmed this number to us. The Chinese brothers and sisters were expecting a million Bibles, and had spent months preparing to receive that many.

That afternoon Daniel Kwang visited us, and saw that we were in a state of confusion and mild panic. We asked him to pray over our dilemma. The young man gently and calmly called upon the name of Jesus, 'Lord, I know that you can make the Bibles fit on the barge. And I know that you want all one million to go into my country to feed your sheep. Please, Lord, may your will be done on earth as it is in heaven.'

We continued to load the blocks into position. Twenty-five years later, I am still unable to explain what happened. I don't know if the barge stretched, or the Bibles shrank in size. All I know is that when we completed the loading all the Bibles had somehow fitted on the barge!

Inside China months of preparation for the delivery were reaching a climax as the delivery date of 18 April neared. Multitudes of house church Christians were setting out from a dozen or more different provinces throughout China, making their way by train, bus, donkey cart and bicycle towards the city of Shantou in Guangdong Province. There was abounding joy as they contemplated receiving the Word of God for the first time in decades, and they were thrilled at the prospect of taking boxes of Bibles home with them to share with their local believers. A tremendous amount of work had gone into setting up a complex and far-reaching distribution network inside China. We had sent $75,000 into China so our contacts could purchase or rent buses, trucks and other vehicles for the distribution. We also paid the train and bus fares for hundreds of those who were traveling long distances to Shantou. Part of the money was used to construct simple storage facilities. The plan was to fill these storage places with some of the Bibles and distribute them little by little in the weeks and months after the delivery.

Many people have asked how we communicated so clearly with the Christians inside China during the whole process of organizing Project Pearl. In the early 1980s China was still very much a closed and xenophobic country, and every citizen was encouraged to spy for the state and report any suspicious activities. The authorities screened all letters and phone calls going into or out of China. One stray word could easily sink the whole delivery and result in terrible consequences for the Chinese believers.

The bulk of communication for the project was handled by the Kwangs and by Brother Joseph. Few people know, however, just how they got their messages in and out of China. To communicate accurately and quickly with our contacts, seven blind Chinese Christian ladies couriered all the messages, typed in Braille, in and out of China. The two main ladies were Florence and Margaret. They made frequent trips together by boat from Hong Kong to Shantou. On average, Florence and Margaret made one trip to China for Project Pearl every week for a nine-month period. It was amazing how God used them for His kingdom! The Chinese authorities never suspected these blind ladies could be involved in something like this, so they were never searched. If they had been searched, it is unlikely the authorities would have known what the Braille messages said. These precious ladies reminded me of what Jesus told his followers: *'Behold, I send you forth as sheep in the midst of wolves: be ye therefore wise as serpents, and harmless as doves'* (Matthew 10:16 KJV).

Now that all 232 blocks of Bibles were safely aboard, the whole load was covered in extra waterproof sheeting. We filled up the tug's massive fuel tanks with $50,000 worth of diesel, and stuffed the freezer with $10,000 worth of steaks, pork chops, hamburgers, fruit and vegetables, ice cream, and other food and snacks.

Terry Hickey was appointed our cook. As an Air Force commander during the Vietnam War, Terry had flown on over 250 bombing missions and was a fearless brother with a heart to serve God. The other crewmembers lovingly nicknamed him 'Mother Hickey'. Our one complaint was that he seemed to enjoy cooking spaghetti, and offered three different varieties for us to choose from. I ate so much of the stuff during this time that I hated the sight of spaghetti for years to come!

One week before the delivery, Papa Kwang made a final trip into China to check on the preparations. He went down to the beach and observed the surroundings, and watched the lighthouse in the center of the harbor entrance. He told us how many soldiers were on duty in the lighthouse, the time they took their breaks and meals, and so on. He discovered that at 9 p.m. every evening the shift changed in the lighthouse. The new guards would commence their shift by sitting down on the floor and spending an hour enjoying a dinner of chicken, fish and rice. During this time they paid no attention to what was going on in the harbor. We were delighted with this news, and believed we had a decisive advantage for the element of surprise. We planned our delivery for just after 9 o'clock in the evening.

Papa Kwang returned to Hong Kong and gave us the green light for the project. We were ready to go.

The construction of our submersible barge Gabriella *in the Philippines.*

The miracle tug boat Michael, *in Singapore (above) and crossing the South China Sea.*

第三十七章

耶和华答复约伯

第三十八章

第三十九章

Top: *Pages from one of the million Chinese Bibles printed for Pearl.*
Bottom: *Loading the Bibles into containers in San Francisco.*

Loading the blocks of Bibles onto the barge in Hong Kong (top), and one of our crew members walking across the one million Bibles after they were successfully loaded.

Top: *Beishan beach near Shantou, China, where the Bible delivery took place.*
Bottom: *The twenty crew members.*

With great Chinese Church patriarch Wang Mingdao and his wife (top); *and with Brother Andrew in Hong Kong in 1980* (left).

Top: *Meiling and I with the late President Richard Nixon.*

Bottom: *In 1993 I brought a delegation of Chinese officials to the United States to study religious freedom. Here President George H.W. Bush shares his faith with the group.*

Meiling and I in 1999 (top) and recently in our home (below).

Chapter Twenty:

The Taste of Death

Captain Bill trained our crew hard during the day, while our boat and barge were docked at the Western Anchorage in Hong Kong Harbor. We rented a room at a nearby hotel and used it as our command center, where we went over all the details of the operation and received communications from the Chinese believers.

After the Bibles had been successfully loaded onto our barge we received confirmation from the Kwangs that the delivery was on. We would be departing for south China on 18 April. With a mixture of apprehension and excitement, the crew gathered for a thanksgiving service on board the tugboat. We worshipped God, prayed and took the Lord's Supper together. It was a somber and holy time, as we consecrated ourselves anew to Jesus, and dedicated ourselves for the task ahead.

On the afternoon of Thursday, 16 April, I was busy trying to tie up some of the many loose ends that had to be completed before the departure 48 hours later. The telephone rang. I picked it up and heard the familiar voice of Brother Andrew, calling from Holland. I thought he wanted to assure us of his prayers and to ask how all our preparations were coming together for the delivery. After a few seconds, however, I sensed something was different in Brother Andrew's voice. The normal joy and encouragement was missing.

'David,' he said. 'I want you to stop the mission.'

A few seconds of silence ensued, before I asked, 'Are you kidding?'

'No, David. I want you to call it off.'

A numb feeling engulfed my body as I began to explain that everything had been organized and we were ready to go. 'Andrew, thousands of Chinese believers are waiting for the Bibles. Some are already traveling thousands of miles to the beach to receive them. We just can't stop the mission now.'

Andrew was adamant. He wanted Project Pearl called off.

Keith Ritter, Dr Jim and Brother Joseph were in the hotel at the time and I immediately told them that we had been instructed to cancel the delivery. They were incredulous, and didn't know what to say.

I called Brother Andrew back and asked him what the reason was for canceling the mission. He replied, 'David, I have twenty things against you. We need to sort these out.' I asked what they were, but he said he didn't want to discuss them on the telephone.

After the call I felt devastated. I told Keith, Jim and Joseph, then went into my bedroom and lay down on the floor weeping. I just couldn't understand why this was happening. While I was pouring out my grief before the Lord, I was reminded of what Jesus said: *If you are offering your gift at the altar and there remember that your brother has something against you, leave your gift there in front of the altar. First go and be reconciled to your brother; then come and offer your gift'* (Matthew 5:23–24).

God was telling me that if I did not reconcile with my brother, we would not be worthy to present our gifts upon the altar. We had a large altar – a barge loaded with one million Bibles. The boat, barge, Bibles and other equipment had cost a total of nearly 3 million dollars.

We went down to the boat and told the crew members to stop working and to come together. 'Men,' I said. 'Brother Andrew has instructed me to cancel the delivery.' My heart bled for these young men. They had sweated and strained for weeks and months, and now their hopes were dashed just as they were about to be fulfilled. They were in shock, and after a while the shock gave way to anger.

Some of the men told me to ignore Brother Andrew, and said we should proceed with the delivery. Others said I should obey him. The most confusing aspect was that I could not give them any clear reason for the cancellation.

The cancellation was one of the most difficult things I have ever had to do in my life. The worst part for me was knowing how disappointed the Chinese brothers and sisters would be when they were told. I wondered if they would ever be able to trust us again. Every day for six months the believers had gathered together and prayed on the beach where the delivery was planned.

The more I thought about it, however, the more I couldn't escape the fact that Jesus taught if I was presenting a gift and remembered a brother has something against me, that I had to leave the gift and go to him and be reconciled, regardless of my personal feelings and strong desire to deliver the Bibles. I called Holland again. Andrew said he was about to depart on a ministry trip to the United States, so we arranged to meet together several days later at Palm Springs, California, to discuss the situation.

I again returned to the boat to inform the crewmembers of the latest developments. Everyone gathered around me in the bridge of the tugboat, but Brother Cor – our only Dutch crewmember – was missing. The others told me he was extremely upset about the delivery being called off and refused to come. I went down and put my arm around Cor and asked him to come to the meeting. He refused, but I said he could stand outside the door if he wanted and just listen to what I had to say.

We stood in a circle around the perimeter of the wheel-house, and Keith opened in prayer. After he had finished, one of the men said he had a gripe, and I let him pour his heart out. A second man complained and vented his frustrations, then a third, fourth and fifth.

Cor stepped inside the door, and I asked if there was anything he wanted to share. 'Yes, David,' he said. 'I don't want to be like Jonah. I don't want to be thrown into the sea and end up in the belly of a fish. I just want to obey God.' Cor's statement seemed to have a chain effect on the other crew members and many of them expressed their desire to be right with God and united with one another. Only then did I start to share the details of my call with Brother Andrew, and the reason why the delivery had been called off. I told the men they would have to wait in Hong Kong while I went to reconcile myself with Andrew.

We all stilled our hearts together, and set up a table for the Lord's Supper. Keith read from the Word of God, then broke the bread and served us. We then shared from a cup of wine. The following day we began the painful process of informing the Christians inside China that we were not coming. We knew they would be bitterly disappointed, but we encouraged them to keep trusting the Lord, and someday we would make it.

We all gathered together again at dawn on Easter Sunday. We sat on top of the million Bibles and had an Easter Sunrise Service. We then read about the Resurrection of Christ and shared the Lord's Supper together. It was a powerful time. Gone was the anger that many of the crew had felt earlier. The whole incident had broken and humbled us.

A few days later Keith Ritter, Dr Jim and myself flew across the Pacific and made our way to Palm Springs, California, to meet with Brother Andrew and the Open Doors board of directors. Before the meeting commenced I received a phone call from Chuck Smith. He told me he was with us in the project, but said to tell the board if we didn't deliver the Bibles he wanted his church's $380,000 returned.

The meeting commenced with a prayer and then I was asked to explain to the board what I had done. I told them we had left the gift on the altar so that I could come and reconcile with my brother. The brother who was in charge of the meeting asked Brother Andrew to share the twenty things he had against me in front of everybody in the meeting. The Lord impressed on my mind that I should *'be quick to listen, slow to speak and slow to become angry'* (James 1:19).

Most of the twenty things were ministry-related matters and rumors that had been circulating around Open Doors. One of them was that I hadn't sought permission to build a new bathroom at the Open Doors guesthouse in the Philippines. This had been done because we had so many guests coming through Manila and our facilities were too small to cope, so we had to put many of our guests up in hotels instead. By expanding the facilities we would actually be saving money.

Andrew also asked me if the rumor was true that I planned to build a printing press inside China some time in the future. I replied it was true, and asked him if he remembered the time we had spent together in the Philippine town of Baguio, when Andrew had told me to consider building a printing press inside China. He had forgotten. As each of the items was presented, I calmly answered each point.

After our discussions, we all had a time of prayer. We asked the Lord to forgive our sins and to bind us together in unity. Before concluding, I told the board that I wanted their permission to complete the Bible delivery without anybody stopping it again. They gave me the authority to complete the project, and promised there would be no more interference.

The first thing I did was to call Captain Bill in Hong Kong and tell him the outcome of our meeting. I then told Papa and Mama Kwang, and they were very gracious about the news. Unexpectedly, they told me not to worry because the Bibles had 'already been delivered'. They meant that in the spiritual realm they were certain the Bibles were already as good as in China. They believed the prayers of so many Christians for this project had already caused a spiritual breakthrough, and it was just a matter of time before the delivery became a reality in the material world too!

I was relieved that the issues that caused the postponement to the project had been resolved, but also frustrated that we had not dealt with them earlier. The devil is good at bringing disharmony and disputes between those involved in the work of the kingdom of God.

We did not know when we might be able to set a new date. There was much work to do, and we had to start the whole process again with the believers in China. The delay was not cheap. With Hong Kong port fees piling up at approximately $1,000 per day, and all kinds of other expenses, the delay ended up adding half a million dollars to the cost of the delivery.

***

In his 1996 book, *The Calling*, Brother Andrew described how he woke up in the middle of the night in 1981, just a week before the scheduled Project Pearl delivery. His heart was pounding and he was upset. He had had a dream in which he found himself crashing down a steep hill in the Alps because the brakes of his truck had failed. The more he thought and prayed about it, the more convinced he became that God was warning him through that dream. By the morning he was so sure that the Lord wanted the project stopped that he phoned me in Hong Kong, where the crew was in the act of loading the Bibles onto the barge.

***

Brother Joseph: It was a huge blow to the Christians inside China when the delivery was cancelled. They had been preparing for months and had all the vehicles and believers ready to receive the Bibles. Some had traveled from other provinces on the arranged date, only to be disappointed. The crewmembers were devastated, and some of us thought we should consider disobeying the order and doing it anyway. We thought we had done nothing wrong, and that others did not comprehend the level of hardship and effort we had already been expended to launch the project. In our own eyes we were right, and we could not see why we had to build bridges or try to ask forgiveness.

At that time the Chinese leaders sent a message to us from Genesis 22, about when Abraham went to sacrifice Isaac. Isaac did not fight against his father's authority, and did not try to get away. He freely surrendered and laid down his life. The implication from our Chinese brothers and sisters was that we, too, should surrender to our authority and don't move until the issues had been resolved. We realized later that the suffering church had ministered to us deeply, showing their depth of commitment and humility.

***

Edward Dean: When I first went to South-east Asia to be a part of Project Pearl, I still understood it from a narrow perspective. I thought that God was only interested in delivering one million Bibles to China. After being involved for three-and-a-half months, I gradually saw the wider picture of what God was intending to do.

God never separated the objective of the mission from the work He was doing among all of us who were involved. The crew came from extremely varied backgrounds, from different walks of life and countries. Apart from captain Bill we all had just one thing in common – we had absolutely no experience at sea! Due to the emotional roller coaster and countless frustrations and changed plans over the months, our nerves were stretched and we often struggled to get along.

Many of the crewmembers were leaders in their churches or jobs, and it was difficult to humble ourselves and take orders, especially while living in extremely cramped quarters away from our loved ones. We all lived and slept in one room on the boat, and there was a solitary toilet on board for twenty men. A shower pipe protruded out of the wall above the toilet. We showered in salt water, so we never really felt clean the whole time. We could only use fresh water for drinking and to brush our teeth.

Despite the stress of living in such close quarters and all the subsequent personality clashes, the Lord showed that He wanted us to love one another, to be in unity, and to come to a place of submission, humility, and consecration in order for the Bible delivery to occur. We could not operate as individuals. We had to serve one another and in humility consider others better than ourselves. When we did this, God was glorified in it.

We all felt devastated when the April delivery was stopped. David had to go and sort out some grievances with Brother Andrew, and we were angry. The Chinese Church had a tremendous need for the Bibles, months of planning had already gone into it, and I felt we had totally let them down. Despite this, at our darkest time, the brothers and sisters in China encouraged us from God's Word. Amazingly, they were willing to sacrifice Project Pearl if it meant we would be reconciled with our brothers. They encouraged us to honor God's biblical principle of authority and submission. The church inside China recognized the submission required of David with Brother Andrew. They agreed that he should go and reconcile, and that if we failed to get our house in order we would not be able to complete the project.

Looking back, this was our 'death' experience. Jesus

said, *'I tell you the truth, unless a kernel of wheat falls to the ground and dies, it remains only a single seed. But if it dies, it produces many seeds'* (John 12:24). Before He would allow us to experience God's resurrection power, we first had to taste death.

Chapter Twenty-One:

A Breath of Fresh Air

After the meeting in California, Keith and Jim flew back to Hong Kong and rejoined the crew, while I traveled to Britain. For months, journalists Dan Wooding and Sara Bruce had been working on a book with me, recounting my experiences in taking Bibles into China, although not a word was mentioned about Project Pearl.

Dan met me at Heathrow Airport and we held three days of meetings with the British press, book-signing sessions in bookstores, and two radio interviews with the BBC. The subject of the book, which was entitled *God's Smuggler to China*,* seemed to strike a chord with readers. Seventy-five thousand copies sold in the first week in Britain alone, and it ended up being translated into fourteen different languages. The BBC asked me what I would say if I had the opportunity to meet the Chinese premier, Deng Xiaoping. I replied, 'I would tell Mr. Deng that the greatest need China has is for its people to know Jesus Christ as Lord and Savior. And secondly, I would ask him to please consider allowing Bibles to be printed freely in China.'

I was later told that the broadcast went to China.

I left London on the third evening and returned to Hong Kong, without having told my co-authors anything about Project Pearl. From the time we established the project on a 'need to know' basis I had been careful not to divulge a

---

* Brother David with Dan Wooding and Sara Bruce, *God's Smuggler to China: A Cry to the Chinese to Let us Love Them* (London: Hodder & Stoughton, 1981).

word of information to anyone who didn't need to know it. Even my own office staff in Manila had no idea that Project Pearl was being planned. They presumed my heavy travel schedule was part of my normal work with Open Doors. Whenever I needed to travel down to Mindoro where the training was taking place, I flew by helicopter. The forty-five-minute flight allowed me to spend as little time as possible away from the office. Later, when my staff found out what had been happening, they were shocked and some were a little upset that such a large project had unfolded right under their noses without their knowledge. I figured that if my own staff didn't know about it, then in all likelihood the Communist authorities in China didn't know either.

I arrived back in Hong Kong to discover that six of our crewmembers had returned home. I did not blame them. They had given months of their time away from their jobs and families, and the postponement had been too much for them to bear. We set up a new command center in a different hotel, and started the long process of planning a new schedule for delivery.

We needed to recruit six more men to join the crew. I called our contacts in New Zealand and Australia, and said we needed three men from each country to come to Hong Kong as soon as possible. Within a week the six men had joined us. They were a breath of fresh air. They brought new life and enthusiasm to our heavy hearts, and reminded us of the importance of getting God's Word into the hands of the Chinese brothers and sisters. They were also experienced intercessors who realized the battle was primarily spiritual in nature. Eddie Cairns and another brother walked over every inch of the Bibles and the tugboat, pleading the blood of Jesus and praying for a breakthrough among the crew.

At this time the nature of the spiritual battle we were involved with became clear. Satan had tried hard to bring division, confusion and discouragement to us. We came to realize that our enemy was not the Communists, but Satan and his fallen angels. We knew what the Bible said in Ephesians 6:12: *'For our struggle is not against flesh and blood, but against the rulers, against the authorities, against the powers of this dark world and against the spiritual forces of evil in the heavenly realms,'* and the Lord taught us that the only way to win this struggle was found in the next verse: *'Therefore, put on the full armor of God, so that when the day of evil comes, you may be able to stand your ground, and after you have done everything, to stand'* (Ephesians 6:13).

Every afternoon we held a meeting on the tugboat, during which we briefed the crew about developments that day. It emerged that some of the men had become so discouraged they had almost given up on the project and had been saying it would never take place. This defeatist attitude spread like cancer and had a major effect on the morale of the other crewmembers.

One evening Eddie told me that he had seen a vision of a dragon climbing up the outside of our hotel, which served as the operations center for Project Pearl. He said, 'I bound that dragon in the name of Jesus and it burned up and fell into the harbor.' That very same evening, Captain Bill handed me a three-page letter. I waited until I returned to my room to open it. Bill apologized to Keith and me, and said he had been fighting us behind the scenes, telling the other men that the mission would never be completed. He asked for forgiveness and said he would like to have a reconciliation meeting with Keith and me. There were tears shed by the three of us, and many heart-felt apologies were made. The Lord did a mighty work that evening, and He restored the unity in our team. The dragon really had lost his grip and been defeated.

The work of the kingdom of God cannot be accomplished unless those involved are in unity with one another.

If two oxen are pulling a plough in different directions, not much will get done. Now that we had cleared the air, God's blessing came upon us in an almost tangible way. It reminded me of what King David had written:

> How good and pleasant it is
>> when brothers live together in unity!
> It is like precious oil poured on the head,
>> running down on the beard,
>> running down on Aaron's beard,
>> down upon the collar of his robes.
> It is as if the dew of Hermon
>> were falling on Mount Zion.
>> For there the Lord bestows his blessing,
>> even life forevermore. (Psalm 133:1–3)

After the postponement, our contacts inside China found they had 'lost face' with their connections, and they had to spend time re-establishing those relationships and earn their trust again. It had been impossible to notify people inside China about the postponement, and thousands of Christians turned up on the beach at the scheduled time, only for their hopes to be dashed when they were told the delivery had been stopped. Our Chinese friends told me their credibility had been stretched to the limit. We had to twice send Joseph into China to work through the issues with the leaders and to assure them that we were serious about completing the delivery. The Chinese believers let us choose the new delivery date, but said they needed at least three weeks' advance notice.

We studied the tide charts and found that only two timeslots were available for another delivery. We needed to arrive at the beach when the tide was high. The first window was between 17 to 20 June, and the second was around 30 June. After much prayer we felt that we needed to take a step of faith, and told the Christians in China that our new target date was the evening of 18 June 1981.

At the beginning of May the Hong Kong government told us we could no longer stay in the Western Anchorage. They had been suspicious of us since we arrived in their territory. It was highly unusual to have a crew of Westerners, with a huge submersible barge, hanging around for weeks while conducting daily training exercises with high-powered speedboats. We were instructed to depart from the Western Anchorage, but we were determined not to return to the Philippines. We asked the Lord for divine guidance. We were then told about a secluded bay north of Hong Kong, on the coast of the New Territories. The bay was surrounded by mountains and was an ideal location for us to train while we waited for the delivery. We requested permission from the Hong Kong Port Authority to move our tugboat and barge to the sheltered location, and it was granted. The new berth was a tremendous blessing for us. We could sit on top of the Bibles and hold worship services as loudly as we wanted, with nobody watching or bothering us. We found a deserted beach nearby and were able to practice driving our three Zodiac speedboats up onto the sand.

For weeks Captain Bill drilled us until we had improved our speed, accuracy and teamwork. Each crewmember had a walkie-talkie, and we used our night-vision goggles to help familiarize us with a delivery in the dark. We estimated we could unload all the Bibles onto the beach in between one-and-a-half and two hours. During the day, the men did jobs on the tugboat and barge, and relaxed by swimming in the warm water. By the start of June we had become a scary-looking bunch. Some of the men had not cut their hair for nine months, while others sported long beards.

One night we got a big shock, just to remind us that our trust had to be in the Lord, and not in our own training. While practicing in our remote bay, three British Air Force helicopters suddenly swooped down from the sky and fixed their powerful spotlights on us. They could see everything we were doing. We decided it was time to stop our training exercises, as we didn't want to risk revealing our secret mission.

***

Eddie Cairns: From the time the Lord first revealed to me that Project Pearl involved taking a million Bibles to China by boat, I asked my wife Betty to pray with me that God would allow me to be involved with the delivery. When Brother David visited New Zealand I told him, 'I would like to be in on the delivery of the million Bibles.' David looked me in the eye and said, 'Eddie, it could cost you your life.'

He explained that they already had a full quota of crewmembers, but assured me if anyone pulled out he would contact me. As the delivery date – 18 April 1981 – approached, I prepared for the operation as though I had already been accepted. I filled out my will so that everything would be transferred to Betty if I was killed. Still, as the delivery date approached, I had not received a call from Brother David. This was strange, for I had prayed a lot about it and was sure that the Lord wanted me to be involved. Easter morning – the delivery date – arrived and I was still in New Zealand. I almost felt like God had abandoned me, so I went downstairs to pray. A few minutes later I ran back upstairs and told Betty, 'Honey, I'll be on the boat! The Lord has shown me that the Bibles were not delivered! I saw a vision of a plate in China, but the plate had no bread on it.'

For the next two weeks I waited patiently, waiting to hear some news about Project Pearl. Then a friend from Open Doors called me and said, 'Eddie, the Bibles didn't go in, and I have received a call from Hong Kong asking for you and two other New Zealanders to come immediately.'

Not long after seeing the tug and barge, laden with its 232 tons of Chinese Bibles, another crewmember and I climbed atop one of the blocks and prayed together. The Lord showed me by His Spirit that Satan had personally come to fight against this project. These revelations made me acutely aware of the seriousness of the battle.*

***

Captain Bill Tinsley: Even though the crew had no experience, it was one of the finest I have worked with at sea because we had one common aim. Every now and then a problem would come up, but it was always handled nicely. The crewmembers didn't like to take orders. Most of them were what I would call executives. In a sense they were all decision makers who simply weren't used to taking orders. When the six Australians and New Zealanders joined us, they brought a fresh spirit with them that helped revive the old crewmembers' morale.

When the April delivery date was cancelled, the morale of the crewmembers plummeted. I knew that when June came around we would be at the start of the typhoon season, when seas can change in an instant and ships much larger than ours end up in watery graves. I was faced with a serious dilemma. I had earlier promised that I would complete the task regardless of the circumstances. Yet now it seemed we had gone completely beyond reason. Personally, I felt I would have been justified to quit. But if I did, I knew the project would never be completed, and I didn't want to be the one responsible for scrapping the delivery. I prayed, and the Lord led me to 1 Chronicles 28:20, when King David told his son Solomon: *'Be strong and courageous, and do the work. Do not be afraid or discouraged, for the Lord God, my God, is with you. He will not fail you or forsake you until all the work for the service of the*

---

* Eddie Cairns later wrote a book which included two chapters on Project Pearl. See Eddie Cairns and Dan Wooding, *To Catch the Wind* (Orange: D/W Publishing Co, 1992).

temple of the Lord is finished.' The meaning for me was obvious. God had spoken. I could only say, 'Yes, Lord'. I sat down and wrote a note of apology to Brother David for adding so much to the heavy burden he was already carrying.

During the weeks we waited in Hong Kong Harbor, I kept the men busy by putting them to work on the tugboat and barge every day, starting at eight o'clock in the morning. We also conducted numerous training exercises in the bays around Hong Kong, where we familiarized ourselves with the procedures needed to unload the cargo safely and quickly. We trained and retrained until we knew that all three inflatable Zodiac speedboats could be lowered into the water and be operational in just four minutes.

Our training caused the Hong Kong authorities to grow suspicious. One day an official boarded our barge and had a look around. He stared at the one million Bibles, tightly packed inside the waterproof blocks, and began to ask us what we were transporting. As he did so, he placed his hand down on a spot where one of the crewmembers had just finished welding. He burned his hand, and we rushed him back to the tugboat, applied first aid, and took him back to land as quickly as we could. We never saw him again!

Early one morning the Sergeant of the Harbor Police boarded the tug and said, 'Those are pretty fast boats you have there,' pointing at the Boston Whalers. 'Why do you need such powerful engines?' In those days smugglers of people and goods attempted to enter Hong Kong from mainland China every night. They normally used fast 'Snake Boats' to evade the authorities.

The Sergeant continued to focus his attention on the sleek Boston Whalers, so I offered to take him for a ride on one. He agreed, and his patrol boat followed behind as we sped away. The patrol boat kept behind us for a time, but when we hit the rough water our Whaler surged ahead, leaving the military craft in our wake. I believe our friend-liness and openness helped to disarm the Hong Kong authorities, and even though they had no idea why a commercial tug was doing the things we did, they left us alone. And as a side note, today the Hong Kong Navy uses Boston Whalers for their patrol craft!

Chapter Twenty-Two:

The Green Light

I made a visit to the tiny, humble apartment of Papa and Mama Kwang, and told them how the Lord had brought reconciliation, and we were ready to deliver the Bibles. They immediately called China and asked the leaders if they were ready to receive the gifts. They said yes, but that a final decision on whether they could be ready by the date we had proposed, 18 June, still had to be made. They would let us know.

The days and weeks went by, and we still hadn't received confirmation for the delivery from inside China. The suspense was eating us up. Keith, Bill and I spent the afternoon of 14 June on our knees praying, but still no call came. We had to leave Hong Kong the following day; otherwise the delivery would be cancelled. Even at this late stage the Chinese were undecided whether we should deliver our cargo directly onto the beach, or to transfer it to another vessel out at sea.

The typhoon season was already underway in Southeast Asia, and if we missed our scheduled delivery date of 18 June we would have no option but to cancel the whole operation and put the Bibles in storage. The earliest we could consider for another delivery was at the end of the year. This prospect sat very uneasily with me, especially when I thought about the countless ways the Lord had guided us through the whole process. It was heartbreaking to think that He could have opened so many doors, shown us miracle after miracle, only for us to falter at the last step.

That evening the three of us went outside into the dark and we quietly discussed the situation. We had no choice but to make a decision to either cancel or proceed with the delivery. Bill said, 'It's up to you David. It's your call.' I spoke softly to my two dear friends, 'I want to take one final step of faith. I just can't give up until all avenues have been exhausted.' I told Bill to return to the boat and complete the paperwork so we could depart the following day.

When Bill arrived back at the boat, Pablo immediately asked him, 'What's the story?' Bill explained the situation to the men, and they went to work preparing for a departure. By faith they set the process in motion by notifying the Hong Kong Harbor authorities that we were leaving the following day.

Keith and I remained in the hotel room in case the call came from China. At about nine o'clock the phone rang. The impossible became a reality. We were told the Chinese Christians were ready, and we were given a green light to go! Through a translator, the main leader inside China then asked us to make an agreement with them before the Lord. They asked us to agree that if things went wrong, and people got hurt or killed during the delivery, that we would never blame one another for it.

I agreed. We were doing this delivery unto the Lord, and the result was in His hands. If we were successful, we would thank Jesus. If things went wrong, we would still thank Jesus. Our life was truly in His hands.

The Bible says, *'You do not have, because you do not ask God'* (James 4:2). Keith and I got down on our knees and thanked God. Then we felt impressed to pray for something very specific. We read in the Scriptures how two angels – Michael and Gabriel – seem to be the most powerful of all the angelic hosts. We were about to risk our lives to take these Bibles to China, and we didn't want to do it without leaving any stone unturned. We simply asked, in faith, 'Lord, can we please borrow Michael and Gabriel for 72 hours, to help us deliver your Word to your precious children in China?'

Keith and I returned to the tugboat and told the men we would be departing for Shantou the following day, 15 June 1981. Our delivery was scheduled for the evening of 18 June. Immediately shouts of 'Hallelujah!' echoed throughout the harbor. This was the announcement many of the crewmembers had been waiting months to hear. Captain Bill mumbled under his breath, 'Now we have our work cut out for us.' He asked if we would be doing a sea transfer. 'No,' I replied, 'they want us to deliver onto the beach.' Bill fell silent with the news, knowing this meant a greater risk. Then he said, 'Well, at last we are on our way!'

We had a time of prayer together and Keith shared a message from God's Word. The men were hungry, so we grilled about fifty T-bone steaks. Some of the men ate two, while others were able to down three. That night the men spent some quiet time alone, gathering their thoughts together before the departure. We all knew there was a cost to pay, and we were willing to pay it. It wasn't a highly emotional thing for us. We made a measured decision to be involved with full knowledge of the potential risks, and we committed ourselves with the assurance that God, and not man, had called us to do it. None of us sat around wiping tears from our eyes. We had been given a task to do, and we were focused and determined to do it. My fellow crewmembers were real men, battle-hardened and ready. Even the two youngsters with us matured into men during Project Pearl.

Although first and foremost we trusted the Lord to grant us a successful delivery, we also had contingency plans in place if something went wrong. Our strategy was to hope and pray for the best outcome while preparing for the worst. This may sound like a contradiction to some, but we didn't see it that way. For example, we decided that if a Chinese patrol boat stopped and boarded our vessel, the captain would punch Keith Ritter in the mouth to make him bloody, and Keith would fake a heart attack. We were reminded of how David feigned insanity while fleeing King Saul (1 Samuel 21:10–15).

If the Chinese boarded our vessel, we would claim that Keith had suffered a heart attack and we were making an emergency landing so that he could be taken to hospital. The rest of us would head back to the Philippines, hopefully with our cargo, and plan for a later delivery. Keith was chosen for this task because he had a pre-existing heart condition and took a dozen pills each day. We all knew, however, that if we were caught while unloading the Bibles on the beach there would be no excuses. If this happened, we instructed the crew not to resist in any way, but to co-operate with the authorities and to pray quietly.

I was reminded of what Brother Andrew once told me. He said, 'Jesus commanded us to go into the world with the gospel, but where does He say we will come back home again safely?' Many missionary organizations will only send workers to a certain country if their safety can be guaranteed. Jesus never promised such a thing. Andrew also asked me, 'David, when you were trained as a Marine, did they guarantee that if you went off to fight in a war they would bring you home safely?' I saw his point. If we focus on worrying about whether we will be safe or not, we will never really enter the battle with the energy and commitment required to succeed.

While for us Westerners the idea that we may literally have to lay down our lives for the gospel was new, for the Chinese it was a daily reality. Our involvement would hopefully be confined to just a few hours in China unloading the Bibles, but for the Chinese the risk would continue for weeks and months afterwards as they distributed the Bibles throughout the country. We wanted to make sure that our brothers and sisters were fully aware of the risks and consequences. They assured us they were, and reminded us that they had lived this way for years. All of the top Chinese leaders of Pearl had spent years in prison for the gospel. They had experienced beatings, torture and stared death in the eye because of their devotion to Jesus. They assured us they were completely willing to die for the gospel if necessary.

I called Brother Andrew and gave him the message that we were about to depart. He in turn sent an urgent prayer request to all the Open Doors offices around the world, asking for fervent prayer for Project Pearl. Within a few hours thousands of Christians had been mobilized to pray for 72 hours during the delivery, but the only information they were told was that a team was delivering Bibles.

***

Brother Joseph: Project Pearl was an intense time for me personally, as I was married just prior to the scheduled delivery date. I decided it was best for my new bride to be with me in Hong Kong, rather than to be left behind by herself in the Philippines. We were staying in a hotel in Hong Kong, and we had a huge struggle trying to decide whether I should go on the boat or not. It was a very difficult decision, but in the end we concluded that it was God's will for me to go. My wife and I had a strange honeymoon, but a special one nonetheless. Despite the circumstances, we really enjoyed our time together, and there was a sense of purpose and mission.

Because I speak Chinese, I was the one who received the telephone call from inside China on 14 June. Our contact excitedly announced, 'Okay, we are ready.' A few moments later I was told, 'We are ready, but we want you to agree to one condition.' I listened carefully to what that condition might be. 'If you inject the patient, and the patient dies, will you accept that we will not blame each other?' In other words, if our delivery went wrong and the church inside suffered, or if we were stopped and the crew arrested, we should agree that we were all doing it unto the Lord and no blame should be attributed by either side.

We accepted the condition.

One of the main tasks I had spent months on before the delivery was helping the Chinese to understand the massive size of the project. I spent hours explaining just how many one million Bibles was, and how difficult it would be for the believers to take them all away safely. The realization of the scale of Project Pearl gradually dawned upon our brethren, and they were confident that they were able to successfully take delivery of 232 tons of Bibles. Storage rooms were prepared, and much equipment was purchased, hired, or borrowed, including trucks, vans and other vehicles that would transport the Bibles from the beach to various points.

Thousands of believers were mobilized to help in the initiative, and planning went on throughout many parts of China as God's children prepared for the delivery.

We had the green light to proceed, and everyone was ready.

There was no turning back.

***

Eddie Cairns: As we waited for the go-ahead from inside China, a powerful typhoon bore down on Hong Kong and the South China Sea. It had already killed twenty-nine people in the Philippines, and any chance we had of delivering the Bibles for the next several days seemed doomed to failure. At that time one of the men I had travelled over with from New Zealand, Ivan, received a vision from the Lord. He said, 'I see a tunnel of light through the storm. I believe God is going to take us through safely.'

We prayed for hour after hour, as the waters outside started to get choppy from the approaching typhoon. Then just as quickly as the storm had come, the angry winds dispersed. Two hours later we turned on the radio and heard that the typhoon had unexpectedly changed course and was now heading towards Taiwan. God had heard our prayers and the prayers of thousands of people around the world who were interceding for Project Pearl.

After receiving the green light from the Christians in China, we all took Communion together and worshipped the Lord. To me this was a very powerful moment. I realized the risks involved and it dawned on me that this might really be my last supper on earth. We were each given a waterproof bag, and told to tie it to our bodies with our passports inside in case we were captured or shot. I realized I might never have the chance to see the faces of my wife and children again in this world. The prospect of dying made me appreciate God's goodness in my life even more. It strengthened my resolve to rely totally on Him, and Him alone.

Chapter Twenty-Three:

Twenty-one Cups of Tea and Eighteen Bowls of Rice

Our minds were focused on the delivery of the Bibles, but the journey north to Shantou turned out to be one we would never forget, as the devil threw everything he could at us. We all very nearly ended up in a watery grave on the bottom of the South China Sea, along with our one million Bibles.

We weighed anchor after lunchtime on 15 June 1981, and slowly made our way through the congested Hong Kong harbor, dwarfed by towering skyscrapers and fifty-story apartment blocks. The water was calm and I thought it was the answer to many prayers. We headed east from Hong Kong out into the South China Sea, looking like we were heading towards the Philippines. When we had traveled 40 miles, Captain Bill changed course and headed north as if we were going to Taiwan.

We were guided by our satellite navigation system and sonar, and were in frequent radio contact with our radio controller, Dino, back on land. At any stage during the delivery the Chinese leaders could have called it off, and we would have turned around and made our way back to Hong Kong.

Just before we departed, a letter was received from a believer in China that touched our hearts, and reminded us of the reason we were involved in Project Pearl. The letter said:

*Today as if I were standing before you and beseeching you,
I beg you to labor hard for the sake of our lack of Bibles
among nearly 90,000 believers in our county. Among us we
have only 30-odd Bibles, and even these are incomplete and
worn out copies. If it is possible for you to send us some
Bibles, we will be more than glad to send whatever amount
of money is needed for this purpose. If you want me to go
down to Guangzhou, I will gladly go, whatever the cost, as
long as I can bring back some Bibles, which are more precious than anything in the whole world. Whatever you
write and tell me to do I will do. For the sake of the 90,000
believers in our county, I am willing to offer the strength of
my life. So long as brothers and sisters can obtain Bibles,
I am willing to offer the last drop of my life's energy and
with it end my life. May you bear this heavy burden
together with me. May you also do it willingly and with a
joyful heart, running with patience the path that the Lord
has placed before you. I am now 64-years-old, but am still
in good health. In these last years of mine, I want to dedi-
cate myself to the Lord until the day when he receives me
to his eternal love. In summary, I beg you to send some
Bibles to us. Amen.*

Our tugboat strained as it pulled the massive barge, laden
with 232 tons of precious Bibles, through the water. We
progressed at a rate of only three or four knots per hour.
The next day was beautiful and the surface of the water the
calmest we had experienced since we purchased the tugboat in Singapore. The trip from Singapore to the
Philippines had seen us tossed around in 20-foot waves.
The journey from the Philippines to Hong Kong had been
similar, but now that the time had finally come to deliver
the Bibles, the sea was as flat as glass. The crew relaxed
during the day. When they were not on duty they read their
Bibles or just chatted with the other men. There was a
peaceful calm resting on us.

From time to time we passed Chinese fishing boats,
some with large beautiful red sails. When I took the wheel
on the first day I don't think I have ever felt more alive.

Occasionally I caught a glimpse of flying fish skimming along the surface of the water. The gentle rise and fall of the tugboat *Michael*'s bow over the calm swells, coupled with the bright sun and cool ocean breeze created a wonderful and peaceful atmosphere.

Captain Bill was always busy, reviewing tide charts and plotting the course. Even he had to rest, however, so he had trained some of the men how to read the instruments and maintain a steady course. On the second day we received a report of a storm heading our way. We radioed our support worker Dino and asked him where it was. He told us it was still centered in the Pacific Ocean, east of the Philippines, and in all likelihood would take three days to reach us. This gave us enough time to deliver the Bibles, so we weren't unduly worried.

Captain Bill called a meeting in our mess room. As I looked around at each of the men, they seemed to me like a combat unit ready to go into battle. They were going to fight for our Commander in Chief, the Lord Jesus Christ. He gave us peace in our hearts, and there was no fear or anxiety, for *'perfect love casts out fear'* (1 John 4:18). Bill began to brief the men on what their responsibilities were during the delivery. These had been modified because of the late withdrawal of some of our experienced crewmembers.

Brother Joseph, Keith and I would be the beach team. We would coordinate all the communications and liaisons with the Chinese brothers and sisters on the beach. Open Doors have a policy that they will only deliver Bibles in person, to any country. They don't just leave them somewhere for people to collect, but insist on having personal contact with the believers receiving them. This same principle applied to our delivery. We were not coming to dump the Bibles into the ocean and leave. We would step onto the beach, greet our family members in Christ, and work with them during the delivery.

The other men each received their instructions from the

captain. Two were placed in charge of operations on the barge. Another was responsible for the actual offloading of the blocks into the sea. The one-ton blocks would then be fastened to a Zodiac boat and pulled to shore. Each of the three boats was to be manned by two men. Two of the more elderly brothers, who were known as intercessors, were given the important responsibility of remaining on the tugboat, overseeing the whole operation and covering it in prayer.

As we chugged our way northeast into the open sea, we decided it was time to make contact with the believers inside China for a final confirmation. The coded message said, 'We're going to have a dinner party. We're expecting so many people that we have arranged 21 cups of tea and cooked 18 bowls of rice.'

This meant we were coming on 18 June at 21.00 hours.

They simply responded: 'Praise the Lord. Welcome to the party!'

***

Captain Bill Tinsley: I set the course and we were on our way up the China coast, although we were progressing at just three knots. There was a feeling of nervous excitement on-board. We were relieved to finally be doing what we had waited and trained for so long, but the risks were very real. It's not every day that a group of people sail uninvited into a Communist seaport to deposit unconsigned cargo. The Chinese authorities were not known for their benevolence. The end fate of apprehended smugglers had been well publicized in the Hong Kong newspapers during our stay. Their policy was to line up the captured vessel's crew and execute the captain and the owner of the cargo. They then sent the vessel back to Hong Kong with a warning. We might have been less tense if we had missed reading those accounts.

It was really beautiful going up the coast, because a storm was approaching and the seas were getting flatter and flatter. By the time we reached the Shantou area the sea looked like a pond. The other men couldn't believe it. There wasn't even a ripple on the surface. It was like we were in a giant swimming pool. I knew this meant trouble, because I realized there is a huge storm coming once it gets that still.

***

Brother Cor: When I first left Holland I knew nothing about Project Pearl. My wonderful wife remained at home and graciously allowed me to go. When I first told her about the possible dangers she said, 'I will stand with you whatever happens.' I still maintain that I have the best wife in the world. If anyone disagrees, they can come and talk to me about it!

Many times during the preparation and training stages we experienced God's protective hand. Being novices at sea, and working around heavy machinery and loading tons of Bibles, one or more of us could easily have been killed. In the end several bad accidents did take place, yet each time the Lord spared us, and nothing more than injuries resulted.

The closer we got to China, the more we began to pray. It was quite tense, because we were heading straight into the lion's den. At the same time the sea was very beautiful. In the mornings we witnessed magnificent sunrises, and during the day we saw many flying fish and some seals. Even the storms were impressive to me. When I saw the waves going over the boat, I realized that the boat was really like a small matchbox, and that the ocean is so huge and mighty. It made me think about how enormous the universe must be. It humbled me to see God's wonders of creation.

***

Brother Joseph: On the second night at sea, as we slowly made our way towards China, I was at the wheel between one and four o'clock in the morning. Everything was pitch black and the compass had such a tiny light that I was barely able to see the direction on it. A brother called out for me to come and help him do something. I thought we were headed in the right direction, and didn't realize that the boat was slowly turning towards the barge. When I looked out the window and saw a large object right in front of us, I asked, 'What's that?' and someone shouted, 'That's the barge!' We were moments away from a head-on collision. Orders were immediately sent to the engine room to cut the engines, and a disaster was averted.

Eddie came up from the sleeping quarters and said the Lord had not let him go to sleep. He had been interceding intensely. Eddie said that just before the collision was to take place he had a vision of a serpent, which swung down as if to grab a wooden knob. When he saw that, Eddie started to rebuke Satan, pleading the blood of Jesus. Moments later he heard the engines cut and came running up on deck to see what had happened. The Lord had truly intervened.

***

Eddie Cairns: On the second night I finished my watch and retired to the bunkroom. I was tired and lay down, but sleep proved impossible as many thoughts were filling my mind. Four hours later I was still awake.

When I finally closed my eyes to get some sleep a shudder shot through me. I saw, in my spirit, a serpent coming down and touching a wooden knob with his nose. I knew that the serpent was the devil, and he was planning something. I bolted upright in my bunk and began to pray with

191

great intensity. I prayed for all the crewmembers and their families, but I couldn't figure out what the wooden knob was.

I finally sat down on my bed again and the tugboat's engines cut off. I raced to the deck and to my horror saw that we were heading straight towards our own barge that carried all the Bibles! In the nick of time the captain was able to avoid a disaster. I later realized that the boat's steering wheel had a wooden knob attached to it to help us steer. The vision had to do with the enemy interfering with the boat's direction.

Once back on the correct course, I returned down below and was finally able to grab some sleep. The enemy had tried to destroy our mission, but the Lord rescued us once again from a watery grave.

Chapter Twenty-Four:

The Sun and Moon Stand Still

The morning of 18 June dawned with a spectacular sunrise. The sea was even flatter than on the previous days. By late afternoon I had never seen anything like it. It was like we were gliding our way through a giant swimming pool. We knew that God was helping us and we could feel His presence. We were thankful, and realized that before the day had concluded one of three things would have taken place. Either we would have delivered one million Bibles to the Chinese Christians, we would have been shot, or we would be in prison.

As we crept up the coast of China's Guangdong Province, Captain Bill again went over each man's responsibilities. He had much experience as a deep-sea diver off the coast of California, and he knew that the success and safety of any mission at sea depended on the men's abilities to follow orders. He listed the following instructions for the delivery:

1. After entering Chinese territorial waters the crew was to stay out of sight as much as possible.

2. No more than six men were allowed on the bridge at any one time, especially during the navigational approach.

3. During the delivery, we must all act calmly but quickly. We must move with a purpose but not appear frenetic. We should pay little attention to the surroundings, beyond what was needed to get the job done.

4. If anyone approached us, be friendly but do not stop work until called to a halt.

5. The six men in the bridge of the tugboat each had a specific chain of command. Bill would communicate with each leader, who would then manage their responsibilities. No one was to anticipate new orders (Bill had learned this during his work with the Fire Service).

6. If any of us was seriously injured and required urgent medical care, we would be left behind on the beach in the hands of our Chinese brothers and sisters.

Bill concluded his briefing by reminding us of the hundreds of hours of prayer that had gone into the project since its inception. The outcome depended on the Lord Jesus Christ, and we should always act in dependence on Him at all times.

Bill asked if there were any questions. Most of the men were lost in their thoughts. They had been thoroughly trained in their tasks, and their minds were focused on their responsibilities.

I asked Keith to close the meeting in prayer. Then each of the men poured out their hearts before the Lord Jesus. We each knew Him more intimately than before. He had been our loving friend, and now He was our Commander in Chief, leading us into battle for His kingdom.

During the day we felt the tension grow like the slow tightening of a violin string. Bill busied himself with the navigation, calculating our approach to Beishan Bay and the village of Gezhou. We gave the codename 'Mike' to the beach where we would unload our precious cargo. It is located just two miles, or three kilometres, from the mouth of Shantou Harbour.

We arrived at the mark on the navigational chart from where we turned westward and headed straight for China. The final countdown had begun.

At this stage Bill gave the order for the engine speed to be increased to 900 revolutions. Our slow cruise up the coast was over. Now for the first time in days we unleashed the full power of our tugboat engine. As the captain called out the new course for Beishan Bay, Brother Joseph joined us on the bridge. He was the only one of us who had previously seen the area and photographed it.

We entered Chinese waters and could see the outline of the mountains of Guangdong Province straight ahead. A huge ship was sitting just off to the side of our intended path. As we drew nearer, our hearts were in our mouths when it was identified as a Chinese Navy troop ship. Bill decided to maintain a steady course, and not to raise suspicions by veering away from the ship.

The sun began to set behind the mountains as we continued on past other large vessels anchored way off the coast. All of a sudden we were stunned by the sight of a high speed Chinese military gunboat crisscrossing the entrance to the bay as the twilight turned to darkness. We watched intently as the gunboat drew near to our port side.

For a moment the lights from our tug illuminated the gunboat. It was no more than 60 feet from us. We saw three Chinese soldiers, each armed with a machine gun, standing on the deck. Those of us standing on the bridge set our gaze straight ahead, trying to appear nonchalant as the patrol boat drew even closer.

I took a deep breath. 'Lord, there's nothing we can do,' I prayed, the most sincere prayer of my life. 'Only You can take control of this situation. We know you love the believers waiting on that beach and we know how much You desire them to have Your Word.' I calmly ended, 'We rest in Your hands, Lord. We can only stand back and watch you work.'

When I opened my eyes I saw that the patrol boat was still alongside us. It was so close that I could have easily thrown a stone onto its deck. Captain Bill continued to steer straight ahead, his eyes fixed on the coastline. He quietly mumbled, 'If you don't look at me, I won't look at you.'

We had Western men on the bridge of our tugboat, and some of the crew was already stationed on the barge. For some reason the soldiers never turned their heads to look at us. We kept going straight, and the gunboat didn't follow us or try to make radio contact. I won't be surprised if we will get to heaven and find out that an angel of the Lord protected us at that moment. It was surreal, as though the Chinese soldiers were blinded and didn't know we were there.

'I can see the lighthouse! Or I think I can see it,' Joseph exclaimed as we searched for the lighthouse that marked the navigation channel. A minute or two later the signal from the lighthouse became apparent to all of us. We were nearing the entrance to Shantou Harbour. Bill's stomach was in knots. He told us to be quiet so he could concentrate on the job at hand. Bill and Joseph put on night vision goggles. Our charts showed there were numerous underwater rocks and reefs to navigate around, and even sunken ships near the entrance to Beishan Bay.

Bill gave the order, 'Shorten the tow line,' and we reduced speed.

The huge cable between the tugboat and barge had dragged our one million Bibles through the South China Sea at a length of about 100 feet. The powerful winch started to turn, shortening the cable to 25 feet. This made us more compact, but also left us with a smaller margin for error. After several minutes Pablo's strong voice crackled over the radio, 'All completed, captain.'

The crew began to lower the largest of our Zodiac speedboats. This was the boat that would take Brother Joseph, Keith Ritter and myself on to the beach to meet the Chinese brothers and sisters.

'I see the beach!' Joseph shouted. He pointed his finger and said, 'There it is, captain.' Off into the distance we could just make out the line of sand on Mike Beach. Just behind the beach was a line of hundreds of fir trees.

Waiting among those trees were thousands of Chinese Christians, hungry to receive God's Word.

By now the moon was shining brightly as we made our final approach. Behind us the last rays of the sun was still lingering on the horizon. The surface of the water remained as flat as a pancake. The conditions were perfect for us to complete the delivery.

It was just like the day when Joshua had prayed that the sun and moon would stand still.

***

Captain Bill Tinsley: We kept a speed of about six knots, and we just held her steady. Then we passed a troop ship. I couldn't imagine why a troop ship was anchored so far out. We passed by no further than a quarter of a mile from its stern. I didn't want to change course and arouse any suspicion, so we just played the part of a commercial tugboat making its way to the port of Shantou. When we were about five miles from the beach we could see Chinese navy gunboats racing across the horizon. Their guns, torpedo tubes and crew were visible for a few seconds as they sped along under the illumination of our deck lights. They were fast. Our Boston Whalers would never have been able to outrun them.

As we prepared to enter the bay I slowed down to about three knots, as it takes a long time for a vessel and heavy barge like ours to reduce speed. At this stage a gunboat pulled up alongside us, no more than 60 feet away. I didn't even look sideways. I vowed that if they didn't look at me, I wouldn't look at them.

When we saw the beach in the moonlight, everyone got excited like it was some kind of miracle. I had navigated the whole voyage and knew exactly where the beach was according to our charts and instruments, but now the crew could see the beach with their eyes it was as if they had discovered it! I told them all to be quiet; otherwise they would have to go down below.

According to the charts, the bay had all kinds of underwater wrecks and obstructions in it. I prayed for God's help as we navigated. I needed to know precisely where everything was in relationship to us so we could get past all these obstacles. We dropped anchor in about 11 feet of water. The problem was that we drew nine feet of water with the weight of our tugboat, so we only had about two feet of water under the keel. The worst scenario I could imagine would be if we got stuck on the bottom and were unable to leave.

***

Brother Joseph: I had first visited the beach one-and-a-half years previously. On that day the waves were high and crashed against the shore. But on the evening of the delivery the sea was very, very calm. Before us we could see the moon, and behind us was the sun. There was no wind at all and we were enveloped by an unusual peace.

As we moved in closer to shore, a small patrol gunboat drew up alongside us. I could see soldiers with machine guns. I must confess that I was scared when I saw them because they could have easily identified us. We were a foreign-looking vessel with two Boston Whalers on-board, and a huge barge trailing behind us with a gigantic load. Each time I looked at the patrol boat fear swept over me. It felt like butterflies were literally flying in and out of my stomach. But then I would look at nature and the glassy sea and the peace of the Holy Spirit would return to my heart. We passed the gunboat and nothing happened.

As we neared the beach I looked through the telescope and could see the sand-line for the first time. I could also see people moving. I told the captain, 'There it is!' As we got closer I could even identify the two believers who had planned the whole project with us, standing on the beach.

***

Brother Wu (one of the Chinese leaders waiting on the beach): I arrived at Shantou early in the morning of 17 June and found the key workers waiting for me. They asked me if the delivery could be delayed because the previous day a robbery had taken place at the home of a prominent official who lived in a village near the beach. In response, the authorities had been called in, and many police and army officers were lining the road leading to the beach! All people coming to or leaving the village were being stopped and questioned. I told my co-workers there was no way to stop the delivery. The boat was already on the way and we would have to pray and trust God to overcome all the obstacles the devil was placing in our way.

During the day of the 18th, our co-workers went around the communities that had agreed to help us collect and remove the Bibles when they came. One brother went to ten different villages recruiting Christians to help.

In the afternoon I went to the beach with four other believers. As we neared the beach we saw a small group of soldiers walking in front of us, so we cautiously followed behind them and tried to look inconspicuous. At about 7.00 p.m., at the prearranged time, all the people who had been recruited to help collect the Bibles came down to the beach in small groups until they lined the entire length, some 20,000 people in total.

At about 7.30 we started to pray with great fervency. We poured our hearts out to the Lord for almost an hour. The Holy Spirit told us that the boat would arrive on the beach in front of the place where several fishermen's houses stood. We waited, along with the large crowd, many of whom were crouching behind the bushes and trees that line the road along the beach.

At 9.00 p.m. we saw the boat coming in. My heart pounded as it came in close to the shore. At the time there were several Christian fishermen aboard their boats in the bay and there were some other believers waiting on the beach. The fishermen had been waiting for the boat to arrive since the afternoon. When we all saw the boat coming in we started to pray and give thanks. Our hearts were full of praise and joy. Praise the Lord!

Chapter Twenty-Five:
Welcome to China!

We had a prearranged signal with the believers on the beach. Brother Joseph gave three sharp flashes of a hand-held light. Almost immediately three responding flashes came out of the shadows at the end of the beach.

The tug and the barge together were more than 200 feet in length, so manoeuvring in the bay was not an easy task for Captain Bill. 'Lord, I need your help now,' he prayed as he slowly turned our vessel into the best position for unloading. When he was happy, Bill gave the order for the anchor to be dropped. An ear-splitting 'clang, clang, clang' noise reverberated around the bay as the anchor rattled against the side of the boat and into the water. We had heard this sound many times before, but it never seemed as loud as now. We could be heard for miles around.

The crew began unloading the largest of our Zodiac speedboats into the water. Michael Bruce was the driver and got into the boat first, and then four of us climbed over the side of the tugboat and into the Z-boat. Our boat surged onto the beach and Joseph, Keith and I climbed off while Michael and Pablo returned to the barge. The three of us were greeted with warm embraces from our Chinese friends. They had been practicing an English phrase for this moment, and boldly declared, 'Welcome to China, Uncles! Praise the Lord!'

We had a short time of prayer together, thanking God as we stood on the beach with our Chinese brothers and sisters, whose eyes were moist with appreciation. By the time our prayer ended we looked up to find that hundreds of excited believers had surrounded us, displaying broad smiles across their shining faces.

We gave them 50 large cutting shears, and explained how to use them to cut the thick ropes from around the blocks of Bibles and then to remove the waterproof covers. The Chinese learnt quickly and indicated that they knew exactly what to do when the Bibles arrived.

The leaders then told us they wanted the barge to move closer to the shore. I tried to reach Bill on my radio, but for some reason it didn't work at first. The Chinese called a fisherman on a bamboo raft to take me back out to the tugboat. When we reached the tug I shouted to Bill, 'They want us to move the barge closer to the shore.' They wanted our barge as close as possible so we could complete the delivery and get out of there quickly. We found out later that police and soldiers had covered the beach earlier in the day after the home of a local Communist Party leader was robbed. Dozens of troops were stationed in a nearby village during the exact time we were unloading the Bibles! There could not have been a more dangerous time. Looking back, I believe the Lord Jesus Christ wanted to demonstrate His great power so that we would know beyond a doubt that God and His angels had protected us during the mission.

After telling him that the Chinese wanted us to move in closer to the beach, Bill replied, 'David, it's going to be very difficult to move now.'

I responded, 'we don't have time to discuss the pros and cons of such a move. I'm sorry, but they insist that you move in closer.'

As I was still standing on the bamboo raft, the captain started to inch the barge closer to the beach. 'How's that?' he asked. 'They say you're to come even closer. They say the water is deep enough,' I replied.

Bill wondered how they could judge the depth of the water, and was sure they had not taken into account the extra nine feet that the barge dropped below the surface. When the Chinese were happy, they took me on the raft back to the beach to join Keith, Joseph, and the Chinese believers.

The two other Zodiacs had been lowered to the surface, and the process of fully flooding *Gabriella* with water commenced. Now that we had anchored, our plan was for the massive 60-feet-long, three-ton steel doors on the side of the barge to be fully lowered into the sea. As the water flooded in, the whole barge would submerse, and the one-ton blocks of Bibles could then be easily pulled off the barge and onto the beach by our speedboats. The whole sinking process was estimated to take only about 40 seconds.

At least this was the plan. The door on the port side opened without a problem, but the starboard side door jammed. The men used all their strength to try to get it open, but it just wouldn't budge. The Captain was demanding to know what was going on, but we again had radio problems and we couldn't communicate with them. This was soon forgotten as enough water finally flooded into the barge to enable the blocks of Bibles to float. The first ten blocks were strung together like a daisy chain and the Zodiacs pulled them to shore. Keith and I gazed through the moonlight as we watched the whole process unfold from the beach.

Pablo and Michael Bruce were in charge of the first Z-boat. My son Douglas and Edward Dean manned the second, and Todd Martin and Amando Reyes from the Philippines were driving the third. Within minutes they had many blocks of Bibles strung out behind their boats, linked by ropes into groups of five, six, or even a dozen blocks.

When the Chinese believers on the beach first saw the size of the blocks of Bibles, they were awestruck. We had 232 blocks on board the barge. After opening the first block the believers began to place the individual boxes on their backs and ran them up the beach to beneath the line of fir trees, where vehicles were waiting along with thousands of believers. Others waded into the water up to their necks to help pull the blocks onto the sand.

Trucks, vans, cars, motorbikes, donkey carts, tractors and bicycles had all been mobilized to whisk the Bibles away. Others strung boxes on either end of a pole, and scurried away with the precious cargo.

In total we had more than 11,000 boxes of Bibles, and we were later told the number of believers there to help may have been as high as 20,000. Other sources suggested the number was lower, at 5,000 or 10,000. However many there were, they descended on the Bibles like an army of ants, removing them one box at a time in remarkably quick fashion. Some were loaded onto vehicles in the shade of the trees, while we saw others being transported along a dirt road to the village of Gezhou where more vehicles were waiting.

After an hour and a half of unloading the scriptures, the Chinese believers suddenly told Joseph it was time for us to leave. I radioed Captain Bill and told him, 'The people here on the beach are getting nervous. They want us to leave now.' Bill radioed back, 'Standby for a few minutes more, David. We are almost done unloading everything into the water, but there is much towing yet to be done.'

There was a few minutes of silence, during which our brothers and sisters on the beach grew more agitated. They told us that as soon as all the blocks of Bibles were floating in the water we should leave, as they had fishing boats standing by which could tow them in after we had departed.

The voice of Captain Bill crackled over my radio: 'David, if you grab a ride on the next Zodiac we should just about be done by the time you get here.'

We hugged our Chinese brothers and sisters again. Keith said a brief prayer asking the Lord Jesus to keep them safe and secure. As the Zodiac came in to retrieve us, we turned to our dear friends and said, '*Zai-Jian!*' (Good Bye!). I climbed in first, followed by Joseph and Keith, and we made our way back to the barge. When we arrived, we found the crew struggling to pull the last blocks into the sea. Because the barge had not been properly submersed due to the jammed door, the final blocks positioned at the front of the barge were proving difficult to get off.

Finally, after a 15-minute struggle that seemed like an eternity, all remaining blocks were floating in the sea. The Zodiacs were hoisted onto the tug, and Bill gave the order for the pumps to start removing the water from the barge so we could head back out to sea.

I glanced at my watch. It was just after 11.00 p.m. We had managed to unload one million Bibles in two hours – the two most extraordinary hours of my life since the time I met Jesus Christ at the Los Angeles Coliseum eighteen years earlier. Even though things did not go as smoothly as we had hoped, we were all aware of a tangible peace from the Lord during the whole delivery. We knew that we had just been part of a miracle. God had answered the prayers of thousands of Christians around the world and the deep longings of His children in China.

The Chinese believers later testified that they had seen angels on the beach and on the water before our boat arrived that night. I believe God had answered our prayer for Gabriel and Michael to help us. We later learned that from the time the location was chosen for the delivery six months earlier, Chinese Christians had stood on the beach and prayed for a successful delivery every single day.

My eighteen-year-old son Douglas did an outstanding job. After the delivery he said, 'Dad, I want to tell you something. Jesus was right there with me the whole time in the boat!' He hugged me, placed his head on my shoulder, and wept. The reality of God's presence during Pearl was so powerful that it changed Douglas' life.

I was reminded of a verse God had given to one of our Australian crewmembers: *'Others went out on the sea in ships; they were merchants on the mighty waters. They saw the works of the Lord, his wonderful deeds in the deep'* (Psalm 107:23–24).

***

Captain Bill Tinsley: All of a sudden I was told on the radio that the Chinese wanted us to pull the anchor and move closer in to the shore. I argued that this was crazy because we might get stuck and I didn't know if we would have enough water where they wanted us to go. But they wanted us to move, so we did. We pulled anchor and our old chains rattled with a loud clang. I moved in as close as I dared. We might have only had six inches under the keel for all I knew. I manoeuvred the barge into position. It was pretty hectic.

People have asked me if I sensed the Lord's presence at this time. To be honest, all I was thinking about was completing the delivery and getting out of there. Others may be more spiritual, but I didn't sense the Lord's presence. My concentration was wholly on the technical side of things. Anyway, whether or not I felt God's presence is not the important thing. My heart was crying out to Him the whole time.

***

Brother Joseph: My main job during the delivery was to translate. I boarded the small boat with Brother David and Keith and went to see the Chinese leaders on the beach. They expressed their thanks and joy, and had practiced a little speech in English: 'Welcome to China, Uncles!'

I was very, very happy. I could feel the joy of the Lord when we landed on the beach. I hugged our friends and shook their hands. We could see a large number of people moving behind the bushes and trees. I was told there was a 'multitude' of helpers waiting for God's Word. After talking for a few minutes it was time to get to work. We instructed them how to cut the ropes and open up the waterproof covering on the blocks, and how to take the individual boxes of Bibles out.

The feeling was a mixture of joy, excitement, anxiety and fear. But joy surpassed everything. We witnessed the power of God that night, manifested right there on the beach.

***

John Everingham: I will never forget when a Chinese believer, on a little raft made of eight or ten bamboo poles strapped together, paddled up to the barge and hopped aboard. He couldn't speak a word of English and we couldn't speak Chinese. Then he saw for the first time the enormity of the load we had. I can best describe him as being like a lion that had been on a chain for six months while being denied meat the whole time. His mouth fell open and he just couldn't believe what he was looking at! He wrapped his arms around one of the one-ton blocks. It occurred to me that all the effort, prayer and fasting, and all the giving of countless people around the world was worthwhile. Perhaps this man had been praying for ten or twenty or even thirty years, that he might own just one Bible. Now here he was standing on hundreds of tons of them.

I will never forget that sight. Everything became worthwhile.

***

Keith Ritter: I was privileged to be one of those who went onto the beach to meet the Chinese believers. It was beautiful. They hugged us and said a few words in English. The captain's voice then broke across the radio, 'The door won't go down. The door won't go down.' I watched all of this from the beach. There was no fear, more a feeling of euphoria and calmness.

When the first blocks of Bibles were pulled ashore, we showed the Chinese how to cut the ropes off. At this time about 100 believers had come out of the shadows of the trees and were surrounding us on the beach. When the first block was opened to reveal the many boxes of Bibles, there were many 'ohhhs' and 'ahhhs'. They could hardly believe that this day had become a reality. After being deprived of Bibles for almost thirty years, there were now tons of them inside China!

After about half an hour the blocks of Bibles were being pulled ashore rapidly. The thousands of people who had been standing in the tree-area formed huge human chains and passed the boxes from the beach into waiting vehicles. Others were taken to storage houses in the area for delivery at a later time. Finally at around 11.00 p.m., the captain radioed everyone to come aboard for departure. We had finished our job, and it was time to leave.

***

Brother Wu (A Chinese leader waiting on the beach): At 9.15 a small craft left the boat and came in to shore. Three brothers climbed out and shook our hands. We gave them a warm welcome, but it was also a stressful time because a group of non-Christian fishermen had seen what was taking place and were tempted to report us to the authorities. Some of our Christian fishermen pleaded with them to stay and help with the unloading, and they were persuaded to do so.

You already know how the precious cargo was unloaded. By 11.00 the boat had gone. At that time almost one-third of the load had been transferred to the tree area and 25 per cent of the Bibles had been loaded onto trucks, carts, and other vehicles. As soon as a vehicle was fully loaded it drove away to its prearranged destination. It was a difficult task carrying the Bibles to the trucks because of the distance, and all of our helpers were needed. By 2.20 a.m. all of the Bibles (one million) had been moved to the tree area, and I made my way into Shantou City.

Chapter Twenty-Six:
Power in the Blood

The door on the port side of the barge had jammed when we tried to open it to flood the deck at the start of the delivery, and it still wouldn't budge. A closer inspection revealed that the cable had snapped. Bill said that of all the things that he had imagined might happen, dragging the barge out to sea with the side door hanging open wasn't one of them.

Our Chinese friends on the beach were flashing their lights at us, trying to get us to depart immediately. Bill calmly told me, 'We will leave as soon as possible.' He knew that we would only be able to move at a snail's pace while the door remained open, and the list to one side would attract attention at a time when we were trying to be as inconspicuous as possible.

The crew furiously worked at trying to shut the door. Finally a voice on our radio announced, 'We've closed it, captain!' We saw the men on the barge climbing down the ladders and boarding the two Zodiacs to return to the tugboat. When they arrived, some of the men expressed concern about the twenty-nine blocks of Bibles that remained floating in the bay. The other 203 one-ton blocks of Bibles had already been carried up into the tree line behind the beach and were being taken away. The men didn't know that the Chinese had arranged to bring the remaining blocks in with their fishing boats.

The door was now closed on the barge, but we still had to pump the tons of seawater out of the port side. The barge looked like the leaning tower of Pisa, as one side was empty and the other still contained a huge amount of water. The captain radioed around to ensure that all twenty of our men were on board, then gave the order to pull up the anchor and fire the engines. We needed to get out of there, and the captain figured we could pump the water out as we dragged the barge away from the bay.

All of a sudden the voice of one of the men cut across the tension. 'We can't get any suction on the port side!' he yelled. This was very bad news. The men didn't know what the problem was. 'Keep trying!' Bill instructed them, 'We're going to have to tow the barge out to sea and work on it there.' The captain eased the throttle lever into gear for a few seconds, and we could feel the gentle surge as the propeller cut through the water beneath us. Bill added more power to the massive engine, and we started to move out of the bay. The unstable barge veered off in a wide arc as the sunken port side functioned like a giant rudder.

It must have been a strange sight as we inched away from China. We were essentially going sideways, dragging a barge that was perhaps 10 feet higher on one side than the other. Captain Bill wisely kept in the shadows of the mountains as we slowly progressed. Fortunately, no Chinese ships noticed us. As the beach faded out of view, one of the Australians shouted, 'Hallelujah!' Bill motioned that it was not time to start celebrating, and prayed, 'Lord, please help us to get out of here safely.' The rest of the crew went down into the mess room for a time of praise and thanksgiving to the Lord. We all slumped down and a tremendous sense of relief and joy enveloped us. We felt every imaginable emotion, all at once! We somehow felt both exhausted and exhilarated. There was a mixture of laughing, weeping and shouts of exultation. We had spent many months training, thinking and praying about this night, and now it was all over in just a few hours. There was also a sense of great awe. We knew that Almighty God had come down from heaven and was with us during the delivery. His presence was tangible. I guess only those who were there and experienced it can fully understand.

In a couple of hours we reached the open sea and were out of Chinese territorial waters, still dragging the lopsided barge. Looking back, it would have been easy for the Chinese navy to come after us, but God had another plan to thwart any thoughts they might have had to pursue us. All of a sudden we felt the swells of the South China Sea smash across our deck. Our smooth ride was over and we were heading right into the teeth of a storm. Celebrations were cut short, as each man battened down for what was to be an unforgettable four-and-a-half-day trip back to the Philippines. At sunrise the next morning Bill cut the engine and we stopped and managed to pump out the water that remained in the barge. Once *Gabriella* was floating level, we set the engine at full power and headed as quickly as we could towards the Philippines.

For the remainder of our journey the sea heaved up and so did the men. At times the mountainous waves were so high that we were unable to see the barge, even though it was just a short distance behind us. Looking back, I believe the storm was a blessing from the Lord. The weather was so rough that the Chinese air force and navy were unable to chase us.

We finally caught sight of land off the northern coast of the Philippines. As we passed by the U.S. military base at Subic Bay, three American fighter jets passed directly overhead and tipped their wings to salute us. They then did a 360-degree turn and passed over again. We thought this was very strange, and wondered what it meant. Later, a United States Marine Corp pilot came to my office in Manila and told me that they had tracked our whole operation by satellite from their operations center at Subic Bay! He even told me they had listened to our radio and walkie-talkie communications the whole time, and had been inspired by our courage. They were so relieved when we successfully got out of Chinese waters that they decided to honor us in a unique way by sending the three jets out to welcome us home.

Despite the secrecy surrounding the delivery, we later found that the Holy Spirit had revealed our plans to a number of intercessors. One little old lady in Holland came up to me and said, 'I was involved with the 72 hours of prayer and God showed me there were angels with you.' Others said they had been promoted to pray for safety at sea.

Each of the crewmembers was later asked to write a report on their experiences of Project Pearl. Here I would like to share a selection of their testimonies about the delivery and the journey home.

***

Captain Bill Tinsley: The moon was so bright that night, and because of all the patrol boats and other vessels around I wanted to keep the tugboat and barge in the shadows of the mountains. When the first blocks hit the water everyone was celebrating, but I knew we had two very critical and stressful hours ahead, and I wasn't in a party mood. Only when we were on our journey back to sea did I allow myself to relax a little.

Because of the problem with the barge doors, that night we just dragged the barge out to sea, hoping to get as far away from China as possible. Progress was extremely slow because of the extra weight caused by the dragging. At sunrise we stopped and got the water pumped out of the barge and everything was fine. Once we were in international waters again I went to sleep. The others had been celebrating downstairs the whole time, right from the time of the delivery, while I was upstairs sweating it out and trying to get out of that place!

I heard radio reports that a storm was heading north and would make a direct hit on us. This was the same storm that had caused the calm seas on our journey up and during the delivery. We had rough seas all the way back.

For most of the way I stood at the wheel with my legs apart for better balance, straining to keep on the correct course. The brothers laughed at me, standing barefoot, sliding back and forth across the floor as the tugboat heaved this way and that.

***

Brother Cor: After 11:00 we had finished unloading the Bibles and we started to head out into the South China Sea. There was great joy and thankfulness as we praised and worshipped the Lord. After the seas became choppy many of us were seasick. I remember seeing John Everingham hanging over the railing, vomiting into the water. In between each time, he called out, 'Hallelujah! Praise the Lord!' On another occasion Alistair, from England, lost his false teeth over the side while he was throwing up!

I had grown a long beard and when I flew back to Holland my wife didn't recognize me when I came out of the immigration area at the airport. One of my children recognized my shoes, and told the others that the wild man must be me!

In the weeks and months after I returned home I started to realize that Project Pearl had involved thousands of intercessors all around the world. Many people prayed non-stop for 72 hours during the delivery, and I know that Brother Andrew battled and wrestled in prayer for weeks about the project. Letters came in from people who knew nothing about the details, not even that we intended to deliver a million Bibles by boat. They had just been asked to pray for an important need relating to getting God's Word into China. Despite this lack of knowledge, the Holy Spirit had clearly revealed the nature of our delivery to many intercessors. One letter arrived from a prayer partner who quoted Isaiah 43:2: *'When you pass through the waters, I will be with you; and when you pass through the rivers, they will not sweep over you.'* Other faithful prayer warriors later told me that at the time the typhoon threatened to scuttle our delivery the Lord had shown them that a dark cloud was hanging over us, but after praying they saw that it wasn't allowed to advance any further and was turned away.

It is tremendous how the Lord worked. All glory and praise to Him!

***

Jack Cole: As we departed for the open sea, with all one million Bibles having been successfully unloaded, I felt so happy. It was a feeling that's hard to describe; a sense of knowing that God was close and that we had seen Him at work in a very personal way.

All the crew testified of God's greatness and rejoiced as we offered praise to His majestic name. While I was on watch the following morning I found myself in tears as I reflected on what God had done. I was overwhelmed by His almighty power and deliverance. It is hard to imagine the consequences if things had gone wrong. We could have been arrested and imprisoned for a long time, or worse.

After we left China the weather started to deteriorate and the sea began to rise up. My diary entries from this point on simply read, 'Sick again, rough weather'. I was reminded of Psalm 107, which I believe was really a word for us from the Lord as we prepared for the delivery. Practically everything in the Psalm happened to us, and we could all relate to the verses that say, *'They loathed all food and drew near the gates of death.... For he spoke and stirred up a tempest that lifted high the waves. They mounted up to the heavens and went down to the depths; in their peril their courage melted away. They reeled and staggered like drunken men; they were at their wits' end. Then they cried out to the*

Lord in their trouble, and he brought them out of their distress' (Psalm 107: 18, 25–28).

I was truly at my wits' end, and every cell in my body screamed out to get off that boat. They were the longest days of my life. As I lay on my bunk bed Satan threw everything he could at my mind. I did all I could to resist him, but it was a dreadful experience. I don't hesitate to say that if the storm was the price we had to pay to get the Bibles to our beloved Chinese brothers and sisters, it was all worth it!

As three of us boarded our flight home to Australia we were quiet within our spirits, meditating and reflecting on the events of the last few weeks and wondering what God had in store for us in the future.

***

John Everingham: When I look back I am still utterly amazed at the fact that He had me involved with Project Pearl at all. Out of all the people in the world there are many who were more qualified and suitable to be there, yet the Lord had me there, one of the twenty. He had brought me all the way from my farm in Australia, and because of that opportunity I praise Him.

Being a farmer, I was used to rising early and going to work. I'm the greatest of land lovers and I never imagined that I'd ever be steering a boat in the middle of the ocean with no land in sight! I marvel at the situations and predicaments the Lord gets us into sometimes. I'll never forget the day of the delivery. Just before sunset the sea was as smooth as glass. There was no white water to be seen, not even a single movement. I believe God was showing that He was with us and that the very elements of creation were acknowledging His presence. It was a tremendous experience.

When the side of the barge jammed, Cor and some other men grabbed long pipes and tried to lever the door open with all their strength. It was to no avail. Then a couple of us gathered together and held hands. As we said, 'In the mighty name of Jesus, we command you to open,' Cor and the others fell flat on their backs as the door suddenly opened. We just praised God. Because of seasickness, I hadn't eaten anything for three days prior to the delivery, yet I don't think I've ever had as much strength as I did that evening.

My low point was the journey back to the Philippines. I lay flat on my back the whole way and was more ill than I had ever been before. Satan really attacked me with everything. I was so sick that I couldn't pray, nor could I read the Word. All I could do was lie there, shut my eyes, and think of the words of that beautiful song, 'There's power in the blood, there's power in the blood'. As I focused on those words the Lord gradually gave me a great victory.

I praise God for every moment of seasickness even though it was such a loathsome thing and I hated every moment of it. Blessing the Chinese believers made it all worthwhile. I was also overwhelmed by the love of the crew. They all prayed for me and encouraged me to take fluids. I gained a whole new appreciation of Bible verses like, 'I can do all things through Christ who strengthens me' (Philippians 4:13) and 'My grace is sufficient for you, for my power is made perfect in weakness' (2 Corinthians 12:9).

I strongly believe that God had much more in mind for us than just delivering the Bibles to China. He taught us so much about His character and about what is important to Him; things like humility and serving with a willing heart. I came out as a much stronger disciple of Christ than when I started. It sends shivers of excitement up and down my spine when I think of what God did in us and through us.

I have never been so happy as when we sighted the coastline of the Philippines. The sea had calmed down again and I was reminded of the tremendous promise God had given us before we left Australia. These were the verses I held on to the most during the whole experience: *'He stilled the storm to a whisper; the waves of the sea were hushed. They were glad when it grew calm, and he guided them to their desired haven. Let them give thanks to the Lord for his unfailing love and his wonderful deeds for men'* (Psalm 107:29–32).

Back on dry land Brother David treated us all to a wonderful steak dinner, and after I called home and assured my family I was all right I quickly returned to normal.

I want to say how much I appreciated the leadership of Brother David. I don't think I've ever met a person before who could be a leader and yet at the same time manifest the love of the Lord as much as he did.

***

Keith Ritter: First we tipped the barge one way and then the other, but the door would not go back up, and the winch didn't work. As we slowly pulled away from the bay back out to the open sea, we were the silliest sight you can imagine. Anyone looking at us must have thought we were towing a sinking ship. Captain Bill wisely stayed in the shadows of the cliffs, so that we could not be easily seen in the moonlight. We passed several ships that were close enough to see all of us on the bridge, but they didn't do anything. It was as if God blinded and confused their minds. We passed right by the troop ship again with our barge almost on its side and the front up out of the water like a water-skier, but nothing happened.

As we put distance between ourselves and China a great sense of relief and jubilation swept over us. We wept and prayed and hugged one another. When the adrenalin died down we were all exhausted. I have never seen anything like it. Just a few minutes earlier we had been so full of energy that groups of four of five men were able to physically manoeuvre blocks weighing one ton each. Now that it was over we basically collapsed into one another's arms.

When the rough seas struck our celebrations concluded and our minds refocused simply on surviving the ordeal and getting back to dry land. We had two very dangerous incidents during the terrible journey home, either of which could have easily resulted in someone being killed.

Being inexperienced seamen, we had tied the spare diesel and gasoline drums to the deck with nylon line. When the line got wet it stretched, and the 50-gallon drums came loose in the huge seas. There were also some oxygen tanks rolling about. If those things had exploded they would have become like torpedoes. It was really dangerous. Edward Dean – who had been a professional tennis player and an accomplished swimmer – was our fittest crewmember, so the captain sent him onto the deck to secure the drums and tanks. He could have been crushed at any moment, or his head could have been blown off by one of the exploding oxygen tanks. In the end he bravely managed to tie them all down securely.

***

Eddie Cairns: We left the bay having successfully unloaded a million Bibles and with the Chinese believers carrying the remainder up onto the beach. We prayed fervently for them. As we pulled away, one of the crewmembers who had been on the beach reported, 'That's truly amazing! The Chinese brothers and sisters told us they were not sure if we would come, but as they looked out at the sea they saw a vision of the Lord standing on the water. We dropped anchor exactly on the spot where they had seen Him standing.'

As we passed through the 12-mile territorial zone into international waters, I brought out a fruitcake that my wife Betty had given me, to be eaten only when the delivery was completed. The cake was decorated with the words, 'He has done all things well.' He certainly had. Prior to the delivery a Chinese Church leader had told us, 'If you complete this task it will be as great a miracle as Moses crossing the Red Sea, and one of the greatest moments in China's history.'

We soon ran into a severe storm. The waves were so high that for much of the time we couldn't even see the barge we were towing behind us. On one occasion I asked Captain Bill if we would reach port by 23 June. That day was my Silver (25th) wedding anniversary, and I had promised to call Betty. The captain replied, 'No, we are only moving at two knots.' 'But we have to be there by the 23rd,' I protested. 'I'm supposed to be home for the celebration and my wife and kids don't even know if I am dead or alive.' The following day the storm started to abate, and we were able to increase our speed. My continual prayer was, 'Lord, please let me call Betty in time for our anniversary.'

My spirit soared when one of the men shouted, 'Land ahoy!' I went on deck with Brother David and we watched as we approached the northern tip of the Philippines. It was 23 June 1981. A number of whales and their young calves accompanied us down the coast and escorted us into the harbor. It was a remarkable sight.

As soon as we dropped anchor in Paradise Bay, I told the captain that I was going ashore to call my wife. 'No you're not!' I was told. 'You have to complete the customs inspection first.' I waited impatiently as the Filipino officers went through the formalities. The moment they had finished I headed straight to the nearest telephone, trying to work out the time in New Zealand. I hoped it was not already after midnight. The telephone rang a number of times before Betty's beautiful voice answered.

'Sweetheart,' I said. 'Happy anniversary.'

'You made it! Praise the Lord, you made it!' she sobbed on the other end.

It was 10.15 p.m., New Zealand time.

Chapter Twenty-Seven:
A Job Well Done

The first thing we did after reaching dry land in the Philippines was to go to a restaurant and have a celebratory feast. I told the men they could order as many steaks as they wanted. Because of the heavy seas most of us hadn't eaten for days. There was a sense of relief and overwhelming joy, and also a tinge of sadness that we would all be heading our own ways the following day.

I was so proud of the contribution each of the twenty crewmembers made to Project Pearl. Many others had also been involved before the delivery, each one sacrificially giving of themselves so that God's name would be known among the one billion Christless Chinese. After a final time of prayer and thanksgiving, the crewmembers dispersed and returned to their home countries. For many of them it was the first time their families had seen them for months. I wrote to each of the men, thanking them for a job well done, and asking them to send feedback about what the Lord had taught them during Pearl. Most responded with letters, while some sent messages recorded on cassette tapes. It soon became apparent that God had done much more than just enable us to deliver Bibles to His children in China. He had revealed His character to each one of us, and when Jesus is revealed, those who see Him cannot help but become more like Him.

Following is a selection of recollections of the unforgettable experience from several of the crewmembers.

***

Edward Dean: Project Pearl involved many tens of thousands of Christians around the world. Multitudes of believers in China were praying for months, and multitudes more in our home countries were interceding, even though they didn't know any of the details of the project. My home church stood by my wife and two-year-old son. They didn't question why I had to leave home for so long, but they were excited to stand with us and honor our step of faith. My church really poured out their love, and this was during a time when the pastor unexpectedly resigned. They also lost an elder, several deacons and many of the congregation went elsewhere. But during this time of upheaval the believers continued to rally behind us in prayer and in giving. They later told me one of the main reasons the church survived was because they got their eyes off their problems and followed through with their commitment to Project Pearl.

My time away from home was a tremendous trial for my wife, but she grew closer to the Lord in many areas and saw God work wonderfully in her life. Pearl was a tremendous building block for our marriage. It bore fruit in our character both individually and as a family, and the whole experience renewed our purpose in Christ.

The first time I saw the boat and realized how cramped we would be, I started to question if I would be able to handle it. After weeks at sea, my appearance was very grimy and dirty. I showered only every second day, as I figured I got so dirty there was really no point washing all the time.

We all got very weary of the stormy weather. Our plates were always moving when we tried to eat, and everything shifted from side to side for days on end. I longed for just five minutes when there would be no rocking, but it never came. I was worn out from the constant upheaval of being in stormy weather, but I also learned that discipline and perseverance are part of a being a soldier.

I believe the Lord wanted to know if Christ was in us in

such a way that we were able to minister back to our brethren in China. When lives were on the line, would Christ use our faith and the things of the Spirit? I believe that He did, because the Chinese told us when they saw our boat sitting in the bay they were encouraged and they knew that we loved them. We sensed their burden, and the intense pressure they were under from the fact they were risking their lives to receive the Bibles. This was a tremendous lesson for me. Many times before the delivery I was frustrated and said, 'I wish I could have fellowship with some of the believers in China. If I could, it would be as precious to me as the delivery of the Bibles.' God saw my heart's desire, and on the night of the delivery I was able to hug several of the believers on the beach.

Before the delivery took place, God showed us that it could only be accomplished by the same power which raised Christ from the dead. Without His power we had absolutely no chance at all. At one time all of us were worn down to a frazzle emotionally, physically, mentally and spiritually. Then the Lord sent six new intercessors to join the crew. They lifted our burden and helped us refocus our enthusiasm and energy on the task. Looking back, I believe if those prayer partners had not joined us we would not have completed the delivery.

I would like to say how much I appreciated Brother David and the other leaders. They treated the crew respectfully, such as always helping us call our loved ones, getting us plane tickets back home for the two weeks break we had, and also making sure we got home after the actual delivery. It was a privilege to serve God and to see the needs of the suffering church met in their request for a million Bibles.

***

Barnabas Schwartz: One of the things that touched me the deepest about Project Pearl was the realization that God had thousands of people involved whom we had never met. The Lord used His whole body to glorify His name. Sunday school children gave up their coins so that their Chinese brothers and sisters could have God's Word, and others gave thousands of dollars, even though they didn't know any of the plans. They gave unto the Lord in faith.

One thing I learned from the project was that God was more interested in the people involved with Pearl than the project itself. He wanted to work in each of our hearts, changing us so that we would be more like His Son. He showed us areas of pride in our lives that needed to change. I believe it was God's mercy that the first delivery was cancelled because as a crew we were not spiritually ready. The Lord wanted to do more work in us and to make us unified in direction and intention. I think it took quite a bit of patience on God's part to finally get us to the depth of unity and love for one another that He needed in order to accomplish a project of this magnitude.

I found it difficult to be away from my wife and children for such a long time, but I learned that God was pouring His grace out on them. The Lord took care of them and gave me a deeper love for them through it all. Later, Christians from our home church told me what a strong woman I had married, and commented on what a good mother she was. That blessed me.

Keith Ritter, our chaplain, always made me laugh. At night he would don his sweater, then put on his life jacket, raincoat and a crazy-looking hat before grabbing his Bible and heading up to the lookout to pray. With all his gear on it looked like he weighed 450 pounds! Because of the constant rocking of the sea he couldn't walk in a straight line and looked like the proverbial drunken sailor!

The delivery was exciting and memorable. I really felt that angels were with us. It was almost like God Himself had taken time out from a lot of other things just to be with us at that time. For me there was a very personal feeling of God's presence on the boat with us.

***

Captain Bill Tinsley: I had known Brother David for many years before the delivery, and count him as a very close friend. At times the stress levels went up and some angry words were exchanged, but on each occasion one or both of us apologized and we moved on. Most of this happened during the waiting and delays, and not during the actual delivery. David is a former Marine and I am a sailor, so our thinking is quite close. Maybe that's the reason we had so many conflicts. Two hard heads.

Because I was the captain and the only person with experience at sea, I saw it as my personal responsibility to ensure the safety of the crew and vessel. Somehow, by God's intervention, this occurred. On one occasion a man was knocked overboard and could easily have been killed after a towline collected him on the stern deck. I had told the crew many times that the stern deck is sacred territory, especially when there is a tow line under tension or in angry seas. It can take your head off when it snaps.

Another one of the guys was trapped by the towline and knocked off his feet. An experienced crew would have kept well clear of the stern deck under such circumstances, but our guys didn't think much about it. Nobody was seriously injured, and nobody lost his life. Good grief, we could have lost lives so easily. It really was a miracle.

I thought a lot about what would happen to us if we got arrested during the delivery. I figured I would get to lose some weight in a Communist prison. I was a little concerned because I was the captain and would subsequently be treated more harshly if we were caught.

From all the adventures I have had at sea over the years,

I'd have to say Project Pearl was the biggest one. Looking back, I'm glad for all the training I had received beforehand, as many aspects of the delivery were really technical and expertise was required.

***

Jack Cole: My whole experience of Project Pearl started when I received a phone call on the evening of 3 June 1981, asking me to come from Australia to Hong Kong. I was quite emotional on hearing the news because I knew God had already given me the answer that morning. I had been reading Hudson Taylor's biography, and he spoke about how we should not make excuses to God about how inconvenient it is to preach the gospel, but that we should always be ready and willing to do whatever God asks us to do. When the call came, I knew my answer was 'yes' as soon as I heard the request. It would have been easy to say 'no', as there were some genuine inconveniences at the time. My wife was expecting a baby around 23 June, and we were in the process of negotiating to buy a house. I said 'yes' and we never regretted it. That night I could hardly sleep because of excitement and a sense of purpose.

Before I left Australia everyone was so supportive, even though they didn't know any of the details about what was going on. My mother came down to look after my wife and son while I was away. She agreed to come at short notice, and didn't ask any questions. She realized the situation was important and made great sacrifices to support us at the time. All kinds of problems presented themselves, but the Lord smoothed the way. For example, we called the airlines for tickets, but were told there were no seats available to Hong Kong at such short notice. We prayed, and just 30 minutes later Qantas Airlines called us back to say three seats had just become available!

After arriving in Hong Kong we saw that the morale of

the long-term crewmembers was at a low ebb. They had spent months on-board and had experienced much discouragement and opposition. They were under great strain. We prayed that God might use us to bring encouragement and spiritual relief to the crew.

My initial excitement about departing for China was dampened when we started to get tossed around and I grew seasick. On 18 June, however, the Lord marvelously worked a miracle, in accordance with His promise in Psalm 107:29, *'He stilled the storm to a whisper; the waves of the sea were hushed. They were glad when it grew calm, and he guided them to their desired haven.'* When the sea became dead flat, a great improvement took place among the crew physically, emotionally and spiritually as we realized we were witnessing God at work. He knew that a calm sea was crucial for the successful unloading of the Bibles.

As we began to maneuver the barge into position to unload the Bibles, we let down the anchor, which made a tremendously loud noise in the still night air. People must have heard us for miles around! It could have attracted a lot of attention, but God was in control. There was no sense of fear.

We worked as hard as we could to unload the Bibles, and in the end we saw some wonderful miracles. I witnessed four or five fellows on the beach move a one-ton block of books. This would be impossible by mere physical strength. Many times I had asked the Lord to assist the Chinese brethren with His angels, and to help pull the Bibles off the sand and into the waiting trucks. And He did.

Chapter Twenty-Eight:
The Dragon's Roar

Children of God are often called to suffer for the Lord's sake, because one's strength and the reality of one's belief can be clearly seen during suffering. God always gives Christians firm hearts.... Not everyone can be trusted during trials, and not everyone can stand firm when he goes through fire. Some Christians even readily curse and murmur, so the Master must carefully choose some who can really stand firm.... And so the Lord assigns some people to preach, some to handle the task, and allows some to suffer. – F. B. Meyer

From the early days of Pearl, indeed from the start of my involvement with China, I knew that the Chinese believers always faced the greatest risks. While we foreigners were able to come and go, the Chinese had to remain behind and deal with the consequences if anything went wrong.

In all my travels inside China I had been as careful as possible, preferring to take options that raised minimal attention. Being a Westerner, and a large one at that, I stood out like a sore thumb in China, and on many occasions I chose not to fellowship with my Chinese brothers and sisters when I had an opportunity to do so. Even though my heart longed to spend time with them, I knew it was not always wise to follow my heart's desire.

During the planning stages of Project Pearl, the Chinese leaders fully realized that there would be a major retaliatory crackdown by the Communist authorities after the delivery. They knew that their involvement carried major risks and consequences, and that they might even have to literally lay down their lives for the Lord. Every single Chinese Christian we were involved with said it was a risk they were willing to take, and that they were ready to die if it meant one million Bibles would be placed in the hands of God's children throughout China.

On many occasions the Chinese believers quoted scriptures the Lord had given them in relation to Project Pearl. Whereas our crew members had been encouraged by verses relating to the sea and God's sovereignty and power, many Chinese received promises from the scriptures like:

'For it has been granted to you on behalf of Christ not only to believe on him, but also to suffer for him.' (Philippians 1:29)

'To this you were called, because Christ suffered for you, leaving you an example, that you should follow in his steps.' (1 Peter 2:21)

'Dear friends, do not be surprised at the painful trial you are suffering, as though something strange were happening to you. But rejoice that you participate in the sufferings of Christ, so that you may be overjoyed when his glory is revealed. If you are insulted because of the name of Christ, you are blessed, for the Spirit of glory and of God rests on you.' (1 Peter 4:12–14)

Thankfully, in the weeks and months after the delivery no Chinese believers were killed, although several of the leaders of the project were arrested and endured terrible persecution and torture.

Just four hours after the delivery, at around three o'clock in the morning, a small squad of soldiers arrived at the beach after they had been tipped off by one of the non-Christian fishermen. By that time most of the Bibles had been removed from the beach area and were either inside vehicles on their way to another part of the country, or had been successfully deposited into one of the many storage rooms set up in advance.

When the soldiers arrived at the beach there were still many believers there, and they thought they had managed to capture the whole load of Bibles. In fact, no more than about 20 per cent of the Bibles remained at that time. The soldiers surrounded the scriptures and tried to set them alight. This didn't work because the books were tightly packed together and surrounded by cardboard boxes and thick plastic wrapping.

Frustrated by their lack of progress, the soldiers then took some of the Bibles and threw them into the water. One of our contacts later said that the sea looked like a bowl of congee, with Bibles and plastic wrapping material floating in the water. At daybreak, officers from the local Public Security Bureau arrived at the beach and took photographs and video footage of the floating Bibles as 'evidence' that the delivery had been a failure. This was no doubt done by the local authorities in an attempt to make themselves look good in case news of the incident reached higher up.

After the soldiers and cameramen had left the beach, however, fishermen went out and brought the Bibles ashore. In the ensuing days and weeks the fishermen sold the rescued Bibles back to the Christians for a few cents each. For days, Bibles were seen on rooftops in the area, drying out in the sun.

One of the Chinese leaders of Pearl later wrote that the soldiers' efforts to destroy the Bibles had actually helped. While their attention was distracted trying to destroy a portion of the Bibles, the majority of the scriptures in the tree area near the beach were taken away unnoticed. One believer later wrote, 'Even the plot of Satan accomplished the will of God.'

***

Brother Wu: At 3.00 a.m. soldiers from the People's Liberation Army arrived at the beach and started to arrest people. One of the unbelieving fishermen had gone to the police station and reported what was taking place. Even after the soldiers arrived our people continued to take the Bibles away, because they were too few in number to stop us. Even throughout the next day believers continued to come and take the Bibles home. Many Christians living in the villages near the beach had taken Bibles into their homes for safekeeping. The Public Security Bureau sent officers to investigate. They ordered people to bring all the Bibles to the local government office, but not a single person did. Almost all of these Bibles that had been taken by the locals were deposited with our co-workers and successfully distributed.

A number of Bibles remained in the water for the next few days. The police had dumped these into the water and took pictures of them. People from surrounding villages came and rescued as many Bibles as they could. Even though the authorities were watching they could not stop them. For the next several days there was a struggle between the authorities and the believers over the remaining Bibles. The police managed to burn some, and others were thrown into a latrine, which caused us to weep. However, brothers and sisters came along and rescued as many of these as possible, drying out the pages and spraying the Bibles that had been thrown into the latrines with perfume.

On the evening of 19 June some of the Christians were caught by the authorities and severely scolded. The government was just starting to get a clear picture about the scale of the operation and were furious when they realized how many Bibles had been successfully taken away before they knew about it. On 24 June the local authorities realized the incident was a major one and decided to get the provincial authorities involved. Three or four days later the

Christians who had been arrested were taken to prison. Despite the heavy pressure they remained stable and strong, but without the Lord's help they would not have been able to endure. The unbelieving fishermen told the police that the three of us had met 'Russians' on the beach and shaken hands, so they started searching for me and the other leaders.

***

Pablo: The local authorities reacted with anger and launched an investigation, questioning many people. They referred the matter to the Guangdong provincial government. Their investigations were thorough and four house church leaders were arrested. Three were from Gezhou village and were relatives of the Kwangs. Heavy pressure was placed on the Christians to reveal the details of the delivery, but they remained strong and did not break. In early August the last of the four was released. Three young people were reportedly beaten during the interrogation process. About ten homes were searched, but this did not cause serious problems. According to one report, the government was making a lot of noise but taking little action.

The soldiers threw a number of Bibles into the sea, and then took pictures and video of them in an apparent bid to show their superiors that the project had been foiled. Many non-Christian fishermen rescued the individual Bibles from the sea. All over Shantou, Bibles could be seen, even on rooftops, drying out. The fishermen then sold the Bibles for ten *fen* (one-tenth of a *Yuan*) in the local market and also to Christians attending the Three-Self Church in Shantou. The immediate response was positive, but the next day the Three-Self denounced the delivery as 'counter-revolutionary' and claimed the delivery was designed to destroy the Three-Self and the government of China. They told their members the Bibles were 'poison' and should not be used. The Three-Self leaders then collaborated with the authorities to discover details of the project and assisted in searching homes.

A great surprise was the number of Bibles that had been stored away by unbelievers, with the motivation of monetary gain. After the period of initial pressure eased, they began to approach Christians, asking if they were interested in purchasing them. Of course they were. Prices ranged from 10 *fen* to one *Yuan*, but the majority were purchased for 20 *fen*. This caused the number of Bibles available for delivery to swell. As of 9 January 1982, a report from our Shantou contacts stated that 95% of the one million Bibles had been delivered. Four percent more were identified and stored, awaiting delivery once the pressure eased.

A co-worker documented that the Pearl Bibles had been delivered to believers in the following provinces: Guangdong, Hunan, Henan, Shaanxi, Anhui, Zhejiang, Fujian, Shandong, Xinjiang, Heilongjiang and Hebei. One of the main co-workers was able to use a truck extensively to distribute the Bibles, although it frequently broke down and ran out of fuel.

A considerable amount of money had been sent to the believers before the delivery to help with transportation costs and other expenses relating to the project. They reported back that the money had been used for the following: to purchase Bibles from unbelievers; to rent trucks and other vehicles; to construct three large store houses which functioned as depositories for the Bibles and were later used as house churches; and aid to families of those imprisoned (e.g. food and medicine).

As word traveled around the country that Bibles were available in Shantou, many believers came to the storehouses to request some. The size of the need for Bibles became apparent from all these visitors, resulting in a new request dated 1 December 1981, for 2 million more Bibles.

In conclusion, the believers in China told us they rejoiced that the ship and crew arrived and left safely. They said the believers are willing to suffer to receive Bibles, and that many churches had been revived because of receiving them. They stated the need remains greater than the supply and requested more Bibles.

***

Brother David: Long after Project Pearl was completed we received a remarkable testimony from an elderly Chinese pastor named John, who had already spent many years in prison for the sake of the gospel.

Pastor John, who was in his seventies, agreed to receive a consignment of 10,000 Bibles on the day following the Pearl delivery. He was thrilled and overflowing with joy to participate in this way, and he looked forward to distributing the Bibles among the many needy believers in his area. When the consignment of Bibles arrived at his home, John wept and hugged them with pure joy, thanking God for allowing them to have so many copies of His precious Word at one time.

After the authorities were notified of the Bible delivery and launched a thorough investigation, the situation became so tense that John decided it was prudent to store the 10,000 Bibles until the pressure eased. The weeks passed but the situation remained tense so he asked a Christian farmer to hide the Bibles under his barn. The authorities were sure John was one of the main participants in the project, so they arrested him and took him to the local prison, even though there was no evidence of his involvement. John realized how serious the situation was when he saw that his interrogators were not local policemen, but special investigators who had flown in from Beijing to deal with the incident.

The infuriated interrogators shouted questions and

abused the venerable man of God, who just closed his eyes and prayed silently. They wanted names of the leaders of Project Pearl, but there was no way John would betray his brothers and sisters in such a way. His refusal to answer enraged the men even more, so they dragged him from the interrogation room into the prison courtyard, where they made him stand on a wooden box about four feet high and less than a foot wide.

Seeing that the old man would not bow to their intimidation, the guards bound John's hands behind his back and placed a noose around his neck. A man climbed up on the roof of an adjacent building and fastened the rope to a beam. 'Now let's see how calm you are, old man!' they sneered. 'The moment you grow tired you will fall off the box and die! This is all your own doing. Get ready to meet your God!'

Two guards remained behind to witness the faithful pastor's death, while the others walked off, mocking John's faith and laughing at his predicament. Instead of stumbling, however, the humble pastor felt a surge of power enter his body. His legs seemed to strengthen, and he boldly proclaimed the gospel to the two guards. When the sun went down, the guards were surprised that the old man had not yet collapsed.

The following day dawned to find John still standing on the small box. His throat was dry, but a shower of rain refreshed him. The guards resumed their positions, sure that any minute the Christian prisoner would collapse and hang himself. The hours passed, and the only sound heard in the courtyard was that of John preaching the gospel in a loud voice. He told the guards that He was not afraid of death because Jesus Christ had already made a place for him in heaven. One of the men laughed and replied, 'Old man, if I get to be your age and look as unhealthy as you do, I won't be afraid to die either!'

The bored guards turned their attention on gambling

with each other. This greatly encouraged John as he thought about the similarities with the Roman guards gambling for Jesus' clothing as He hung on the cross.

Incredibly, the second day ended, and the pastor remained standing.

The same happened on the third day, then the fourth, fifth, and sixth! The other guards heard that the old man was still alive and they came to see for themselves. Other prisoners heard of the incredible miracle and gave glory to God. The longer John remained standing on the box without food or rest, the more the fear of God began to grip all who witnessed the extraordinary event.

As each day passed, John's physical condition worsened. His legs swelled up to twice their normal size and at times they shook uncontrollably from cramp. On the 11th day John started to feel weak and was close to collapse. The Holy Spirit sustained him, however, and he carried on. John had now become something of a spectacle, and news of the miracle had reached outside the prison walls. Some of the leading officials and men of the town came to see it for themselves.

On the 13th day a strong storm swept in and heavy rain lashed John's body, soaking him to the skin. As the box beneath his feet shook from the wind, John realized that he could hold out no longer. Every sinew in his body had been strained beyond endurance. His limbs were numb, and his torso ached for a moment's respite.

John closed his eyes as his legs gave way, and the beloved pastor fell unconscious as the noose tightened around his neck.

About ten minutes later John opened his eyes to find himself stretched out on the prison floor. His whole body was in excruciating pain, especially his arms which had been tied behind his back for almost two weeks. Now that the ropes had been loosened, the blood rushed to his limbs and caused overwhelming pain. Not knowing what was going on, John finally became aware that someone was trying to help him sit up, and a bottle of water was being pressed against his chapped lips. A few minutes more passed before he was able to make out that the person helping him was one of the guards who had been assigned to watch him die. The second guard was standing nearby.

'Please don't die! We want to know your God!' the men pleaded. 'Please, uncle, help us to know your Jesus!'

'Why?' John asked in a faint whisper.

They explained to John that when his legs had finally collapsed in the midst of the storm, his body hung in the air, swinging back and forth from the overhead beam. Then, a moment later, a bolt of lightning suddenly illuminated the courtyard, cutting the rope just above his head and causing him to fall to the ground. Shaking with fear, the two guards dragged the unconscious prisoner inside and tried to revive him.

Pastor John gradually regained his strength and led the two desperate men to faith in Jesus Christ. Dozens of other guards and prisoners who heard what happened also repented of their sins and placed their trust in God. Realizing that they risked the wrath of God if they continued to persecute the elderly Christian, the authorities released him from prison. John returned home, and later dug up the 10,000 Bibles and distributed them among the believers.

Chapter Twenty-Nine:
Friendly Fire

Although we were deeply pained by news that several of our closest brothers and sisters in China had been arrested and tortured because of the delivery, the believers themselves remained undeterred. Indeed, they even began requesting further Bible deliveries. One letter said, 'In order to continue the work, please prepare 2 million pieces for us and send them in.'

On 7 September 1981, Brother Andrew wrote a beautiful letter to Open Doors supporters around the world who had been faithfully praying for Project Pearl as they patiently awaited news of its outcome. While being careful not to mention any specific details about how the Bibles had been delivered, Andrew wrote:

Dear Friends of the Suffering Church,

I have marvellous news for you. Our share of Project Pearl has been completed. One million complete Chinese Bibles have been delivered to China. Hallelujah!

And as impossible as it seems, they were all delivered at one time!... Concerning the actual delivery, our team in Asia told me, 'Andrew, we saw the glory of the Lord in China. Those of us on this delivery experienced the overshadowing presence and protection of the Lord.' While inside China, Chinese believers told our team, 'Before you arrived, we saw visions of the Lord Jesus and His angels in this place.'

And how else can you explain that our team passed undetected past Chinese patrols, not once, but many times! The prayer I have used so often during the past 27 years was answered again... the Lord made seeing eyes blind...

I'm glad to state that hundreds of thousands of these 'Project Pearl' Bibles are now being read by grateful Christians all over China. The Bibles to our brothers and sisters were freely given, but they paid a price for them, and I fear will continue to do so.

But was it worth the price? Chinese believers say 'Yes'. Already, word has reached us that hundreds have accepted Christ since we delivered one million Bibles just a few weeks ago. A letter just received from Chinese leaders has already asked us for a second million. They bear the scars of the first million – but they have found the joy of Jesus in His Word far greater than the rod of a godless regime...

What I want to do right now is shout: 'China – Jesus loves you!' And then I want to send more Bibles in His name.

Yours, on behalf of China,
Brother Andrew

Meanwhile, the first letters started to arrive from believers in China who had received Pearl Bibles. They expressed the absolute joyful exuberance they experienced when their prayers of so many years were finally answered. Among the letters was one that described the desperate lengths the Chinese Christians had gone to because of the shortage of Bibles:

Before when I wanted to read the Bible, I had to walk more than 100 miles to borrow it. Then I had to return it within a short time. Now, after one million copies have been delivered, we obtained some from a sister in Guangzhou, and tens of thousands of hungry sheep have been fed and nourished through God's Word. When the Bibles reached the house churches, the believers sat next to the Bibles. Tears welled up in our hearts of love. We caressed the Word of God with loving and respectful hands. Each co-worker was afraid they would miss out on owning a copy themselves, but when there was enough for all the leaders they felt deeply honored. I went out one day and led 700 people to the Lord. Everybody has the same desire – to obtain a copy of the Bible. I told them to ask the Lord to prepare them for us. May glory and power be unto Him for evermore.

Another letter, signed 'From all the brothers and sisters in China', said:

Because of the one million Bibles the wilderness has become delightful, the desert joyful, and many dry hearts have been moistened. Countless souls who were dying in sin have been saved, and many who were previously walking on the road of darkness have returned to the safe path. The 50 million Christians in our country are well fed by the one million Bibles. The countless saved souls are of immeasurable value, for just one soul is more precious than all the wealth in the world.

The successful delivery of the one million Bibles reveals a mighty act of God. It's a glorious achievement, an unprecedented miracle, a wonderful incident, and an extraordinary witness of God's power and goodness. Hallelujah! Glory be to the Lord's Name. The result of your hard labor has obtained an eternal reward in heaven. The beautiful song of victory sounds everywhere. Hallelujah! Praise the Lord!

And a third letter explained some of the impact that the Bibles were having on whole communities:

Now we have Bibles and everyone can study the Word of the Lord. The flock that is hungry and thirsty now is feeding on the spiritual food, and drinking from the spiritual fountain. Our spiritual lives are now growing like a healthy tree in springtime. Many have believed in the Word of the Lord and have endured trials. Now we have learned to stand firm, discern true from false, and become strong in the faith against the evil one and all his attacks. The Word of God really is a lamp unto our feet and light unto our paths. The Word of the Lord is our foundation and we will stand on it forever. The flock is making great progress in the pursuit of spiritual maturity. They know that prayer provides power, and realize how sweet it is to commune with the Lord early in the morning. Praise the Lord!

We fully understand that the Bibles did not come in an easy way. We know that for the suffering church and the spiritual needs of the flock, you have done your best. Brothers and sisters, your labor will not be in vain. Your love has blessed numerous congregations and has also awakened a multitude of souls who were drunk in this world... We have learned from your example of love, caring for other brothers and sisters in the church, spreading the gospel to the world, and sharing the light and warmth with others so that the church will be revived and grow, glorifying the name of the Lord. Please pray for us often. All brothers and sisters in our church greet you. Emmanuel.

***

Back in the Philippines I kept a low profile, as did the other crewmembers. Our desire was that Project Pearl might pass with as little fanfare and publicity as possible. Then, unexpectedly, I received a call to say that Captain Bill had been arrested in the Philippines and was being held in a small military prison! No charges had been laid against him. I immediately contacted some friends in places of authority, and within a week Bill was released. No explanation was provided as to why he had been arrested, but we guessed the Chinese government had pressurized their counterparts in the Philippines to punish those in charge of Project Pearl. Being the captain of the tugboat, Bill's name appeared on official documents so he was the easiest target for them to locate. Bill was later told that China had asked the Philippines to kill him, but they had been unwilling to do so and held him in the prison instead. Because of the pressure Bill relocated to another country where he continued to serve the Lord for many years.

Apart from this incident, our desire to maintain a low profile seemed to be happening until strong opposition and criticism started to circulate around the world from a totally unexpected source.

In recent years a new expression has emerged on the world's battlefields to describe the worst kind of way for a soldier to die or be injured in battle. Soldiers explain that if they are killed or wounded by an enemy bullet it is considered a great honor, but the worst insult is to be wounded by 'friendly fire'. It is a terrible feeling to be shot by fellow soldiers whom you thought were on the same side!

In the many months of planning for Project Pearl we had seen the Lord Jesus Christ overcome numerous obstacles. We had stood in awe as we witnessed His mighty works during the delivery, and had marveled at the power and reality of His presence. We were prepared for a backlash from the Communist authorities in China, but we were not expecting to be severely attacked and criticized by other missionary organizations when they heard about the delivery.

Unfortunately, and tragically, 'friendly fire' is alive and well among God's people today. To come under fire from fellow Christians, who are meant to be fighting on your side, is a miserable and terrible thing to have to cope with. How sad and grievous this is to the Holy Spirit!

Although the term 'friendly fire' may be relatively new, sadly it has been practiced among believers since the church was born in the Book of Acts. All throughout Christian history we can find God's revival fires being quenched by church leaders, many of who did so out of ignorance and a misplaced zeal to 'protect' the gospel. Others have been motivated by intense jealousy or hatred.

Many of the great Christian leaders throughout history have been the subjects of brutal attacks from other Christians. The great revivalists like Charles Finney and D. L. Moody were strongly denounced by other Christian leaders of the day. The young preacher used by God during the famous Welsh Revival of the early twentieth century, Evan Roberts, was also cruelly attacked and slandered. A large group of leading pastors of the day took out full-page advertisements in the Welsh newspapers denouncing the revival as being 'from the devil' and condemning Roberts as a heretic. It is worth noting that today Moody and Roberts are still respected for their labors for the kingdom of God, but nobody can remember the names of any of their critics.

The first thing we need to realize is who is really behind such undeserved attacks against God's children. The Bible says, *'For our struggle is not against flesh and blood, but against the rulers, against the authorities, against the powers of this dark world and against the spiritual forces of evil in the heavenly realms'* (Ephesians 6:12). Satan knows if he can turn Christian against Christian, he has already gone a long way to winning the battle. Paul pointed this out to the Corinthian believers long ago, when he wrote, *'The very fact that you have lawsuits among you means you have been completely defeated already'* (1 Corinthians 6:7).

The first attack came in September when the American leader of a Christian mission, sent a letter around the world strongly criticizing Project Pearl.

The first I knew about the letter was when I received a phone call from an Open Doors leader in Europe, who asked, 'David, what's going on?' The claims in the letter, which were then repeated by other ministries, were simply untrue. The letter claimed Open Doors had raised millions of dollars but only put 40,000 Bibles into China.

Two hours later Keith Ritter in Japan called and also asked, 'Brother David, what's going on? This letter has gone out all over Japan, attacking us and claiming Project Pearl was a terrible failure.'

Less than an hour later a brother in Australia contacted me: 'David, what's going on? This organization is attacking us all across Australia, saying Project Pearl was a total flop.'

I was taken aback. I knew we would probably receive strong attacks from the Communist authorities and from unbelievers, but I never thought there would be such a strong attack from other members of the body of Christ. Even then, I would not have been so upset if other Christians criticized what we had done, as long as they had been accurate. But here the attacks were quite unfounded. I was also stunned that a fellow Christian ministry, who purported to serve the Chinese Church, would place them at risk by making the details known throughout the world.

Now that Project Pearl had been so strongly attacked all around the world I knew these reports would quickly spread.

We had no plans at all to issue a public statement on Pearl. Ideally, we would have said nothing about the whole project, but in the circumstances, we had no option but to set the facts straight. If the truth is presented, people can weigh up the evidence and make their own judgment. I was concerned that these misleading reports would greatly hurt and discourage thousands of good-hearted believers around the world who had faithfully prayed, given, or otherwise been involved in Project Pearl from the start.

I called my friend David Aikman, a dedicated Christian, who was later appointed the Bureau chief for *Time* magazine in China. At the time he was living in Israel. I called him and said, 'Hello David. Do you want an exclusive story for *Time*?' He asked what I meant, and I told him, 'We delivered one million Bibles into China in a two-hour period on the night of 18 June.'

'What?' David gasped.

He said he was going to hang up and talk to some of his journalist colleagues, and would call me back within 20 minutes. My telephone rang, and David asked, 'How fast can you get to Hong Kong?'

Michael Bruce and I flew from Manila to Hong Kong the next day and contacted a staff reporter with *Time* magazine. When he came to our hotel room we showed him a collection of photos and told him about Pearl. He quickly wrote a two-page article, entitled, 'Risky Rendezvous in

Swatow', and dispatched it to the main *Time* office in New York. It was Friday afternoon and he told us it would appear in the following Monday's magazine. Before leaving, the reporter told us that the only thing that could stop the publication of the article was if a world leader was assassinated between now and then.

The next morning I woke up in my hotel room and saw a copy of the daily newspaper under my door. I opened it and read the headline: 'Anwar Sadat Assassinated'.

I couldn't believe it! The President of Egypt had been murdered on 6 October 1981, and the publication of the Pearl story was delayed until the 19 October edition of *Time*. The article described Pearl as 'A remarkable mission... the largest operation of its kind in the history of China.'

The article in *Time* helped some Christians mellow a little in their criticisms. Four leading mission organizations released the following statement to the worldwide media on 10 December 1981:

> *We are sympathetic to the need for Bibles by Christians in China. The Bible contains the basis for their faith, yet millions do not have access to the Bible.*
>
> *We therefore appreciate the intentions of Open Doors in its 'Project Pearl' to help meet that need. However, we cannot endorse that project's violation of China's territorial waters.*
>
> *In order to meet the need more effectively, we urge the religious authorities in China as soon as possible to speed up the printing and open distribution of Bibles, or to permit the free importing of enough Bibles to meet the need.*

(signed)
Paul E. Kauffman, Asian Outreach International
Jonathan Chao, Chinese Church Research Center
Ted Hsueh, Christian Communications Limited
Kenneth Lo, Far East Broadcasting Co., Inc-HK

Ironically, one of these organizations started smuggling Bibles across the border into China soon after, while another had effectively been 'violating China's territory' for many years by broadcasting the gospel via short-wave radio from another country!

Of course, the Far East Broadcasting Company had been my former employer, and had been so kind to my family and me as they helped us adapt to the mission field. After Pearl, FEBC distanced themselves from Open Doors. They even cancelled a gospel radio broadcast called 'Awake', which Open Doors had been producing and FEBC broadcasting into China.

In the heat of the moment and the overwhelming desire for self-preservation, some Christian ministries forgot that we were team members with them in the body of Christ. I believe Jesus is interested in reaching the lost and He does not always work according to how we think He should work, or how our own mission says He should work!

Time is short and multitudes of people are going to hell, while some sections of the body of Christ spend incredible amounts of time and energy fighting and criticizing one another. In the long term it all amounts to nothing. God is the judge, and He will weigh up every person's work.

***

Meanwhile, reports continued to come in from the believers in China. Brother Joseph and others were heavily involved with compiling a clear picture of the impact of the Project Pearl Bibles. The first indications in the weeks after the delivery was that 90 per cent of the Bibles had been successfully delivered into the hands of believers in China, but that the process was still continuing.

In March 1982 our contacts confirmed that 95 per cent of the one million Bibles had been successfully delivered. In early April, Brother Joseph made a special trip to all the house church leaders who received the Bibles, interviewing them and gathering data. I was in the United States when Joseph called me. He said that upon his return from China he had been able to put all the pieces of the very complex follow-up together. After checking and rechecking the figures to assure accuracy, it was found that only 10,000 Bibles were unaccounted for. This meant a 99 per cent success rate.

Meanwhile in the nine months since the delivery we had continued to send Bibles across the border by suitcase. In that time more than 10,000 Bibles had been successfully delivered, so counting deliveries both by sea and by land, the goal of Project Pearl had been achieved.

A million Bibles were now safely in the hands of our brothers and sisters throughout China.

Chapter Thirty:

Sweet and Sour

In the months following the delivery I continued to work hard at wrapping the project up. We sold the barge for $115,500. Although it had cost almost three times as much to build, its unique features and dimensions made it difficult to find a buyer. The barge was later used by the Philippine government to help construct the metro train line across the Pasig River. The tugboat *Michael* was sold for $300,000. *Michael* and *Gabriella* had served God's purposes well. These sales helped us recuperate some of the costs and outstanding debts of Project Pearl, although it was to take another three years before we had paid back everything that was owed.

An unexpected thing happened in the second half of 1981 and into the following year. As Christians around the world learned about Project Pearl, reaction was split down the middle. In the West many Christian publications were scathing in their criticism. So too was the government-sanctioned China Christian Council and Three-Self Church in China.

Because of the confusion caused by the false information, there are many Christians even to the present day who believe Project Pearl was a failure. For this reason it is important to set the record straight to explain how some of these misconceptions arose.

A few months after the Pearl delivery, the China Christian Council sent a delegation to America. During several interviews Bishop Ding, the head of the Three-Self Patriotic Movement, strongly attacked Pearl, saying those involved were 'unscrupulous', and the whole project a

'humiliating hoax'. His comments were carried by numerous media outlets throughout the country and around the
world, with headlines like 'Chinese Christians Beg Halt to
Bible Smuggling', appearing in the *Los Angeles Times*, *New
York Times*, and other leading newspapers. One Three-Self
Church leader even claimed the Chinese were humiliated
and angered by the delivery, and that they would be willing
to wait another 300 years for Bibles if necessary!

Some of the critics of Pearl initially claimed that 'none'
of the Bibles had reached the hands of believers, and that
all had been destroyed. Later, even some of the harshest
critics admitted that 'around 80 per cent' of the Bibles were
successfully delivered. *Tianfeng* (the official magazine of
the Three-Self Church) published a vitriolic article entitled
'The Self-Betrayal of an Anti-China Clown'. They slandered
the Bible delivery, describing it as 'dirty', 'shameless,' and
an 'uncivilized trampling of the truth in the Bible'. Using
rhetoric similar to the political tirades of the Cultural
Revolution, they even claimed that 900,000 Bibles were
swept back into the ocean because nobody had come to the
beach to get them, while the other 100,000 Bibles had been
intercepted and burned by the authorities!

Brother Andrew continued to be a blessing to me. When
the waves of criticism were crashing against us he wrote
me the following beautiful letter of encouragement:

David,

*You may have wondered about the origin of a pearl: some
sharp object which is accidentally or intentionally inserted
into the sensitive inner part of an oyster; there it causes
irritation and in the end produces beauty. Those living in
Asia know better than the rest of the world that pearls are
not only cultured in Japan but also grow in the oceans and
come in many different shapes and colours, some fasci-
nating, some less so, but usually very expensive – at least
the real ones.*

*You have been working on the real Pearl. There is
enough irritation from those who disagree, but there is a*

*lot of beauty being produced – by the One who is charge of
all those living, God Himself. But as long as the Pearl is
inside, it does not stop growing. We believe the Pearl inside
China is still growing too, becoming more and more beautiful in shape and colour all the time. Maybe it is red right
now, because of all the terrible suffering.*

*For my part, I want to say a very big THANK YOU for
your personal involvement. I am sure proud of you; you've
done a marvellous job; and as I walked on Michael and
Gabriella a few months ago, I looked for your footprints
and found them all over the place! My heart was filled with
longing to have been there with you... But the Lord had a
different plan for me.*

*In closing, we have to continue to bear the load spiri-
tually, so that not only every book but also every page will
count for the kingdom of God.*

*Yours in the longing to see the Book of God in the hands of
every Chinese, until He comes Who wrote the book,
Brother Andrew*

One of the main objections of the critics was that God's
'holy work' should never be mixed with 'smuggling'. In a
self-righteous tone, they boldly denounced Project Pearl
and those involved. Rarely was any mention made about
the desperate need for Bibles in China, and nobody bothered to ask the opinions of the house church Christians. Of
course this was not a 'smuggling' operation in the true
sense of the word. Smuggling is done for profit. We were
giving free gifts to our Chinese brothers and sisters. Our
only reward will be realized when we meet the Lord in
heaven.

I wonder if the critics would also have attacked us if
there had been millions of people starving to death somewhere in Africa with their government deliberately standing by doing nothing to help, and we had delivered a
shipload of food to them despite it being against the will of
the authorities? I think most people would have considered us heroes for such an action, risking our lives to save

others. Well, that is exactly how it was with the starving Christians in China. This world, and some Christians, place more importance on the material realm than the spiritual, but Jesus ministered to both at the same time.

At the same time that the critics were sharpening their knives, dozens of beautiful letters continued to come in from Christians throughout China. The tone of these letters was exactly opposite to the vehement denunciations from the critics, and they helped to keep us sane!

Over the years I have come to love Chinese food! One of my favorite dishes is sweet and sour pork. Asians are skilled at implementing contrasting tastes in their cooking. In the same way, I would like to use the rest of this chapter to reprint a selection of the sweetest letters we received about Project Pearl, and also a selection from those who opposed it. I also hope readers will gain an understanding of how the truth was deliberately distorted so that many people believed Project Pearl had been a dismal failure. Just as the sweet taste offsets the sour, these contrasting words and opinions will help you gain an appreciation for the strong flavor that Project Pearl cooked up!

***

Sweet – A house church leader from Guangdong Province, November 1981:

> *Ink and pen are unable to describe His wonderful works, and words cannot describe his power. How my heart moves! Since the night of 18 June until now, God has performed countless miracles in our midst. That night, God appeared to us on the beach, and He reigned as King. Even the plots of Satan accomplished the will of God. Satan seemed to think he could destroy the work of God by human means, but the wonderful works of God were manifested to us once more. Satan wanted to destroy the rest of the bread (Bibles) that remained in the sea, but the bread sparkled in the water. When people saw that sparkle, they*

salvaged the bread and it is filling many hungry hearts.
Isn't it wonderful?

God had kept His Word safe through the delivery
process. We have already sent the Bibles by mail and ship-
ment to countless cities and villages in the provinces of
Hunan, Shaanxi, Anhui, Guangdong, Fujian, Shandong,
Xinjiang, Heilongjiang, Henan, and Hebei, etc. How grate-
ful the believers were when they received the bread!

As the return of the Lord approaches, hungry souls are
everywhere waiting for the Word to nourish them, espe-
cially in China. We thank Brother David and the other
believers who took part in this ministry, whether it was to
give money, time, strength, prayer, or spiritual support.
Please let them all know that many brothers and sisters
with grateful hearts safely received the bread. How happy
and comforted we are! The Lord richly bless you!

***

Sour – *Tianfeng*, the official magazine of the Three-Self
Patriotic Church:

THE SELF-BETRAYAL OF AN ANTI-CHINA CLOWN

An article entitled 'Risky Rendezvous at Swatow' in the
religious column of the U.S. *Time* Magazine published on
19 October 1981, vividly described the whole process of
a Chinese Bible smuggling incident which took place on
the coast near Shantou. The operation was carried out by
two anti-China organizations that hid themselves in the
robes of religion.... According to the report, these two
organizations worked out the so-called 'Project Pearl'
through conspiracy. They used 'the Chinese Christians
need plenty of Bibles urgently' as the theme to raise a
large sum of money and secretly printed one million
copies of the Bible in the United States. The article stated
without mincing words that Project Pearl was led by an
American ex-Marine...

The large-scale Bible smuggling incident was discovered near Shantou... It was just the opposite of what the

Time Magazine bragged about. The shameless smuggling deed was discovered on time by the highly alert militia. A large portion of the smuggled goods were washed away by the tide. Some were burnt by the angry militia. Those anti-China people celebrated their success too early, for their smuggling act actually ended in shameful failure...

Isn't it an extreme profanation to the will of God to claim that this deed is an obedience to God? Distributing Bibles through this kind of method is the most uncivilized trampling on the truth in the Bible itself. Can this kind of act help the Chinese Christians who need the Bible badly? It is just the opposite!... The mastermind of Project Pearl has destroyed the reputation of the gospel and has insulted the Lord's truth by performing such a dirty action... In fact, they don't have even a bit of genuine concern towards the spreading of the gospel in China, but only attempt to split and subvert the new China by carrying out Bible smuggling activities. Their reactionary political purpose is very clear. Both for the sake of the inviolable sovereignty of our country and for the truth of the Bible which can't be profaned, we Chinese Christians should of course strongly oppose the shameless crime of Bible smuggling.

The 'Risky Rendezvous' near Shantou has already ended in shameful failure. This incident will surely enhance the alertness of Chinese Christians towards this small portion of international anti-China forces who put on a religious robe. It will also provoke a determination and enthusiasm among Chinese Christians to walk the path of 'love country, love church'... All the anti-China clowns will be cast aside by more and more people due to the continued self-betrayal of their crimes.

***

Sweet – From 'A weak brother' in Henan Province, 27 May 1982:

After receiving this Bible I realized that the Heavenly Father really loves me. I am deeply moved and encouraged.

Because of His love you were willing to help us in spite of the risk of losing your life. Oh! I know that I was a seedling in a drought. Now I am like a thirsty and starving man who has found plenty of water and food.

The Bible helped me immeasurably after I possessed it. I found the way, the goal, and the truth of life in it. It teaches me to avoid false teachings. Previously I had been walking on many dangerous paths without knowing it. I depended on my own knowledge and wisdom, which is futile. I have more strength after I obtained the Bible.

During the times before I had a Bible, I had nothing to do at home after work. I read novels, played cards, or chatted with my friends. Now I read the Bible as soon as I arrive home. My spiritual life has grown daily and the Lord is pleased with me more and more.

After I received the Bible, many brethren wanted to have one also. I told them that I only had one, but prayed that the Lord would provide a second one. It's not only me who has benefited from this Bible, but at least 5,000 other brothers and sisters have also benefited. Now tens of thousands of Christians are hoping that they can have their own Bible.

***

Sour – Letter in *Time* magazine, 16 November 1981:

Your report on efforts to smuggle Bibles into mainland China (Oct. 19) reveals incredible insensitivity and lack of understanding regarding the visible re-emergence of Christianity there.

Western Christian missions like Brother Andrew International show callous disregard for the desire of Chinese Christians to be self-supporting, self-governing and self-propagating. Ironically, they pose a far greater threat to the future of Christianity in China than does the present Chinese government.

Spurgeon M. Dunnam III
Editor, *The United Methodist Reporter*, Dallas

***

Sweet – From Liu in Anhui Province, November 1981:

The 25th of September 1981 is a day I'll never forget. On that day the Bread of Life was delivered to me. My dry heart was moistened by God's sweet dew, and my spirit revived like a dead man coming back to life. He sent us, the suffering ones, the bread of life through you, our dear brothers and sisters, who are far away from us but willing to pay the price of even your lives. Countless lost sheep have returned and many starving people have been fed. May God give us new lives through this book and make us the salt and light of the world until He comes again.

***

Sour – Nicholas Read, 'Chinese Christians Don't Want Smuggled Bibles', *Vancouver Sun*, October 1981:

The code name was Project Pearl. The mission: to unload and distribute more than one million Chinese-language Bibles from the port of Shantou on the South China Sea.

According to *Time* magazine, a 232-tonne cargo from the U.S. was smuggled 300 kilometres up the Chinese coast from Hong Kong.

But what the magazine declined to report, says Anglican Bishop K.H. Ting, president of the China Christian Council in Nanjing, was that the mission was an abject failure.

The *Time* report claims that up to 80 per cent of the contraband books ended up in house church groups, some as far as 5,000 kilometres away from the coastal drop-off point. But reports from within China, says Bishop Ting, confirm that most of the Bibles drifted out to sea... Most of the books had disappeared or sunk within hours of the deposit.

'I think the whole thing was a fiasco,' Bishop Ting said.

***

Sweet – From a believer in Henan Province, 23 March 1982:

Because of the ten-year Cultural Revolution (1966-76) and natural disasters, all Bibles were lost. There were only a few copies left in the whole prefecture. Because of our desperate need, we borrowed a Bible and copied it by hand day and night. We finally finished copying the whole New Testament. It is exceedingly precious.

Since the winter of 1980, God has been reviving His churches here, and the number of believers increases every day. Their desire to have a Bible is much more important to them than their daily physical needs. I attended a meeting in a mountain district and my long-standing desire was unexpectedly fulfilled. I obtained a Bible! When I heard how my Bible had come to China, I couldn't hold back the tears in my eyes any more. Clutching the Bible close to my heart, I cried along with three co-workers for one hour. We didn't know how to divide the Bible between the four of us. At last, we agreed that I would keep the Bible and all of us would share it. Glory be to the Lord!

***

Sour – Louise Branson, 'Bibles Smuggled into the Communist World', *Bangkok Post*, 17 January 1983:

Smugglers huddled on the beach of a dark and deserted South China bay, waiting for a tug. As the vessel chugged in to shore carrying one million Chinese-language Bibles, searchlights snapped on and soldiers swarmed down the cliffs.

Operation Pearl had failed...

'Yes, the Bible smugglers have fantastic imaginations,' says Samm Dahlgren of the Geneva-based World Council of Churches. 'They are also often misinformed and naïve and do more harm than good to the people they are trying to help – the restricted Christians in Communist countries', he said.

***

Sweet – A 'Letter from the Brethren in China', 29 June 1982:

Dear faithful and powerful witnesses of the Lord in free countries, greetings! While 50 million seeds in China were longing for a sudden rainfall, while our voices rose to heaven's door, the mighty God revealed the urgent need of Chinese Christians in your hearts.

The arrival of one million Bibles is an historical and miraculous event. It is evident that the Lord was in control at the helm of the ship, and that He worked with each crewmember. Hallelujah! God took care of the brothers and sisters of the suffering Church in China and performed a wonderful miracle. The fire of your love is burning in the hearts of the brothers and sisters who truly love the Lord. Oh, how much we are moved! Praise be to the name of God forever and ever. God is sovereign over the kingdoms of men. He gives wisdom to the wise and knowledge to the discerning. He reveals deep and hidden things.

The fulfilment of Project Pearl has had far-reaching significance. The one million Bibles have been the trigger for the wide spread of the gospel. The Bibles are the guideposts to lead people back onto the right path and are the bread of life to feed people walking on the heavenly road. They are the lamp of God to lighten the journey home. They are living water to quench the thirsty fields that were parched by drought. Now many bitter lives have turned into sweet ones.

We are studying our Bibles every day, but one million is not enough. We are asking for more in faith. We ask the Holy Spirit to continue working in the hearts of all faithful men, until every Christian is able to study his own Bible.

May the Lord, who walks among the seven lampstands, be with you. May His right hand take hold of you until you reach the finish line.

Your co-workers in Jesus.

***

Sour – *Tianfeng*, no. 5, 1981:

AIDING THE GOSPEL CAUSE?
by Xing Wen

The Bible is sacred, but smuggling is dirty. Strange enough, then, that someone has made a combination of both. What is this all about?... Obviously, the motivation of those Bible smugglers is not for the ministry of the gospel, but aimed to condemn and attack the New China. What they have done should be considered a reactionary political enterprise rather than a ministry for the gospel.

Smuggling is an illegal and sinful activity. Nothing is allowed to be smuggled, how much more the Bible we treasure! Bible smuggling does not honor the Bible, but absolutely disgraces the Bible... Therefore, all we Chinese Christians who really love and treasure the Bible stand up and denounce such a sinful act which harms the sacredness of the Bible... Smugglers are characterized by doing things in darkness. They don't bear the fruit of goodness, righteousness, and truth, but only carry out their works through rumors, cheating and defrauding. Their aim can only be to destroy – to destroy the reputation of China, to destroy the Protestant Three-Self Patriotic Movement in China, and to spoil the good intention of many kind foreign Christians simultaneously.

We deeply believe that the Lord of light won't accept their actions in the dark, and we Chinese Christians who walk in the light also firmly condemn and oppose such a sinful act.

***

Sweet – A reply to the above article by a house church leader in Shanghai:

Yes, it's for the ministry of the Gospel!

Only through the Tianfeng report did all the brothers and sisters throughout the country come to know about the delivery of one million Bibles into China. This is huge, marvellous news! This event is actually proof of God's might. To man it all seems impossible, but everything is possible to our God. Man's ability is limited, but in the hands of our God weak human beings can do great things beyond our imagination.

In China hundreds of thousands of faithful Christians gave thanks to God after they heard news of the delivery. Hallelujah! Praise the Lord! Glory be to God. One million Bibles – this is what the Chinese Christians need so badly. If ever another million Bibles come into China, they will be more than welcome too…

In the whole country, Henan Province has the largest Christian population. It exceeds one million. There are three counties in southern Henan with between 120,000 to 140,000 Christians, but they had only 30 copies of the Bible between them. Anyone who needs the Bible must register and attend the Three-Self Church, and they control them under their fist. If they printed lots of Bibles and everyone could obtain them freely, the Three-Self would lose their power to control Christians. If there were plenty of Bibles in China, there would be no need to smuggle them in.

The writer named Xing Wen has distorted the actual situation of the Chinese churches today. He also used the Bible in a wrong way. His article was titled, 'For the Ministry of the Gospel?' I would like to ask him the same question, 'Are you for the ministry of the Gospel?' There's a Heavenly Father who knows everything and controls everything. In the past 30 years, the Three-Self Church hasn't done anything for the gospel. They are against the gospel. The have tried their best to wipe away the gospel. But the gospel has not been destroyed. God controls and protects, for the gospel is the great power of God unto salvation.

The Bible is very precious and important to us. One could even say that without the Bible, Christianity would not exist. The Bible helps Christians to be spiritually strong and have more power to preach the gospel. Though smuggling is not an ideal method, there's no other way because the Three-Self Church won't allow Bibles to be produced legally. The smuggled goods were not weapons or drugs. They were the Book which leads to eternal life! Therefore, this smuggling of Bibles is for the ministry of the gospel. Those who are against the smuggling of the Bibles are against Christianity. They are afraid that the gospel will spread widely and the number of Christians will increase.

All the Christians in China give thanks and praise to God for this great news! God has heard our prayers and met our needs. Thanks to all our unknown brothers and sisters who helped us for the sake of our Lord. You love the Chinese Christians and the people of China. You risked your lives and money for us. God has done a great thing through all of you! It is really a miracle! Thank you!

Only through the Tianfeng magazine did we learn about the respectful servants of God who were so mightily used by God in this generation. We don't know how tall, how old, or what colour their skin is. We don't know where they live, but we believe wholeheartedly that they have our Father's eternal life in their hearts. We don't know why they did such a risky thing, but we believe they must have known the result if the operation failed. What was their motivation for doing this? Was it personal ambition? Was it to conduct a profitable business? Was it a political motivation? Obviously not. We believe they did this because they were touched by the love of God and the heavenly vision to bring one million Bibles into China. God has carried out a miracle through them.

Except for those copies of the Bible destroyed by the authorities, the rest of the one million Bibles are being distributed all over the country under the protection of God. In Shanghai we have also received and distributed some already. Praise the Lord!

We've heard that some Christian organizations expressed their opposition against this smuggling event.

There are even some famous pastors who are against it. Actually, they are not against the brothers who did this – but they are against the gospel. They do things for their own benefit and fame only. The hundreds of thousands of Christians in China don't understand their 'concern'. They have done nothing for us. They never gave us any Bibles. When we were hungry, they didn't give us any food. When we were thirsty, they didn't bring us water. When we were sick, they didn't care about us. When we were naked, they didn't give us clothes. When we were in prison, they didn't pray for us.

May the Lord remember what you've done for Him! Thank you so much for your concern for the Chinese brothers and sisters. Your bold act has really encouraged us. You love the Chinese people so much that we feel moved to love our own countrymen even more. We will always remember you in our prayers.

You, unknown brothers, suffered a lot for sending us the one million Bibles and yet you are now receiving more opposition from men. What you did is for the ministry of the gospel. May the Lord have mercy on you and strengthen you. Amen!

Chapter Thirty-One:

The Path to Revival

Time continued to advance, and the high level of criticism directed at Project Pearl slowly drifted away. My work with Open Doors continued throughout the 1980s, and although we never again attempted such a bold delivery as the one million Bibles by boat, hundreds of teams came to Hong Kong and continued to carry Bibles across the border into China. Hundreds of thousands more copies of the scriptures made it into the hands of believers this way. Several other organizations also started 'Bible smuggling' ministries based out of Hong Kong. Ironically, some of them had been among the fiercest critics of Project Pearl!

For years we continued to receive reports from all over China. Many talked about 'perfume Bibles' being delivered to them.

After moving to the United States in 2002, Peter Xu Yongze, the leader of one of China's largest house church movements, fondly remembered the impact the one million Pearl Bibles had on the church in China. He said that after some of the Bibles were captured by the authorities and thrown into a large tank of human waste, the believers crept back under the cover of darkness, removed the precious books from the waste, and took them home where they lovingly washed each page and dried them in the sun. They then sprayed perfume on the pages, hoping to replace the unpleasant stench. The believers didn't care what their Bibles smelled like, however, for they now had their own copies of the precious Word of God and rejoiced in the sweet spiritual aroma those precious pages contained.

Reports of powerful heaven-sent revival came in from

all over China. Many Chinese believers commented on the role the one million Bibles had played in fanning the flames of the revival. One pastor said Project Pearl was the spark that set many house churches alight, as believers gained strength and faith from God's Word. Looking back with the hindsight of years, I believe the timing of Project Pearl was God-ordained. In 1981 the harvest in China was ripe and the believers were desperate for God's Word. In a sense, if we had done the delivery a few years later the impact might not have been quite as great. Many church leaders have told me the Bibles came at the exact time of their greatest need.

Years after the Pearl delivery we heard about how a young man received one of the Bibles after praying for three years that God would provide a copy. After reading his precious new possession through three times in three weeks, the young man heard God calling him to preach the gospel in China's countryside. He commenced his ministry in Fujian Province, and God used him mightily. Hundreds of people believed the gospel and gave their hearts to Jesus Christ, and small fellowships of hungry believers were established in numerous villages. In 1986 my wife Meiling met with this man and found that he had become the leader of a house church network numbering approximately 400,000 Christians.

In the mid-1980s Eddie Cairns led a group of Christians back into China. One day he and his group decided to visit a city park in central China. Suddenly, as they sat down on a bench to rest their feet, a Chinese woman approached them clutching a Bible from Project Pearl. With a look of intense longing on her face, she held the Bible up and repeated the only English word she knew, 'More! More!'

The Chinese Christians have simple faith. They read the Bible and believe it is relevant for them today. They went out and prayed for the sick, and they were healed. They cast demons out of people, and everywhere the gospel was proclaimed with great power.

In the West we think to make strong Christians we need to first indoctrinate a new believer and fill him with teaching. This intellectual approach tends to create weak believers. In China, the gospel often comes with a demonstration of God's power. People see Him move with their own eyes, and the gospel became a reality in their lives. It is then natural for these new believers to hunger to know more of God's Word. This seems to be the biblical method for creating strong disciples of Christ. The apostle Paul reminded the church in Corinth: *'My message and my preaching were not with wise and persuasive words, but with a demonstration of the Spirit's power, so that your faith might not rest on men's wisdom, but on God's power'* (1 Corinthians 2:4–5).

Although all the Bibles that went into China in the 1980s greatly helped the churches, the need for more Bibles remained acute because of the revival that burned throughout the decade. No matter how many Bibles the various Christian ministries could carry in, the need always exceeded the supply because of the huge number of people coming to faith every day.

A short time after Project Pearl, the government announced that they would allow a limited number of Bibles to be printed legally by the Three-Self Church. Later, the Amity Press was established in Nanjing to oversee this tremendous need. I was later told by a Chinese official that one of the reasons for the government allowing Bibles to be printed was that they didn't want the possibility of another Project Pearl to take place. The Chinese political leadership was embarrassed by the delivery, and it helped them realize there was a tremendous need for Christians to have the Bible in their country. Dr James Hudson Taylor III confirmed this, while speaking at a conference in New York in April 2000. He said, 'Project Pearl put pressure on the Chinese government to officially allow a Bible printing press. Pearl made them realize similar deliveries might happen again unless the tremendous demand for Bibles in China was met.'

The establishment of the Amity Press was the fulfilment of the fourth and final outcome we had prayed for at the start of Project Pearl.

In the early years the house church Christians were unable to get their hands on these officially-printed Bibles. They didn't trust the government or the Three-Self Church, and it was reported that some believers who tried to purchase a Bible from the Three-Self were asked for their names, addresses, when they became Christians, and the name of the person who led them to the Lord. The house church believers are not stupid! They could smell a rat and they stayed away. This resulted in a marked imbalance among Christians in China, for it had become clear that the number of Christians who worshipped in house church meetings far outweighed the number of Three-Self Church members. The privileged minority therefore had access to Bibles, but the majority of Christians were still without. This imbalance was exacerbated due to the fact that Bibles were only available in the large cities of China, whereas the great majority of house church believers live in rural farming areas, often hundreds of miles from the nearest Three-Self Bible store.

As I continued to minister with Open Doors, Brother Andrew asked me to become one of his 'ministers-at-large'. My responsibility was to travel and speak on behalf of the suffering church in China, and I was blessed to minister in more than fifty different countries. The Lord Jesus was always good and faithful, and it was pure joy to see Him touch people's lives. I felt like the ministry had become a two-way blessing, with the suffering church in countries like China and North Korea being blessed by the body of Christ around the world, while those believers in the 'free' world who became involved with ministering to their persecuted brethren also received a great spiritual blessing in return. I know of many churches in the West that experienced a great breakthrough and growth, both inward and numerical, after they started to focus on serving the needs of their brothers and sisters in Asia. The greatest antidote for any church or individual who is absorbed in their own problems is to start serving the needs of others. The Bible puts it this way: *'A generous man will prosper; he who refreshes others will himself be refreshed'* (Proverbs 11:25).

As the atmosphere in China relaxed a little in the mid to late 1980s, I was able to meet more freely with Chinese church leaders, and enjoyed many wonderful times of fellowship with them. I gained a deeper appreciation of them as individuals, and a greater respect for their commitment to God. On many occasions I left such a meeting realizing that I had been with spiritual giants of the faith, although such a giant might be trapped inside the tiny body of a seventy-year-old Chinese sister or a humble pastor who had spent decades in prison for the gospel. The apostle Paul understood this principle when he wrote, *'We have this treasure in jars of clay to show that this all-surpassing power is from God and not from us'* (2 Corinthians 4:7).

I came to understand that suffering is one of the main tools that God uses to transform us into His image and to mature us as believers. In the West we tend to think that persecution is something that only comes upon Christians who live in hostile environments, but this is not true. Persecution and suffering may come to us in the form of criticism, slander, lies, rejection, illness or ridicule. The important thing for followers of Christ is not whether or not we experience hardship or pain in our lives – for they are guaranteed – but rather how we respond to them. We can choose to become bitter and withdraw from others in a bid to protect ourselves from the pain, or we can learn to follow the Lord regardless of the circumstances of our life. Such an attitude, over time, produces humility, gentleness, self-control and many other wonderful fruits of the Spirit. Just after he wrote about the 'jars of clay', Paul said, *'We always carry around in our body the death of Jesus, so that the life of Jesus may also be revealed in our body. For we who are alive are always being given over to death for Jesus' sake, so that his life may be revealed in our mortal body'* (2 Corinthians 4:10–11).

I believe the revival in China these past thirty years has come about because of the steadfast commitment of the Chinese Christians who have paid the price for their faith through incredible suffering and hardship, and through the perseverance and prayers of many saints down through the centuries.

The suffering of our fellow believers in China is incredible. One of our dearest friends, a young lady named Mary, was arrested and thrown into a dung-pit. Because of her unwillingness to denounce Jesus, electric wires were attached to her head and breasts and she was repeatedly electrocuted. She still refused to deny the Lord. After she was released from prison my wife Meiling and I went to meet her. When we saw her we were appalled. She was barely recognizable from the pretty young lady we had known. Her body was battered and bruised, but as soon as she started to talk, the same spirit of Jesus flowed from her heart. It reminded me of what the Bible says: *'Though outwardly we are wasting away, yet inwardly we are being renewed day by day. For our light and momentary troubles are achieving for us an eternal glory that far outweighs them all'* (2 Corinthians 4:16–17).

When you go through times of intense struggle, don't give up! Cling to Jesus and He will see you through. This is the same battle that thousands of Chinese believers have experienced. Most of them had never envisaged spending years in prison being part of their life. Many have told me they struggled for a long time with thoughts that God had abandoned them and didn't love them any more. Over time, however, they learned to *'endure hardship... like a good soldier of Christ Jesus'* (2 Timothy 2:3). They came to realize that nothing could affect their intimate relationship with Jesus. Their spirit belonged to God alone, and no person or hardship could ever take that way. The suffering believers in China were able to declare, *'For I am convinced that neither death nor life, neither angels nor demons, neither the present nor the future, nor any powers, neither height nor depth, nor anything else in all creation, will be able to separate us from the love of God that is in Christ Jesus our Lord'* (Romans 8:38–39).

If we ever catch hold of this perspective on suffering, our lives will be radically transformed! Suffering can cease to be the thing we avoid at all cost and can become a friend to be embraced, for in suffering we can experience part of the character of Jesus that cannot be experienced any other way. This is what Paul meant when he declared, *'I want to know Christ and the power of his resurrection and the fellowship of sharing in his sufferings, becoming like him in his death, and so, somehow, to attain to the resurrection from the dead'* (Philippians 3:10–11).

***

A powerful letter, written by a Chinese Christian who only referred to him or herself as 'a weak member of the Body', was received in Hong Kong in May 1982. This precious document was addressed to Christians around the world, and perfectly summarized the beauty of the suffering church in China and was an insight into the revival they were experiencing. I would like to share the letter with you here:

ALL WHO LIVE GODLY IN CHRIST JESUS WILL SUFFER PERSECUTION

Dear brothers and sisters in Christ,

On behalf of the brothers and sisters in Henan Province I send greetings to the members of the Body overseas!

Today the Church here is being greatly blessed by the Lord and the number of people being saved is increasing daily. The Good News of God is being proclaimed more and more...

The proverb, 'When good is one-foot high, evil is ten-feet high' is true. Yet the growth in the life of the Church has been promoted even by the servants of the devil. Wherever the Church flourishes there are difficulties. The revival has grown up in such circumstances. If Jesus had not been crucified, nobody today could be saved. If there is no testing by fire, then true faith would not become apparent, and if the Lord did not train us, we could not become instruments fit for His use. If the rock was not split open, the living water could not have sprung forth. Therefore difficulties are the means for promoting life and revival in the churches.

Recently the gospel here has once again been greatly promoted, because ten brothers and sisters were imprisoned, beaten and bound. They regarded their sufferings for the Lord as more precious than the treasures of Egypt. They started to preach the gospel in the poorest and most barren areas. One day they went to a certain commune where they met those who attended a Three-Self Church. Those people only believed in the four Gospels and tore up all other books of the Bible. They were not separate from the world. It was a confused situation, so that when our co-workers preached the truth to them, no one listened or received it. The preachers prayed and were greatly moved by God. They split up and went to different places to preach. As soon as they opened their mouths, the power of God came forth. They preached with tears streaming down their cheeks, causing the passers-by and street merchants, Christians and non-Christians, to stand still and listen. Even the fortune-tellers were moved by the Holy Spirit and burst out crying. Many people, after hearing the Word of the Lord, forgot their food, their work, and even forgot to return home. This went on until the evening, and still people had not dispersed. The brothers and sisters preached until they were exhausted but still the crowd would not let them leave...

The authorities made a move and seized the believers, dragging them away one by one. They bound them with ropes and tortured them with electric batons. They also slapped their faces with their shoes and knocked them unconscious, but when they came to, they continued to pray, sing and preach to the bystanders. One little sister, just 14-years-old, was beaten senseless. When she revived she saw that many people were sympathetic to them because of their persecution, so she again began to preach. Her words were few and her voice faint, but the people could not stop themselves from crying out, and they repented and believed in Jesus. When the believers were bound and beaten, many people noticed that their appearance was lively and gracious, and that they were smiling. People asked them why they did not feel ashamed. They asked where these young people's power came from. Many were led to faith in Jesus by their example.

At this point many people who had not accepted the preaching earlier came to listen. Many people who attended Three-Self churches also came to know Jesus. Those who had not received the truth began to understand. The brothers and sisters in that area saw the young preachers bound and forced to kneel on the ground for more than three days without food or water, and beaten with sticks until their faces were covered with blood and their hands were black from the ropes. Yet they continued to pray, sing, and praise the Lord. The watching believers were cut to the heart, and wished to share in the persecution and be bound with them and cast into prison. In this area the flame of the gospel has spread everywhere. There had never been a revival like this before, but through persecution this place has truly received the seeds of life. May everyone who hears of this give thanks and praise for the revival of the church in this area.

Dearly beloved brothers and sisters – in men's eyes this was all an unfortunate occurrence, but for Christians it was like a rich banquet. This kind of lesson cannot be learned from books, and this sweetness is not usually tasted by men. This rich life does not exist in a comfortable environment. Where there is no cross, there is no crown. If spices are not refined to become oil, the fragrance of the perfume cannot flow forth, and if grapes are not crushed in the vat, they will not become wine. Dear brethren, these saints who went down into the furnace, far from being harmed, have had their faces glorified and their spirits filled with power, with greater authority to preach the Word and a far more abundant life. The Lord will have the final victory in their bodies, and will put Satan to shame. In fact, Satan could find no way to make them renounce their faith, and they were released.

Recently our fellow-laborers in three counties here have had greater courage to preach the gospel because of what happened. Those who have not been imprisoned feel ashamed. They see that these ten all carry the scars of the Lord Jesus upon their bodies, so the others are full of regrets and long to receive this kind of punishment so that they too can bring greater glory to the Lord's Name. Dear fellow-workers in the Word, God has placed us in these last days to wage war so that the number of those saved will increase through us, and that His will shall be fulfilled through us in this generation. He desires that we advance into Glory with Him, so making the most of the very short time left, let us continually do the work of the Lord, for there are still many souls who have not been rescued, and many lambs wander in the mountains and high peaks without anyone to seek and find them.

May the Lord's peace place a burden to preach the gospel on each laborer's heart, and give a spirit of prayer to each Christian so they will become prayer warriors. Let no one in the Lord be lazy or idle... May God give you a heart faithful unto death or until He comes. All who have such a heart will obtain a great reward. The Lord will come soon.

Lord Jesus, I desire you to come! Emmanuel!

Chapter Thirty-Two:

Winds of Change

In early 1987 a house church leader whom I had known for many years described his concern for the house churches of China. He asked me to develop a vision in the free world and bring back to China encouragement for the house churches. I told him I was already doing this through Open Doors, but he persisted. In 1989 I began to seriously pray to find if God was behind this brother's request. I was thankful for my time with Open Doors, but life is never static and I realized I needed to be flexible enough to change if that was what the Lord wanted. I was scheduled to speak at a large cathedral of the Reformed Church in Hungary on 3 December 1989. The day before, I asked the two Christian men who were driving me around if the people in that church were saved. 'No. They don't know the Lord,' was their reply.

I told my colleagues that we should pray together for the salvation of the churchgoers, but they told me, 'Don't waste your time, David. They'll never get saved. That church is just full of dead religion.' This was at a time when Hungary was still under Communist control, but I refused to listen to my two friends. That night I got down on my knees and prayed for two-and-a-half hours, asking the Lord Jesus to glorify His name and to send the Holy Spirit to convict the congregation of *'sin, righteousness, and judgment'* (John 16:8). I also 'laid a fleece' before the Lord, and told him, 'Father, if the entire congregation of the Reformed Church stands to their feet and receives you, then I will take it as a sign that I am meant to leave Open Doors.'

As we entered the cathedral the next morning one of my

hosts turned to me with a concerned look on his face and said, 'David, I hope you won't be too disappointed if nobody gets saved this morning.' I told him, 'Listen. My responsibility is just to deliver the message the Lord has given me. God's responsibility is to save the people.'

When it was time to speak I had to climb the stairs to a platform high above the congregation. The cathedral was completely packed with people. I was only given 15 minutes to speak through a translator, and I shared on the message God had given me from the Gospel of John: *'God is spirit, and his worshipers must worship in spirit and in truth'* (John 4:24). I told the Hungarians that the Chinese Christians had learned the meaning of this verse of scripture, and I shared some testimonies from China. I then asked the people, 'Have you made this decision yet? Are you worshipping the Lord in spirit and in truth? Have you heard the Holy Spirit knocking at the door of your heart? Are you saved?'

I explained that God does not favor one nation or one kind of people over another, and that He wanted to do mighty things in Hungary just like He was doing in China. I concluded with these words, 'If you have never heard the voice of the Lord, then listen!' I held my hand up and didn't speak for the next minute. The congregation was absolutely silent, and I could tell that the Holy Spirit was moving in people's hearts. It was a holy moment and I continued in little more than a whisper, 'If you feel that small, soft voice speaking to you, and you need to receive Jesus into your life, then stand to your feet now.' In an instant the entire congregation – men, women, and children – stood to their feet. Many people were in tears as they prayed a prayer of repentance from sin and received Jesus Christ into their lives.

As I came down the stairs, the rector of the church approached me. He was visibly shaken and said, 'Oh, thank you. Oh, thank you.' I told him, 'Brother, don't thank me,

273

thank the Lord Jesus.' We went out for lunch and this dear man leaned across the table and said, 'David, you're a professional preacher, aren't you?' I said, 'No, I'm not a professional preacher at all. I just shared what God told me to. It wasn't me talking to the people's hearts. It was the Lord!'

***

I had a green light from God to begin praying about starting a new ministry in the United States. One of the first people I shared this with was my good friend David Aikman. When I think of David I am reminded of the verse, *'A man of many companions may come to ruin, but there is a friend who sticks closer than a brother'* (Proverbs 18:24). He has been a wonderful friend over the years. At times he has cautioned me, and he has always encouraged me. When I told him about this new possibility, David believed that God was in this calling.

A short time later I received a phone call from the wife of a well-known Christian leader, asking if I would consider finding a position for her son in this new ministry. I agreed, and in May 1991 I handed the presidency of the new organization over to him. We had an understanding that I would continue as the founding President and would head the China operations of the ministry. We established our ministry headquarters near Seattle, Washington.

Because of Project Pearl and my relationships with house church leaders all across China, the ministry soon began to receive requests for Bibles. The need remained huge all across China. We continued to receive many letters like this one, begging us for Bibles:

> *Our family members continue to come from different places asking for more Bibles, but we will soon be out. Therefore, we ask for more help again. At the same time, we are praying that God will supply our needs. Please try your best to solve our problem. All the family members*

[believers] are very thankful when they receive your gifts.
We are all touched by your love for God. In the meantime,
we are very much in need of more, especially for those who
live in faraway places. The need is bigger than the supply.

For the first few years we purchased these Bibles from Three-Self churches and delivered them to house churches, because I didn't believe God wanted me to continue smuggling. Things had changed in China since the early 1980s. While there was still a great shortage of Bibles, the methods of getting God's Word into the Christians' hands had changed and there was an opportunity for our ministry to purchase hundreds of thousands of legally printed Bibles and deliver them to our contacts among the house churches. This way it worked out much cheaper to buy and deliver the Bibles, and the risk to our Chinese brothers and sisters was greatly reduced.

In March 1992 one of the key Chinese leaders of Project Pearl requested another one million Bibles for the house churches. They encouraged me to go to Amity Press and see if I could obtain the Bibles through official channels. The first time my wife Meiling and I went to the Amity Press was quite funny, because at first the people who worked there did not realize who we were. After being warmly greeted by the general manager of Amity Press, Peter MacInnis, and his co-worker, I said to them, 'I'm here to find out how I can get Bibles printed for the house churches throughout China. Can you help me?' The two men wanted to know who I was and what involvement I had in China up to that time. After discovering that we had a mutual friend in Eddie Cairns, who of course had been on the boat during the Pearl delivery, one of the men directly asked, 'Who are you?'

I replied, 'Take a guess.'

Then a look of bewilderment came over his face, and he sighed, 'Oh no! You're one of the guys who took the one million Bibles into Shantou by boat in 1981, aren't you?'

When I confirmed that I was, Peter and his co-worker almost dropped off their chairs! However, when they realized that our motivation both for Project Pearl and for coming to meet with them was simply to get Bibles into the hands of Christians in China, they relaxed and we worked together to meet this need.

I entered negotiations with the China Christian Council and in October 1992 we signed an agreement to print one million Bibles. Over the next three years we printed and successfully distributed Bibles to a host of house church believers in almost every province of China. We began with 250,000 copies in the first year, then 350,000 the following year, and 500,000 in the third year, as the funds coming in increased. Therefore over the three-year period we actually exceeded our goal and printed 1.1 million Bibles for the Chinese Church.

The first time I met Han Wenzao, the President of the China Christian Council, we became friends, even though he had been one of the strongest critics of Project Pearl in 1981. He was a fine Christian man who loved the Lord with all his heart right up to when he passed into the presence of Jesus in 2006. Every time I entered his room, whether in China or on one of his trips to America, I would find him reading his Bible. It pained me whenever I heard Christians say that Han Wenzao was not a real Christian, a conclusion reached solely on the basis that he was a leader of the government-sanctioned church in China.

In May 1995 I suggested to the board of my organization that we ask the Lord for 5 million more Bibles over the next five years – or one million per year. In the first year we successfully distributed 800,000 more Bibles. When I thought about the incredible amount of time, effort and money that had gone into Project Pearl, I was amazed to think we were now able to reproduce the same result, legally, every year as the Lord provided the funds.

On one occasion I was asked to speak at a meeting of

missionaries in Hong Kong. I stood up and declared, 'The era of smuggling Bibles into China is over. The day of working in co-operation to get the Word of God printed and distributed among the Lord's people has begun.'

This statement had the same impact as a bomb! Many of the mission leaders went after me like snakes. They thought I was a traitor, and no amount of explaining could change their belief that I had betrayed the house churches and was in league with the Communists.

The irony is that my motivation for this new approach of printing Bibles legally was simply to get as many copies of God's Word to the house churches throughout China as possible, in the most efficient and inexpensive way. Yet many of the missionaries saw China in very black-and-white terms. Working with the Amity Press was akin to working with the devil in their eyes. They saw it as a disgrace that the man who had led Project Pearl was now cooperating with the 'enemy'.

Various people spoke many nasty words about me, but I forgave them all as fast as the words came out of their mouths. At one time rumors began to circulate that I had apologized to the Chinese government and Three-Self Church for Project Pearl. This is nonsense. God told us to do Pearl, and He provided, empowered, equipped and protected both the Bibles and us. I have never apologized to anyone for Pearl, and I never will.

We discovered that propaganda is not a tool exclusively used by Communists. Some Christians are also skilled at using propaganda to achieve their own purposes. All kinds of silly rumors continue to the present day that the Amity Press prints just a small number of Bibles and not the millions that are claimed, that most of the Bibles are exported overseas, that the Bibles end up being burned by the authorities and so on. I was even told once that a missionary had it 'on good authority' that the Amity Press mostly printed telephone directories on their presses, and claimed they were printing Bibles! As someone who was closely involved with the whole process from start to finish, I can tell you that all these rumors are baseless and foolish.

Some claimed that it was dangerous for the house churches to get Bibles printed by the Amity Press. It was rumored that many believers who received deliveries of Bibles were arrested and thrown into prison. This may have been true in the early 1980s, but things had dramatically changed in the years since then. My wife was responsible for handling all the Bible deliveries to the house churches during those years. She knew exactly where the Bibles were going, how many were sent and when they were picked up. The only problem we had in all this time was when a delivery of 2,500 Bibles was sent to a house church pastor in a remote part of China. The local authorities thought the delivery must be a mistake and held the Bibles for a short time. As soon as we found this out we notified Han Wenzao. He made a call, and the Bibles were immediately released into the pastor's hands.

James Hudson Taylor III, a great grandson of the pioneer missionary of the same name, invited me out to lunch one day in Hong Kong. Jim asked, 'David, how come you said that the era of smuggling Bibles is over?'

I replied, 'First of all, things have changed and we can now legally print Bibles inside China. Secondly, I'm responsible for the deaths of two people because of Bible smuggling. One is a Burmese brother named Gideon who crossed the border into China with Bibles and was caught by the police. They hung him upside down from a tree and beat him to death. The other was a man who traveled from Nepal into Tibet and was murdered by the Chinese military there. Although I don't know of any Chinese believers we work with being killed, I am responsible for several being severely tortured. One was hung from the ceiling and beaten for twenty-one days. Another was imprisoned for ten years. We have pictures of him before he went to prison and after he came out, and it doesn't look like the same person.'

I told Jim Taylor that I carried the burden of these dead and persecuted brothers and sisters in my spirit. I was the one who got them involved, and they had paid the ultimate price. Even though the two martyred men had willingly engaged in this work knowing the possible risks involved, whenever I thought about what happened to them it crushed me, especially when I met the wives and families they had left behind.

Jim leaned forward in a loving manner and said, 'David, I want to tell you something. You are just like my great grandfather. One day the Lord told him, "Your responsibility is to recruit missionaries and send them to the interior of China. My responsibility is to take care of them. If they lay down their lives because I want them to come and be with me in heaven, then that is my choice."'

When I heard these words, the burden of these two men's deaths lifted from me. I realized it was a burden I didn't have to carry around any more, and I gave it to Jesus.

Chapter Thirty-Three:

When All Hope Hit the Floor

A dramatic change occurred in my life at the end of 1995. On 30 November I suffered the first of four heart attacks in seventy-two days. It was a terrible, terrible time. Three doctors, in three different countries, told me that I was soon going to die.

We were in Hong Kong when my first heart attack struck. On the morning of 30 November I awoke to find I had difficulty talking properly. I had just completed a long journey from Beijing to Hong Kong and was exhausted, so I put my symptoms down to the arduous trip. Later that morning I met with the pastor of the Kowloon City Baptist Church in Hong Kong. During our meeting he noticed that I was slurring my words and advised me to rest. I returned to my hotel room and lay down on my bed for the remainder of the afternoon.

At around eight o'clock in the evening Meiling brought me some dinner. I propped myself up in bed and enjoyed a plate of chicken and rice, washed down with a cup of hot tea. About an hour later I had trouble breathing. I asked Meiling to call a doctor, who advised us to go to the Hong Kong Adventist Hospital immediately. With difficulty we climbed into a taxi and made our way up the winding hills to the hospital entrance.

I could hardly breathe during the drive, and as we pulled up at the entrance I was sure my life was about to end. I was rushed to the emergency room where an oxygen mask was placed over my nose and mouth. A nurse took my blood pressure and a team rushed in to administer an exploratory test. Within minutes the doctor informed me I was having a heart attack and I was transferred to the Intensive Care Unit. By this time our good friends Michael and Sara Bruce had arrived at the hospital. They looked more shaken than me, for even though my body felt like it was being dragged through hell, my heart and spirit were filled with the peace of God that surpasses human understanding.

A few days later a leading Hong Kong cardiologist, Dr Ko, administered an angiogram procedure to determine the level of blood flow in and out of my heart. After carefully observing my veins, blood vessels, arteries and heart, he left the room without saying a word to me. I found out later that Dr Ko had been unable to break the news of my condition to me. The state of my heart was totally hopeless. He told my friends in the waiting room that there was little that could be done, and I only had a short time to live.

In the following days the doctor and his staff showed great kindness to me. The hospital chaplain came and comforted me by reading the Word of God out loud at my bedside and praying with me. These were precious times in the presence of the Lord Jesus. News of my heart attack reached the Christians in China, and all across the nation a tremendous chorus of prayer was raised up on my behalf. I was even told that some believers were fasting for me.

After ten days I was discharged, and after regaining some strength, Meiling and I flew back to Seattle. When we touched down I had just enough energy to drive to our home in North Bend, about 45 minutes away. After arriving home, we were surprised by the love of our wonderful Christian neighbors, Dick and Pat Breneman. They had spent hours setting up a Christmas tree and decorating our home for us. Meiling and I spent Christmas Day worshipping the Lord and praying. We collapsed in bed, exhausted from everything that had happened. God had a purpose in all of this, but I was too weak to see it. All of my strength was expended just fighting to stay alive. I believe that if it had not been for the prayers of my Chinese brothers and sisters, I would surely have died. By the grace of God, I am still alive more than ten years later!

Over the next several days we had a wonderful time studying God's Word. Passages about faith came alive to us. This was a time when we needed to have our faith strengthened. We needed to know the Lord Jesus more intimately than ever before. I desperately wanted Him to heal me so I could continue to serve Him and the Chinese Church. Little did we know that just around the corner lay our darkest hour yet.

On 30 December I suffered my second heart attack. The doctors told me I was not a candidate for bypass surgery because the blood vessels around my heart were too small for a successful operation. They told me I should continue to follow a program of medication, rest and a slow rehabilitation.

My third knockout came on 26 January 1996. Meiling and I had traveled to British Columbia, Canada, for a time of rest and to hear from the Lord while attending a mission conference. We were exhausted and needed to get away. We went to lunch on a freezing day and I was again struck with chest pain. A short time later I felt better, so we decided to go to the meetings that afternoon. The pain returned, and I lay down on a couch hoping for relief. Our dear brother Pablo spotted me and came over. We spent the next three hours in wonderful fellowship; recounting the mighty acts we had seen the Lord do in China, both during the Pearl delivery and in the years since. I arranged to meet Pablo again the next morning, but our plans were never realized. Back at the hotel I again struggled for breath and pain pounded in my chest. I was rushed to hospital, my third heart attack in the third different country.

By now, the only hope I had was that I knew Jesus

Christ was my Lord and Savior. Apart from this foundational truth, my life had been turned upside down. My faith was the lowest it had been since I had become a Christian thirty-three years earlier.

After returning home to Washington the attacks on my body continued. These were horrible days for me, and also for my loving wife Meiling. She was stretched to breaking point as I was transported back and forth to the hospital. She suffered incredible agony during these months, and it is only because of the grace of God that she did not collapse.

On 12 February I traveled back to Seattle where I had an appointment two days later. After arriving at the Providence Hospital, however, I suffered my fourth heart attack. My cardiologist Dr James Schneider entered the room. With a stern look on his face he said, 'David, you are going to die. The only thing we can do is to attempt a bypass operation immediately and hope for the best result.'

Meiling was home by herself at the time, and I just couldn't let her know that I had suffered another heart attack and was dying. I told the doctor, 'I am not scared to die, but please don't tell Meiling. Just do your best.'

That evening I searched my soul and confessed every sin I knew I had ever committed. I wanted to be ready to meet the Lord. I knew that I had the assurance of Christ's salvation, and that gave me hope. I also knew that God could do the impossible, for I had seen Him do it many times over the years, from the night he saved me at the Los Angeles Coliseum to the delivery of the million Bibles off the Chinese coast. I wished that Jesus would just heal me with a word, like He healed the centurion's servant.

I finally mustered enough strength to call David Aikman. I asked him to phone Meiling and calmly tell her what had happened. I didn't want to call her myself, because I knew she would hear the strain in my voice and would become scared. She rushed to Seattle to be by my side for the operation. Meiling was unable to drive at that time, so our kind neighbor brought her. A Catholic nun named Maureena entered my room and asked Meiling and I if she could pray with us. I had not had much contact with Catholics before, but I agreed. The nun loved the Lord Jesus Christ, and she brought heaven into our room when she prayed. God's peace encompassed me. Before entering the operating theatre I asked the male nurse if we could pray first, and he said yes. We bowed our heads and committed the operation to the Lord. As my bed was pushed to where family members were not permitted to enter, I told Meiling that I loved her.

It was a surreal moment for me as I looked up at the lights and equipment around me. The operating theatre looked like the flight control of the space shuttle! I had been in dangerous places many times over the years, including in Vietnam during an offensive with bombs falling all around us, and on the beach in China while a million Bibles were being offloaded into the water. Having survived those experiences, I never thought my last moments on earth would be lying on my back as an oxygen mask was placed over my nose and mouth, especially as I was only 59 years old.

The nurse told me to count back from twenty. I can only remember reaching nine. I also recall the pain in my chest, and the nurse saying the pain would soon be gone. I was at death's doorstep, but I had peace knowing that I would soon meet Jesus Christ face to face.

Meiling had been told that the nurses would update her on my progress from time to time. For eight long hours, however, no word came from the operating theatre as the surgical team did their best to save my life. Friends came to the hospital to comfort her, and Christians around the world were praying, fasting and believing in God for a miracle. It was the longest evening of Meiling's life.

My wife finally caught a glimpse of me as I was wheeled back to my room. There were all kinds of tubes and machines attached to my mouth and body, and my arms were taped down to the bed. She couldn't believe her eyes and burst into tears. Before going into the operating theatre, I told Meiling that when I came out I would not be able to speak, but that I would tap three times to say, 'I love you'. I awoke four hours after the operation, and tapped her hand three times.

After returning home, my condition meant I had to be attended to twenty-four hours a day. Somehow Meiling mustered up the inner strength to get through our darkest hour. I often thank God for bringing Meiling and I together in marriage. After Jesus, Meiling is my life. In many ways I see them as one, because I can see Jesus in her all the time. Meiling is a tremendous blessing, and the rare kind of wife the Bible describes in the final chapter of Proverbs.

Seeing our desperation, God sent several Chinese Christians who were living in America to help and serve us. One of these was Dr Rong Wang, who graciously offered to take me to my doctor's appointments. At the start we didn't even know some of those who helped, yet on several occasions the Chinese believers drove more than 100 miles just to take me to the hospital to see my surgeon. These heaven-sent helpers became close friends, and we were able to minister into their lives as they ministered to us.

***

Meiling: When my husband was taken in for open-heart surgery I felt so alone in the world. Each passing hour seemed like an eternity while I waited for news. Various doctors had told us that David was going to die and I didn't want to think about how life would be without him. In the hospital I broke down before the Lord and bared my soul to him. I prayed, 'Lord Jesus, if I have twenty more years left in this world, please allow me to give half of those years to my husband.'

When the doctor came out of the operating theatre it looked like he had been in a fight! He was exhausted and had literally fought for eight hours to keep David alive. Our friends in New Zealand called and asked how the operation had gone. They said that while interceding for David, the Holy Spirit had shown them that his heart had stopped beating. We later asked the doctor and he confirmed that David's heart had indeed stopped beating during the operation.

In the decade since that time there have been many difficulties. A mission leader asked me once what parts of America I had seen during these years. I told him I had seen the inside of many hospitals and doctors' offices, and had become an expert at calling 911 for an ambulance.

I am thankful to God for our wonderful neighbors, Dick and Pat Breneman. Since David's first heart attack in 1996 I have called the 911 emergency services a total of twenty-four times in order to get help for my husband. The second thing I did each time was to call the Brenemans, who told me I should call them whenever we needed help, regardless of the time of day or night. Uncle Dick, as we affectionately call him, always hurries over and handles the whole situation when the ambulance arrives. Every time we travel we leave our home under their care. There is a Chinese saying, 'A close neighbor is better than a distant relative.' They have been a Godsend.

Most of the time I have felt completely exhausted, and few people can understand what it has been like. But Jesus understands, and He has given me the strength and grace to endure. I have so many things to thank the Lord about each new day. I have come to appreciate that every minute and every second of each day the Lord is unfolding His plan in our lives.

***

Brother David: Meiling and I thought we had overcome the worst of our experiences, and we even allowed ourselves to think there was a glimmer of light at the end of the long and dark tunnel. Then, when we least expected it, Satan threw a fiery dart at us that almost destroyed us.

At the time I was still experiencing tremendous physical pain in my left leg where the skin grafts had become inflamed and I had a hard time walking and getting around. I was hoping and praying that God would restore me so that I could once again serve the body of Christ in China. As long as breath remained in my lungs I wanted to serve God in China. China is my call, and my greatest joy.

On 28 March 1996 – four months after my first heart attack – the new chairman of our ministry informed me that I was no longer a member of the board or the ministry team. I was also notified that my salary and medical insurance would be terminated a week later on 5 April. I was told that I had been voted off the board in January. I wrote a letter to the chairman, asking how this was possible seeing I was a life member of the board and the Founding President. No answer was given.

My wife and I were in a state of shock. Because of my illness, my colleagues apparently saw little value in us. We were even sent a letter informing us that we were forbidden to use any of the ministry's stationery or envelopes!

We had been fired from the very ministry we had founded. If I learned anything from this experience, it is this: If God gives you a vision and calls you to a certain work, don't allow an outsider to come in and take over the reins.

Meiling and I now faced massive financial difficulties. I needed a lengthy period of rehabilitation and treatment, but without medical insurance this was impossible. We had only recently purchased a home in the small town of North Bend, Washington, and now we faced the prospect of repaying the mortgage with no income or savings. We felt devastated.

I didn't know of any place we could turn except to God. For some time I struggled with unforgiveness against the brothers who had treated us so cruelly. I could hardly pray or think about what had happened. Then, one day, God in His marvelous grace and mercy opened a window in the midst of the all-encompassing darkness, and His light came in. I began to compare our experiences of betrayal, pain and suffering with those of our brethren in China. Slowly it dawned on me that we were being called to walk through some of the same trials that our friends in the underground churches had endured for many years. Could it be that our Heavenly Father was giving us an opportunity not only to serve the suffering church in China, but also to actually experience something of what they experience?

I later learned that God had allowed all of this for an even greater reason. He not only wanted us to be able to relate better to the Chinese Church. He wanted us to relate more intimately with Jesus Christ. Jesus had suffered betrayal and rejection at the hands of his brothers, and had been sorely tested in every conceivable way. We came to realize that whatever difficulties we faced, Jesus had been there before us and had experienced them all. *'For we do not have a high priest who is unable to sympathize with our weaknesses, but we have one who has been tempted in every way, just as we are – yet was without sin. Let us then approach the throne of grace with confidence, so that we may receive mercy and find grace to help us in our time of need'* (Hebrews 4:15–16).

Over time we learned to forgive those who had wronged us, and the beautiful presence of Jesus returned to our lives.

Today, more than a decade later, I am living beyond the impossible. I have learned that for a Christian to live beyond the impossible requires complete abandonment to

God's will. We need to stop struggling, and just submit ourselves on His altar like obedient children. As long as a Christian continues to limit God by their unbelief, this place of rest and victory will remain elusive.

Maybe you are facing an impossibility in your life right now, and you can't see any light at the end of the tunnel. Be encouraged, for nothing is impossible with God!

Chapter Thirty-Four:

A New Vision

We continued to walk through the valley of the shadow of death in 1996 and 1997, but Jesus did not forsake us. Even at our lowest point, when we were under tremendous stress and despairing of life itself, our gracious Lord visited us and the sweet aroma of His presence filled our hearts.

During the months of convalescence I often remained awake for most of the night praying and reading His Word. During this time I reviewed my entire Christian life and service to God. After being fired by my organization, I wondered if my times of ministering in China had come to an end. If it had, I could not complain. God had allowed me to see and experience so much in China that it could fill a hundred lifetimes.

The more I prayed and waited upon the Lord, however, the deeper sense I had that He had not finished with me in China. The Apostle Paul said, *'God's gifts and his call are irrevocable'* (Romans 11:29). The King James version of the same verse says, *'The gifts and calling of God are without repentance.'* I felt inwardly encouraged as I meditated on these and other scriptures. I came to realize that it was God who had called me to China, and no man or man-made institution could put an end to my call!

One night as I was praying, the Lord Jesus spoke to my heart and told me to begin a new ministry, and to call it 'Love China'. I told him, 'Lord, I don't have enough strength. I have given all of my energy already, and I have nothing left.'

When I told Meiling what the Lord had instructed me to do, she excitedly jumped up and ran to our home office.

She hurried back with a red notebook in her hands and showed me the words, 'Love China', as the name of a new ministry we were to establish. She had written it down months earlier during my operation, but had not said a word about it to me. We shared the news with our closest friends around the world, and they all encouraged us to begin Love China Ministries immediately. Even though I was still under sedation when the Lord showed us to launch this new initiative, we registered it as a non-profit organization with the United States government and invited trusted friends to join our board of directors.

One evening a Chinese friend visited us and stayed until after midnight, talking and praying with us. When he got up to leave, he handed Meiling an envelope. Once he was gone, we opened it and found a sizeable gift inside, marked 'for a trip to China'. We thanked God for His wonderful and timely provision. We knew that despite all our hardships, God had not forgotten us, and He was showing us that He would provide our every need as we stepped out in obedience to His call.

Four months to the day after my surgery, Meiling and I flew across the Pacific Ocean and spent three months ministering in China and Hong Kong. Our trip was a surprise to many people who had been expecting to hear news of my death. Instead, they received news that we had started a new ministry for the Lord! In China we thanked all the believers who had prayed and fasted for us. I felt like a living miracle and a walking answer to their prayers. We also told our friends about our new calling and ministry, and commenced work on several new projects that would benefit the believers in China. One plan was to introduce and distribute electronic Chinese Bibles that included a concordance, a Chinese Greek and Hebrew Lexicon, and historical and biblical encyclopedias. This was the work of Dr Paul Ma, a graduate from Stanford University who has invested years of his life compiling Greek and Hebrew lexicons. We signed an agreement to provide 10,000 computers with software over a period of seven years to Christian leaders all across China.

Another objective was to provide 5 million more Bibles over the next seven years for the house churches. The Bibles would be printed legally inside China, yet all were to be distributed for free to the illegal house churches, such is the strange nature of working in contemporary China.

I also spent three years serving on the Lausanne Committee for restricted access countries in Asia. The tracts I worked on were China and North Korea. I have been to North Korea many times since my first visit in September 1979. My first trip was arranged through a Chinese institution, and the Koreans didn't realize I was an American until I arrived. They were amazed and thrilled, because virtually no Americans ventured into their country in those days. When I first flew into the capital, Pyongyang, cute little Korean girls rushed up to my plane and greeted me with bouquets of flowers. During my many subsequent visits I have been warmly welcomed by North Korean officials and diplomats, and have shared the gospel with all of them. It is only in the past few years that North Korea has gained a fear of America.

Some Christians think it is wrong for us to go to North Korea, and that by going we only strengthen the evil Communist regime. I think such an argument is nonsense. I don't go to North Korea for political reasons, I go there as an ambassador of Jesus Christ, to share the gospel with as many people as possible, most of whom have never heard it before. If we think we can advance God's kingdom by separating ourselves from those who don't know Him, we are greatly deceived. Jesus told us to *'Go into all the world and preach the good news to all creation'* (Mark 16:15) – not just to those places that are friendly or your country's political allies. God loves people in North Korea just as much as He loves you.

Meiling: After my husband suffered a series of huge heart attacks we were not required by the ministry he had founded. I asked him, 'Why don't we start a new ministry for the Lord?' He replied that he was too old.

I told David that I believed we should start a new ministry and leave the results to the Lord. I said, 'If God sends us one dollar, we will be able to do one dollar's worth of work. If He sends a million dollars, we will do a million dollars' worth of work. We should not actively fundraise or promote ourselves or our activities in any way, but just serve the Lord and if God wants to tell people to support what we are doing, then that will be His choice.' The truth is that I believed the Lord had already shown me that we should start a new ministry, and I had even written the name, 'Love China with Brother David', in my notebook, but I didn't tell my husband about it.

After initially saying 'no' to the idea of starting a new ministry, David went to our prayer room one evening. I went to sleep, and when I woke up at about three o'clock in the morning I found my husband wasn't next to me. He was still praying. I went to the prayer room and asked if he was all right. David looked at me and declared, 'God has shown me that we are going to start a ministry.' I asked him what we should call it, and he replied, 'Love China'.

I shouted, 'Wait a minute!' and hurried to find my notebook. I returned excitedly and showed him the place where I had written the name, 'Love China with Brother David'. He smiled, but said there was no need to connect his name with the name of the ministry, so we just called it 'Love China'.

Over the years I have had to learn about forgiveness. It is easy for Christians to say that we need to forgive people who wrong us, but it can be much more difficult to actually do it! My husband and I have been attacked and lied about on countless occasions. Once I shared some of our experiences with Christian friends in China and they said, 'Even though you live in the West, you have experienced your own Cultural Revolution.' Many times we have felt the pain in our hearts of being wronged, but the Lord has taught us not to fight back, and not to repay evil with evil. The Bible says, *'Do not repay evil with evil or insult with insult, but with blessing, because to this you were called so that you may inherit a blessing'* (1 Peter 3:9).

On one occasion I was really struggling to forgive those who had abused us. The Lord woke me up in the middle of the night and started to deal with me, reminding me that unforgiveness only ends up destroying the person who holds on to it in their heart. One preacher has said that unforgiveness is like digesting poison and waiting for the other person to die. That night the Lord Jesus visited me in an intimate and powerful way. It was as though He said, 'My child, why don't you let it go?'

When I forgave every person who had wronged us, a strange thing happened. I heard a choir, outside our bedroom window, singing the beautiful song, 'I see the Lord. He is high and lifted up, and His train fills the temple. The angels cry holy is the Lord.' I had not heard that song for a long time and thought that perhaps some music was playing outside our house, or people were singing.

I looked at my husband, but he was sound asleep. Then I realized it was the middle of the night, and the entire neighborhood was sleeping. I fell to my knees in awe of the Almighty God as I realized the choir I had heard was a heavenly choir of angels.

I believe that forgiveness is one of the most neglected doctrines in churches today. It is so fundamentally important for every believer to walk in freedom and forgiveness. In fact, Jesus tied our forgiveness to whether or not we are willing to forgive others: *'For if you forgive men when they sin against you, your heavenly Father will also forgive you.*

But if you do not forgive men their sins, your Father will not forgive your sins' (Matthew 6:14–15).

Even if someone has done the most terrible things to you, you need to forgive them. Even if they never ask forgiveness or even acknowledge any wrongdoing, you still need to forgive them.

How are we to forgive others? The Apostle Paul told us, *'Be kind and compassionate to one another, forgiving each other, just as in Christ God forgave you'* (Ephesians 4:32), and *'Bear with each other and forgive whatever grievances you may have against one another. Forgive as the Lord forgave you'* (Colossians 3:13).

We are to forgive others the same way that the Lord Jesus forgave us: unconditionally, freely, generously and without keeping a record of past wrongs. Then we will be free!

Chapter Thirty-Five

Serving God

Over the years God has given me a gift to meet and relate to presidents, ambassadors and diplomats from many nations around the world. This has all been the Lord's doing. It has nothing to do with me or any skills I may possess. It is just the favor of the Lord.

One thing God has shown me over the years is that I should never judge a person without knowing them. Once I attended a meeting where a whole group of Russian Orthodox priests came. When they were introduced to the other people in the meeting, two-thirds of the Western missionaries stood up and left the room in protest against the presence of these men. I couldn't believe it, and when the meeting concluded I found a Russian translator and went up to the leading Orthodox priest. I said to the translator, 'Please tell him that I'm his friend and brother. Tell him Jesus loves him and so do I.' When these words were translated the Orthodox leader's face lit up. He was so happy as I was one of the few Westerners in the meeting who had bothered to greet him.

On another occasion I found myself inside the Vatican in Rome, in a meeting with 300 Jesuit priests. I had always been taught that Catholics were deceived and lost, but when these men started to sing 'How Great Thou Art' with all their hearts the unmistakable presence of the Lord Jesus filled that place, and I was forced to reconsider my prejudices. Drawing conclusions before you know someone is immature. The Bible says, *'The Lord does not look at the things man looks at. Man looks at the outward appearance, but the Lord looks at the heart'* (1 Samuel 16:7). Jesus once rebuked the Jews, *'Stop judging by mere appearances, and make a right judgment'* (John 7:24).

In 1993 I had the privilege of bringing a group of Chinese politicians and officials on a trip to the United States. The group came to examine how religious freedom works in American society, and to study the separation of church and state. First we met with President Richard Nixon in New Jersey. He spoke about his relationship with Mao Zedong, and shared stories about how he had helped re-establish diplomatic relations between the United States and China in 1974.

Next we traveled to Houston and met with President George Bush, Sr. It was just a year after he had lost his presidency, but even though he was talking with a room full of Communist leaders, he was joyful and showed genuine care and concern to each one of them. The first thing President Bush said to the Chinese was, 'My daughter Dorothy was baptized at the Chongwenmen Church in Beijing.' This caused them to pay attention, and the President proceeded to extensively share about his relationship with Jesus Christ. In my experience, President Bush and his team are easily the kindest and most helpful I have been with. I have a lot of respect for President Bush and his wife Barbara.

It's been a good experience meeting with these presidents and leaders, but let me tell you that meeting them pales in comparison with meeting Jesus Christ!

I have also been privileged to speak at hundreds of churches, from small Bible studies in homes to the largest church in the world in South Korea. God has given me a wonderful opportunity to see and appreciate the beauty of His body around the world. It is easy to only see our and other Christians' weaknesses and faults, but thankfully God has a different perspective! He sees us not just as we are, but as we will be. The Bible says, *'God gives life to the dead and calls things that are not as though they were'*

(Romans 4:17). The greatest news in the world is that if you are a follower of Jesus Christ, God does not view you in your weakness and failures, but He views you as His precious Bride, redeemed at the cost of His Son's life.

In America today many Christians think they need to possess certain skills or qualifications for God to use them. These can be helpful, but they are not the most important thing. You see, God is always searching for someone who is fully surrendered to Him. He has not changed since the prophet Hanani told King Asa long ago, *'The eyes of the Lord range throughout the earth to strengthen those whose hearts are fully committed to him'* (2 Chronicles 16:9). The greatest ability you can have for God is your 'avail-ability'.

The Lord is not impressed by oratory skills or people who dress smartly and present themselves with an air of confidence. If this is all you think ministry is, you will fall flat on your face. God is not looking for people full of themselves. On the contrary, He is looking for empty vessels into which He can pour His spiritual treasures. We should pray for a similar attitude as John the Baptist, who declared, *'He must become greater; I must become less'* (John 3:30), for *'God resists the proud, but gives grace to the humble'* (1 Peter 5:5).

The Lord Jesus is passionate for you, and He wants to enter into an intimate relationship with you. From that relationship will flow opportunities. This, essentially, is what people call 'ministry'. As you surrender your own wants, desires and plans to Jesus, He can take what you lay on the altar and use your life to bless many for His kingdom. He wants to use you to witness to a hurting world. But first He wants to possess you and make you into a useable vessel. This process usually takes years, but God often works in us *while* we are serving Him rather than us having to wait for a fixed point in time before we can start serving Him.

Serving God is a great joy. It is never a burden. The

Bible says we should *'Serve the Lord with gladness; Come before His presence with singing'* (Psalm 100:2 NKJV). From the first time I set foot in China in 1976, when I saw thousands of earthquake victims weeping in anguish, God has put a great love in my heart for China. I have been to China on countless occasions over the past thirty years, and every single time I have felt great joy. It is as though I belong there. God broke my heart for China many years ago, and I have been so privileged to give my life to serve Jesus there.

The church has experienced incredible revival throughout China during this generation. It is surely the greatest revival in the history of Christianity. I feel so honored to have witnessed this miracle as it has unfolded over the years. Countless millions of Chinese men, women, boys and girls have found Jesus and their lives have been changed in a wonderful way. What a privilege it has been to help them with Bibles and in other ways! I understand what the Apostle Paul meant when he spoke about *'the privilege of sharing in this service to the saints'* (2 Corinthians 8:4).

I was also privileged to spend time with Corrie ten Boom in her latter years. I learned so much from this precious saint. Once I attended her home and she picked a flower and showed it to me and the others gathered there. She said, 'Do you see this beautiful flower? In a few days from now it will be dead. We are like a flower. Our time on earth is very short. We must do what we can for Jesus now because very soon we too will fade away.'

The Bible says that our lives are like a vapor, here one day and gone the next. The Psalmist wrote, *'You have made my days a mere handbreadth; the span of my years is as nothing before you. Each man's life is but a breath'* (Psalm 37:5).

If you are a Christian, and your life ends tomorrow, will you stand before the Lover of your soul with the confidence that you have done everything possible with your time, gifts and resources to make Him known throughout the world?

I'm sure there are many people in heaven now who wish they had spent their lives less for themselves and this world, and more for the kingdom of God. Do you realize that once you are in heaven, all opportunities you have to reach people with the gospel will have concluded forever? That's right. Believers in heaven can no longer impact this lost world for Jesus. That great privilege and responsibility belongs to those of us here now.

We need a passion for God's kingdom on this earth! This kind of passion does not come by trying to hype yourself up through human effort, but rather it comes naturally as you press into an intimate relationship with Jesus Christ. When you know the heart of Jesus, He shares His desires with you. And his desires are for His bride, the church, and for the lost sheep who wander in darkness.

When Jesus shares His heart with you, you will never be the same again.

Christian friend, in all likelihood I will make it to heaven before you do. Would you please set aside some time to do what I have done recently? Would you shut yourself away for a whole day with your Bible and no other visitor except the Holy Spirit? If you, as a child of God, would do that, you will soon either break up or break out in spiritual power and revival.

You see, the price of birth is travail. You and I cannot escape this fact. Just as a mother travails to give birth to a baby, so we must travail in prayer to see new things born in and through our lives.

Let me ask you, where is the travail in our lives, ministries and churches today? Do you think the Holy Spirit delights in all our programs and plans, machinery and equipment, while the cribs where new believers are meant to grow in Christ sit empty? Recently I read that the great missionary Amy Carmichael prayed:

O for a passion for souls, dear Lord!
O for a pity that yearns!
O for a love that loves unto death!
O for a fire that burns!

O for the prayer power that travails,
That pours itself out for the lost;
Victorious prayer in the Conqueror's Name:
O for a Pentecost!

If you are going to be a preacher, a missionary, or a teacher of the Word, you must first have the wind and fire of God in your life. You can afford to be ten times less clever if only you are ten times more spiritual. When the Holy Spirit is free to move and has room and opportunity, He will destroy the dross of sin and purify our lives.

Repentance is not just a few tears at the end of a touching sermon. It's a change of mind and a change of heart towards God and away from sin. Repentance is the irrevocable factor needed for revival – in your own life, in your church and in your nation. James said, *'Come near to God and he will come near to you. Wash your hands, you sinners, and purify your hearts, you double-minded. Grieve, mourn and wail. Change your laughter to mourning and your joy to gloom. Humble yourselves before the Lord, and he will lift you up'* (James 4:8–10).

I have found that when you draw near to the Lord, God will answer from heaven. All you need is to set aside a day of quiet time. Shut yourself away from everything except your Bible and the Lord. The Bible gives us this wonderful promise: *'Since we have a great priest over the house of God, let us draw near to God with a sincere heart in full assurance of faith, having our hearts sprinkled to cleanse us from a guilty conscience and having our bodies washed with pure water.'* (Hebrews 10:21–22)

May I enquire, how are you living today?
Has God given you a vision and passion?

Has the Holy Spirit given you a revelation of His holiness and your sinfulness?

Do you know God's plan for your life?

When I die, I want a revival and not a funeral. How about you? Do you want a revival too? Then begin crying out to God.

Stop shrinking from His will and begin working under His direction.

Take the time to be alone with Him and His Word, and He will begin blessing and giving guidance to you as He has done for me.

Postscript

Our telephone rang on the morning of 18 June 2006 when I was once again in the hospital. It was my old friend Brother Andrew and the current President of Open Doors, Johan Companjen, calling from Holland.

'David, can you believe it?' they asked.

'It has been twenty-five years since Project Pearl.'

We talked about those dramatic days a quarter of a century earlier, when God made the sun and moon stand still and a million Bibles were delivered onto the beach at Shantou.

Much has changed in China and the world since then, but one thing that remains constant is God's love for people everywhere. The church in China has experienced tremendous growth despite – or perhaps because of – years of hardship and suffering.

Many years ago, when I was a strong and healthy young man, God gave me a vision to see 10 million Bibles distributed to the Christians in China. Chinese officials have told me that Project Pearl in 1981 accelerated the formation of the Amity Press in Nanjing. Pearl had been a catalyst in helping Christians around the world realize how desperately their Chinese brothers and sisters need God's Word. In 2006 Amity announced that they had printed 40 million Bibles since their inception. Despite this tremendous figure, the need for Bibles in China remains strong, especially among the house churches in the countryside where tens of millions of people have come to faith in Jesus Christ.

The years have rolled on, and I am still here. In 1996 doctors told me I was dying, but God has been good to me. On 1 April 2005, I celebrated forty years of involvement in Christian ministry in Asia.

Since my series of heart attacks I have continued to serve the Lord. Some people say they plan to retire when they get old, but I don't know how to do that. I don't want to retire, I want to re-fire! I can't think of anyone in the Bible who retired. When God calls us to a work, it is a lifetime call, and a privilege. If you need a rest, wait for heaven. Listen to what Joshua said near the end of his life: *'Now then, just as the Lord promised, he has kept me alive for forty-five years since the time he said this to Moses, while Israel moved about in the desert. So here I am today, eighty-five years old! I am still as strong today as the day Moses sent me out; I'm just as vigorous to go out to battle now as I was then'* (Joshua 14:10–11).

The last ten years have not been easy. After being diagnosed with diabetes, this dreadful disease has gradually consumed my body. In 2002 my vision started to fail so I had my eyes checked out. My right eye required cataract surgery, and my left eye was degenerating and the retina had detached. In 2004 all of the toes on my right foot were amputated, and my weight plummeted more than 60 pounds in less than a year. That was one of the worst experiences of my life. It's no fun lying on an operating table listening to your toes being ground off like in a meat-grinder. It was such a horrible experience that I couldn't even pray.

After the amputation I lay in a nursing home for five months while undergoing physical therapy. That nursing home had the worst food and the most uncomfortable bed I have ever experienced in America. The five months seemed like years. I was going blind at that time, so Meiling came and read the Bible to me every day. That, coupled with listening to Christian radio and being visited by friends, helped me to keep my spirit up and get through the experience.

The following year my doctor started working on my left foot too, cutting off part of one toe and trimming others. I can't imagine how all these struggles would have been without Meiling by my side. She is truly an angel from heaven, and has sacrificially served me while I have been sick. It has been incredible, and I see the love and beauty of Jesus radiating through her every day.

At the end of 2005 Meiling and I made another trip into China. Although I was confined to a wheelchair and my sight was failing, it was a wonderful opportunity to catch up with my dear Chinese friends. We had walked hand-in-hand through many battles together, and we wept as they hugged me and reminisced about old times. Many people wondered why I went back to China in my condition. The main reason is simply because God called me to China, and that has never changed. We also have many projects that we still support.

Today we continue to help out in China in a variety of ways as the Lord provides funds to Love China Ministries. We continue to print Bibles, and we also support the Chinese Church through various initiatives.

As long as I remain alive I want to keep serving the Lord. I may not be able to see much, and I need to be pushed around in a wheelchair, but that's okay. I can still share the gospel and encourage those I meet. If it becomes too hard to push me around, I can still ask God to give me the strength to call people on the telephone or share with visitors. While the fire of the gospel remains inside of me, I have no alternative but to share Jesus Christ with people. I don't do so merely from a sense of duty, but rather it is my greatest joy and privilege. Jeremiah put it this way: *'If I say, "I will not mention him or speak any more in his name," his word is in my heart like a fire, a fire shut up in my bones. I am weary of holding it in; indeed, I cannot'* (Jeremiah 20:9).

How about you? Have you ever experienced the fire of God inside of you?

As you have read my story, centered on Project Pearl, I pray that you have realized I am nothing without Jesus

Christ. You see, if the truth were told, I am just a football-loving former Marine who has made plenty of mistakes throughout my life. I am no spiritual superman whatsoever. Sometimes I feel like I have been a spectator on an extraordinary journey with God. Jesus told Nicodemus, *'The wind blows wherever it pleases. You hear its sound, but you cannot tell where it comes from or where it is going. So it is with everyone born of the Spirit'* (John 3:8). It is a wonderful journey when Jesus is your driver! He is amazing, awesome, and oh, so faithful. He always has love in His eyes towards His children, and delights in surprising us with new and wonderful blessings.

Jesus means everything to me. He is my life, my Rock, my Savior and my soon-coming King. He has been so good to me, and the greatest thing I can do in return is to simply give Him glory and to tell the world that He is real, and the answer they seek. In 1963 Jesus Christ took me by the hand and led me down to the front to commit my life to God at the Los Angeles Coliseum. He has never let go of my hand since.

There have been plenty of difficult experiences in my life, but Jesus has never left me or forsaken me. At times I have stumbled, but Jesus has always picked me up and helped me continue walking.

If you don't know Him yet, please don't wait any longer! If you sense the Holy Spirit knocking at the door of your heart, inviting you to repent of your sins and start on a journey with Jesus Christ, do not delay. The Bible says, *'In the time of my favor I heard you, and in the day of salvation I helped you. I tell you, now is the time of God's favor, now is the day of salvation'* (2 Corinthians 6:2).

If you don't yet know Jesus Christ as your best friend, talk to him now and ask Him to use your life for His glory and kingdom. Come to him humbly and ask forgiveness for living your life for your own desires. Determine in your heart that you will no longer live for your own name, but for the name and reputation of Jesus Christ. The Bible puts it this way: *'He died for all, that those who live should no longer live for themselves but for him who died for them and was raised again'* (2 Corinthians 5:15).

After you have taken your first step, go and tell other Christians what you have done. You might know a friend, a relative, or someone who has started the journey before you. Connect with them and they will be able to help you. Get a Bible and start to read it, especially the four Gospels of Matthew, Mark, Luke and John. These will help you to know the character and teachings of Jesus.

Don't be content to just read the Bible, but obey it. This is a key. Christianity isn't some kind of race to gather as much head knowledge as you can. Your life should be shaped and molded by God's Word, and not just your head enlarged by it. This occurs when you step out and start to serve Jesus Christ. God's heart is for the whole world, and so yours should be too.

I recently turned seventy, and I am bedridden. I can't see much, and it is a struggle to go anywhere because of my illnesses. Because of my chronic heart disease I live with an Implantable Cardioverter Defibrillator. This little device inside my chest monitors my heart twenty-four hours a day and jolts it back into action when it fails. It has done so several times.

There is so much more I want to do for Jesus, and my condition often frustrates me. If you have your sight and two legs, please don't waste them! Our time on this earth is short, and getting shorter every day. There are so many people whom Jesus wants to reach out to, and He wants to do it through people just like you.

God Bless You, and thanks for giving me your time so that I could share my story. I look forward to getting to know you in heaven.

Your brother, David.

At 1.42 a.m. on 8 May, 2007 – as this book was being prepared for publication – Brother David passed away at a hospital near his home in North Bend, Washington.

There are many people whose lives were deeply impacted by the life and ministry of this warrior of God, who has gone to his eternal reward. He is now happy, whole and safe in the embrace of Jesus Christ.

'For when David had served God's purpose in his own generation, he fell asleep; he was buried with his fathers' (Acts 13:36).

Contact Information

Brother David's wife, Meiling, continues to lead Love China Ministries International, a mission committed to serving the persecuted church by publishing the Word of God in China and other initiatives for the gospel. You can contact her at:

Love China Ministries International
PO Box 1775
North Bend, WA 98045
USA

E-mail: LoveChinaIntl@aol.com

Paul Hattaway is a New Zealand-born missionary who has authored many books about the church in Asia, including the best-selling *The Heavenly Man*, *Back to Jerusalem* and *Operation China*. He is married to Joy, and they have two sons, Dalen and Taine. Hattaway is also director of Asia Harvest, an inter-denominational ministry which serves the church in China and around Asia through various strategic initiatives, including Bible printing in China, and supporting the families of persecuted believers. To receive the free Asia Harvest newsletter, go to www.asiaharvest.org, or write to the address below nearest you:

Asia Harvest
1903 60th Place, Suite M1204
Bradenton, FL 34203
UNITED STATES

Asia Harvest
PO Box 181
Te Anau, 9640
NEW ZEALAND

Asia Harvest
Mill Farm
Wesham, PR4 3HD
ENGLAND

Asia Harvest
Clementi Central PO Box 119
SINGAPORE 911204

Asia Harvest
36 Nelson Street
Stepney, SA 5069
AUSTRALIA

Asia Harvest
PO Box 8036
Pejabat Pos Kelana Jaya
46780 Petaling Jaya
Selangor
MALAYSIA

The Heavenly Man is the intensely dramatic story of how God took a young, half-starved boy from a poor village in Henan Province and used him mightily to preach the gospel despite horrific opposition.

Brother Yun is one of China's house church leaders, a man who despite his relative youth has suffered prolonged torture and imprisonment for his faith. Instead of focusing on the many miracles or experiences of suffering, however, Yun prefers to emphasize the character and beauty of Jesus.

This book is like reading a modern-day version of the book of Acts.

– Rev. Dr Mark Stibbe

ISBN: 978-1-85424-597-7 (UK)
ISBN: 978-0-8254-6207-8 (USA)
Available from your local Christian bookshop
In case of difficulty, please visit our website: www.lionhudson.com

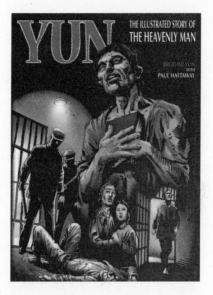

This is a graphic retelling of *The Heavenly Man*, which has sold over half a million copies in English and has been translated into at least 30 languages.

ISBN: 978-1-85424-744-5 (UK)
ISBN: 978-0-8254-6128-6 (USA)
Available from your local Christian bookshop
In case of difficulty, please visit our website: www.lionhudson.com